Actors of Globalization

Library of Economic History

General Editors

VOLUME 10

The titles published in this series are listed at *brill.com/lehi*

Actors of Globalization

New York Merchants in Global Trade, 1784–1812

By

Lisa Sturm-Lind

BRILL

LEIDEN | BOSTON

Cover illustration: 1797 oil on linen of the Tontine Coffee House, Merchant's Coffee House, and Wall Street, leading down to the East River. By Francis Guy (1760–1820).

Library of Congress Cataloging-in-Publication Data
Names: Sturm-Lind, Lisa, author.
Title: Actors of globalization : New York merchants in the global trade, 1784-1812 / by Lisa Sturm-Lind.
Description: Leiden ; Boston : Brill, [2018] | Series: Library of economic history, ISSN 1877-3206 ; VOLUME 10 | Includes bibliographical references and index.
Identifiers: LCCN 2017053695 (print) | LCCN 2017054554 (ebook) | ISBN 9789004356412 (E-book) | ISBN 9789004344389 (hardback : alk. paper)
Subjects: LCSH: Merchants--New York (State)--New York--History. | Business networks--New York (State)--New York--History. | International trade--History.
Classification: LCC HF3163.N7 (ebook) | LCC HF3163.N7 S78 2018 (print) | DDC 382.09747/1--dc23
LC record available at https://lccn.loc.gov/2017053695

Typeface for the Latin, Greek, and Cyrillic scripts: "Brill". See and download: brill.com/brill-typeface.

ISSN 1877-3206
ISBN 978-90-04-34438-9 (hardback)
ISBN 978-90-04-35641-2 (e-book)

This book is printed on acid-free paper and produced in a sustainable manner.

For Patrick & Matilda

Contents

Acknowledgments

This book has grown out of my doctoral dissertation submitted at the European University Viadrina Frankfurt/Oder in 2014. I am deeply indebted to a great number of scholars and especially to my supervisors, Reinhard Blänkner (European University Viadrina Frankfurt/Oder) and Michael Mann (Humboldt University Berlin), who have both been a part of this project early on and encouraged me to consider the global in historic writing. I am thankful for their support and assistance. Klaus Weber and Gangolf Hübinger both from the European-University Viadrina were also immensely helpful with their input and suggestions.

My research was generously supported with a dissertation grant from the European-University Viadrina and a research grant from the German Academic Exchange Service. For this I am grateful.

Peer Vries has been a mentor to me throughout my graduate studies and has always had an open ear, advice and encouragement.

The following programs provided an intellectual community for my dissertation. Most importantly the Summer Dissertation Workshop 2011 at the World History Center, University of Pittsburgh with Patrick Manning, Heather Streets-Salter, Adam McKeown, Peer Vries, Sönke Bauck, Paromita Das Gupta, Emily Gioielli, Shawna Herzog and Violetta Ravagnoli; the Spring School *Global History: Connected Histories or a History of Connections* at the German Historical Institute London 2011, the *Humboldt India Project* at the Institut für Asien- und Afrikawissenschaften at Humboldt University Berlin 2012 and the Workshop *Identifying new themes in South Asian History* at Zentrum Moderner Orient, Berlin 2010.

I am also indebted to the librarians, archivists and staff at the New York Public Library, especially the Manuscripts and Archives Division, the New York Historical Society, the Brooklyn Historical Society and Columbia University who provided so much assistance.

Thank you to Adam McKeown for inviting me to come back to New York as a research scholar at Columbia University, which allowed me to continue my research.

Reinhard Spindler provided valuable information on New York's India trade.

Anne Sophie Overkamp, Manuela Jäger, Birgit Tremml, Forrest Kiliminik and Sadia Bajwa have helped with readings and support. Christiane Bauer provided companionship in the libraries and made long days of studying so much better.

Thanks is also due to my editor Kim Singletary for her great work and input, to the Brill editors Jennifer Obdam and Wendel Scholma for their assistance as well as to the anonymous reviewers at Brill whose comments were immensely helpful. With all this help of great minds, all errors are of course mine.

Last but not least my thanks goes to my family. To my parents and sister for their continuous support throughout all the years and to my husband Patrick Lind for being so much more than my first reader and critic. Without him, this book would not exist.

List of Illustrations

Figures

Tables

Merchant Biographies

This chapter offers a brief overview of *the merchants*' biographies; some are longer than others based on the amount of available source materials.

William Constable
was born in Dublin, Ireland, in 1752. At the age of ten his family immigrated to America and settled near Schenectady in upstate New York. Constable's father, Dr. John Constable was a surgeon in the British Army during the French and Indian Wars. William's brother James, who would later join him in the business, was born shortly after the family's arrival in Schenectady. Young William became good friends, and later business partners with Alexander Macomb, who lived close to the Constables.[1] After returning to Dublin to attend Trinity College, Constable came back to America in 1771 where he served as an apprentice in the New York business Phyn, Ellice & Company, which was active in the fur trade. The firm was connected through family to the Constables: James Phyn had married William's sister in 1768.[2] For the first two years as an apprentice, Constable was sent to the Northwest posts of Detroit and Michillimackinac.[3] There he most likely met Alexander Macomb again as well as two of his other later associates, William Duer and William Edgar who were both active merchants in Detroit's fur trade. After a few years, Constable decided to settle himself in New York City as an independent merchant, from where he engaged in trade with the West Indies and Ireland.[4] During the revolution he transferred to Philadelphia where he was an aide-de-camp to General Lafayette. He also established the firm Seagrove & Constable with James Seagrove in Havana, Cuba. The firm was active in the West Indies and European trade with Holland and France.[5] In 1781, he joined the Society of the Friendly Sons of Saint Patrick in Philadelphia, an Irish society, which proved to be an excellent networking opportunity.[6] Upon his return to New York City in 1783, he helped to

1 R.C. Murphy and L. Mannion, *The History of the Society of the Friendly Sons of Saint Patrick in the City of New York, 1784 to 1955*, New York, The Society of the Friendly Sons of Saint Patrick, 1962, p. 9.

2 R.H. Fleming, 'Phyn, Ellice and Company of Schenectady', *Contributions to Canadian Economics*, vol. 4, 1932, p. 14.

3 W.A. Davis, 'William Constable. New York Merchant and Land Speculator, 1772–1803', PhD Thesis, Harvard University, 1955, p. iii.

4 Davis, *William Constable*, p. iii.

5 D. Tailby, 'Chapters of the Business Career of William Constable', PhD Thesis, Rutgers University 1961, p. 83.

6 Murphy and Mannion, *Society of the Friendly Sons*, p. 42.

establish a branch of the society in the city with Dr. Thomas Cochran, director of Hospitals for the Continental Army and Captain Thomas Randall, merchant and ship-owners.[7] Back in New York, Constable married Ann Maria White[8] and established the merchant firm Constable & Rucker with his business partner John Rucker. Gouverneur Morris, Robert Morris, and William Edgar were silent partners. Rucker was the son of a wealthy merchant family from Hamburg who had connections with the British Parliament and mercantile and banking firms in England, France and Germany.[9] He had come to America in service to the Philadelphia merchant Jonathan Nesbitt before he joined with Constable. Rucker's contact helped the firm to obtain solid credit foundations in Europe. Constable's connections to Phyn, Ellice & Company, who had transferred their firm to London in 1774,[10] also proved to be valuable.[11]

In 1784, Constable and Rucker decided to send their schooner *Betsy* on a voyage to China. With the help of Constable's contacts in England and other international connections, they were able to obtain first-hand information about trade in several ports around the world. The *Betsy's* voyage was a full success and she brought home a profit return of 25 percent.[12] Encouraged by the *Betsy*'s expedition, the firm continued to send ships on voyages to the East Indies in the 1780s and 1790s, providing Constable with most of his money at the time. Within a few years, Constable's trade developed into a business of considerable size and magnitude, apparent as early as 1787, when he began exporting India goods to the British West Indies competing with English merchants in the sale of teas and nankeens. During the 1790s, Constable took advantage of the European Wars and achieved great profits in the carrying trade from the West Indies to Europe. In 1791, Constable ceased business with Morris who Constable believed was involved in too many speculations that could potentially endanger their business and joined with his brother, James Constable (Rucker died in June 1788). The new firm William & James Constable, opened a counting house at 51 William Street.

In November 1791, Constable went to England, where he spent five years coordinating the European concerns of his firm and the sale of his land in the

7 Murphy and Mannion, *Society of the Friendly Sons*, p. 43.

8 W.C. Duyckinck and J. Cornell, *The Ducyckinck and Allied Families*, New York, Tobias A. Wright, 1908, p. 18.

9 M. Schulte-Beerbühl, *Deutsche Kaufleute in London: Welthandel und Einbürgerung 1660–1818*, München, Oldenbourg Verlag, 2007, p. 176. John Peter Rucker left London in 1774 and settled as merchant in New York. He kept his connections to the house in London. John Anthony Rücker, Sr., also possessed several sugar plantations in the Caribbean.

10 Fleming, *Phyn, Ellice and Company*, p. 23.

11 Tailby, *Chapters*, p. 203.

12 Davis, *William Constable*, p. 124.

United States. Upon his return, he discovered that under his brother's charge the company had incurred great losses; Constable spent the next years reorganizing and saving his firm. In the end Constable managed to partly correct his brother's failures and was even able to direct new grand business ventures profiting off of the Haitian Revolution.

The shipping business was not Constable's only concern; he was also vice-president of the Chamber of Commerce (1785), director of the Bank of New York (1787–1792), president of the Society of Friendly Sons of Saint Patrick (1789), and member of the New Jersey Society for Establishing Useful Manufactures (1791).[13] Civic concerns accompanied his business interests and as an active member of the city he preoccupied himself with moral and humanitarian issues as well as cultural and philanthropic life. Constable became one of New York's most well established merchants with considerable influence in mercantile, political, and social affairs. He strengthened his societal standing with strategic marriages of his children to the children of others within the business community.[14]

In his last years, Constable quit most of his mercantile business activities and focused solely on land speculations. In 1787, he already began speculating in the lands of Ohio, Kentucky, Virginia, and Georgia.[15] He also acquired huge amounts of lands in upstate New York and with Daniel McCormick took over the management of Alexander Macomb's land after Macomb was taken to debtor's prison.

William Constable died in 1803 at the age of 51, leaving a considerable inheritance to his wife and seven children, four of whom were born in the 1790s. After his death, his brother James was appointed guardian of his infant children. When James died ten years later, Hezekiah B. Pierrepont was appointed guardian with John Pierpont and William Bell as his sureties.[16]

William Edgar

was one of New York's most influential and affluent merchants during the 1790s. He was born in Northern Ireland in 1739. His family was originally of

13 Tailby, *Chapters*, p. 158.

14 Ann Marie Constable married Hezekiah B. Pierrepont. Three other Constable children married into the McVickar family, John McVickar was an Irish shipowner and commission merchant. Murphy and Mannion, *Society of the Friendly Sons*, p. 145.

15 B. Moffat, *Pierrepont Genealogies: from Norman times to 1913, With Particular Attention Paid to the Line of Descent From Hezekiah Pierrepont, Youngest son of Rev. James Pierpont of New Haven*, New York, L. Middleditch Co., 1913, p. 20.

16 *Records of the Chancery Court Province and State of New York, Guardianships 1691–1815*, Cited by K. Scott, The Holland Society of New York, p. 198.

English descent but had settled in Ireland around 1688.[17] Edgar served in Detroit as a financial agent for the British Army post[18] and arrived in New York around 1760, where he went into the fur business between Detroit and Montreal. In 1779, he joined the firm of Alexander Macomb who supplied provisions to the garrison, goods to the India department and acted as paymaster for post personnel, militia, volunteers, and interpreters.

Edgar married the sister of Constable's wife Isabella White, in 1784 and in 1785, joined the East Indies trade as a silent partner and brother-in-law of William Constable.[19] Edgar accumulated a fortune and rose to become one of the city's most prominent businessmen. Like William Constable, he was involved in a variety of business activities in addition to his involvement in the oversea trade, such as land development and infrastructure.[20] He enjoyed a great reputation among his fellow citizens, which he maintained by holding important administrative offices. He served as president and vice-president of the Society of the Friendly Sons of Saint Patrick, was treasurer in the Mutual Insurance Company, the first insurance company in New York, and was an original stockholder as well as director of the Bank of New York. Contemporaries mentioned his famous white marble palace at 7 Greenwich Street as a sign of his great wealth.[21] Although it is not certain if he had actually lived in the white palace because his address was registered at 39 Broadway in 1799, he might have died there in 1820 when his son William Edgar, Jr resided there.

Hezekiah Beers Pierrepont

was born on 3 November 1768, in New Haven, Connecticut. He was the son of John Pierpont and Sarah Beers (he changed his name later to Pierrepont). In college, he was dissatisfied studying Greek and Latin and decided to quit his studies. He first entered the firm of his uncle Isaac Beers in New Haven where he was introduced to business.[22] He left Connecticut in 1790 and went to New York, where he started as a clerk at the Custom House. After one year he moved to Philadelphia where he acted as an agent for Watson & Greenleaf

---

17 Murphy and Mannion, *Society of the Friendly Sons*, p. 60.

18 *William Edgar papers, 1750–1870*, Manuscripts and Archives. The New York Public Library. Astor, Lenox, and Tilden Foundations.

19 Duyckinck and Cornell, *The Ducyckinck and Allied Families*, p. 17. In 1794, after his first wife passed, Edgar married Ann Van Horn the daughter of David Van Horne a well-known New York City merchant.

20 F.B. Hough, *A History of Lewis County, in the State of New York: From the Beginning of His Settlement to the Present Time*, Albany, Munsell & Rowland, 1860, p. 135.

21 W. Barret, *The Old Merchants of New York City*, New York, Carleton, 1864, p. 250.

22 Hough, *Lewis County*, p. 243.

of Philadelphia and made a small fortune in the speculation of national debt. He returned to New York after three years and, with his cousin, established the company Leffingwell & Pierrepont. The firm quickly made a fortune delivering supplies to revolutionary France. After some time, Pierrepont debated joining the East Indies trade. He purchased the ship *Confederacy* and went on a voyage to India and Canton in 1796 as part owner and supercargo. He recorded a 78-page journal on the common trade practices of the East Indies trade. The journal, which contains valuable insights into the trade business, including routes, statistics, commodities, evaluation of profits, and other details, is preserved at the New York Public Library.[23] On his return from Canton in 1797 French privateers seized the ship, which was a violation of both international law and the treaty between the United States and France. Pierrepont stayed in France for several years, attempting to collect his claims but never succeeded. However, he was successful in retaining some of his lost value from his British insurance company. Because of the high risks, Pierrepont decided to abandon the East Indies trade dissolving his firm in 1800.

Upon his return to New York in 1802 Pierrepont married Anna Maria Constable, daughter of William Constable. He had met William Constable and Robert Fulton during his stay in Europe. The same year he and Anna were married, he bought the old Philip Livingston distillery in Brooklyn and became actively engaged in the development of the surrounding village. His residence at Brooklyn Heights, on the old Benson farm, later known as the Pierrepont Mansion, stood at the conjunction of Pierrepont Place and Montague Street and constituted an important landmark in Brooklyn. In 1815, he was on the committee to incorporate Brooklyn as a village and hired a surveyor to create a new plan for streets and blocks. The plan laid out the basic grid structure of today's Brooklyn Heights. Pierrepont, who was known to row himself to Manhattan in a small boat every day, assisted his friend Robert Fulton in establishing the Fulton Ferry, for which he served as one of the directors until his death. Besides his interest in the progress of Brooklyn, Pierrepont also became a famous developer in upstate New York. When Constable died in 1803 he inherited parts of his land possessions. Pierrepont died in 1838 leaving behind his wife and ten children.

William Bayard

was born in Greenwich Village in 1761, the son of Colonel William Bayard and Catherine McEvers Bayard. He was a descendant of Balthazar Bayard, a

---

23 Notes on the Trade of China made at Canton 1796, Hezekiah Beers Pierrepont Miscellany, Constable-Pierrepont papers. Manuscripts and Archives. The New York Public Library. Astor, Lenox, and Tilden Foundations.

Hugenot who came to New Amsterdam in 1647.[24] His mother Anna, widow of Samuel Bayard, was the sister of Peter Stuyvesant who served as the last Dutch Director General of the colony New Netherlands. Colonel William Bayard was a merchant and landowner who was a British loyalist during the revolution and was eventually forced to move back to England. His son William stayed in New York City and married Elizabeth Cornell, daughter of the wealthy merchant and landowner Samuel Cornell.[25] After the revolution, Bayard decided to embark on the international shipping business and founded the firm Le Roy, Bayard & Co. in December 1786 with his partner Herman Le Roy, each investing £2,000.[26] Bayard's cousin James McEvers later joined the company. A trip to Tenerife, Spain, for liquor was their first enterprise. Trading extensively around the world from Europe to the East and the West Indies, Le Roy, Bayard & Co. managed a world-spanning enterprise, taking advantage of global events and crises. Their merchant house was located on Hanover Square and many of New York's later merchants started their careers as clerks there. In 1800 they were the largest commercial house in the city.[27] In 1822, during the Latin American revolutions, they engaged several ships in the trade with South America, with great profit returns.[28]

While still continuing their shipping business, the firm's focus later shifted toward land speculations in upstate New York after the Embargo Act in 1807. Bayard was also a prominent character in New York City and served as director of the New York Chamber of Commerce, the president of the Bank of America, and as president of the Morris Canal Company. He was engaged in the development of roads and turnpikes and held stock in the Oswage Lumber Association. His remaining documents reveal him to be a fan of art and architecture, containing various descriptions of French and Italian cities, including palaces, churches, and monuments, which he collected during travels to Europe. Bayard

24 Balthazar became prominent in the affairs of New York. He died in 1705. He was an ancestor of John Jay. Biographical Notes on William Bayard. Bayard Family Papers 1659–1898, Bayard-Campbell-Pearsall families papers. Manuscripts and Archives. The New York Public Library.

25 Biographical Notes on William Bayard. Bayard Family Papers 1659–1898, Bayard-Campbell-Pearsall families papers. Manuscripts and Archives. The New York Public Library. Astor, Lenox, and Tilden Foundations.

26 S.C. Steward, *The Le Roy Family in America 1753–2003*, Boston, Randall Publishers, 2003, p. 22.

27 *Ships and Shipping of Old New York: A Brief Account of the Interesting Phases of the Commerce of New York and the Foundation of the City to the Beginning of the Civil War*, New York City, Bank of Manhattan Company, p. 36.

28 Biographical Notes on William Bayard. Bayard Family Papers 1659–1898, Bayard-Campbell-Pearsall families papers. Manuscripts and Archives. The New York Public Library. Astor, Lenox, and Tilden Foundations.

owned the Greenwich Village house, where Alexander Hamilton was taken after being wounded in a duel and where he died on 12 July 1804.[29] Bayard passed away in 1826, leaving the firm to his two sons Robert and William.

Herman Le Roy's
father Jacob Le Roy came to New York City in 1753 from Rotterdam, the Netherlands, and became a successful merchant operating the firm Jacob Le Roy & Sons. In 1770 he was one of the ten wealthiest residents of the city.[30] During the revolution he fled to Rhinebeck, Dutchess County. When Jacob Le Roy died in 1793 his sons Robert and Jacob continued the firm.[31] Herman, the third son, was born on 16 January 1758, in New York.

After diplomatic relations were established with the Netherlands under Washington's administration, Herman Le Roy became Consul General for New York and New Jersey.[32] On 19 October 1786, he married Hannah Cornell at William Bayard's House on Queens Street, now 89 Pearl Street.[33] He founded the company Le Roy, Bayard & Co. with his brother in law William Bayard two years later. In 1803 he was appointed president of the Bank of New York.

Le Roy lived at 4 Bowling Green until he moved to 7 Broadway where he built a white marble house. The house had the same design as the one he constructed for his daughter Cornelia, at 7 Greenwich Street. Cornelia married William Edgar, Jr. on 29 April 1809, at Trinity Church. Le Roy also owned a country home in Pelham, New York, where his daughter Caroline married Daniel Webster in 1829. In 1815, Le Roy was one of fifteen New Yorkers who owned a carriage. He died on 31 March 1841, leaving behind seven children.

Samuel Gouverneur's
biography is very limited as only little information on his life can be retrieved from archival records. The remaining records of Gouverneur & Kemble provide little information on biography. Only with the help of ancestral research was it possible to fill in some of the gaps. Gouverneur (1759–1847) was head of the firm Gouverneur & Kemble along with his brothers Isaac (1749–1800) and Nicholas (1753–1802)[34] and his brother-in-law, Peter Kemble, who was married to their

---

29 Steward, *Le Roy Family*, p. 22.

30 Steward, *Le Roy Family*, p. 18.

31 Steward, *Le Roy Family*, p. 19.

32 *The National Cylopaedia of American Biography, Volume III*, New York: James T. White & Company: 1967.

33 Steward, *Le Roy Family*, p. 21.

34 Nicholas Gouverneur, Jr. married Hester Kortright, sister of Elizabeth Kortright Monroe who was First Lady from 1817 to 1825. Their son Samuel L. Gouverneur (1799–1865), a lawyer

sister, Gertrude Gouverneur. They were the sons of Samuel Gouverneur, Sr., (1720–1798) and Experience Johnson (1720–1788). Samuel Gouverneur, Sr., was brother to Isaac Gouverneur, Sr. and Nicholas Gouverneur, Sr., all prominent New York merchants.[35] Their father, Isaac Gouverneur, (1677–1728), descended from a French Huguenot family and was born in Amsterdam in 1677. He immigrated to America where he was an active merchant trading in the West Indies. The family was tied to the Dutch Caribbean island Curacao through Nicholas Gouverneur Sr., who married Maria Winkler, the daughter of Herman Winkler and Gertrude Van Kinswilder; Herman Winkler was born in Batavia and later worked for the Dutch West India Company there and Gertrude was born in Curacao. Nicholas and Maria had two children, Isaac Gouverneur (1746–1794) and Gertrude. Isaac continued business on the island and was an important trade partner of the firm Gouverneur & Kemble in New York, along with Gertrude's husband, Captain Anthony Rutgers.

Peter Kemble's

grandfather Richard Kemble was a merchant in Smyrna (modern day Izmir), Asia Minor. His father Richard Kemble, Sr., was born there on 12 December 1704.[36] In 1712 Peter Kemble, Sr., was sent to London for his education; in 1718 he was sent to Rotterdam to be introduced to mercantile life at George Kemble's merchant firm, who was a distant family relative active in the wine business. From there Kemble Sr. went on his first trading voyage to Guinea in 1720 and afterwards returned to London.[37] He conducted business in London during the following years until he moved to America in 1730.[38] There he married Gertrude Bayard, a daughter of Samuel and Margaret Bayard on 13 June 1731,[39] and the newlyweds settled in New Brunswick, New Jersey, where Peter Kemble, Sr., rose to success in business and politics and became one of the most preeminent people of colonial New Jersey and a good friend of Governor Lewis Morris.[40]

---

and civil servant later married the daughter of President James Monroe who was also his first cousin, Maria Hester Monroe.

35 Isaac Gouverneur Sr. died in 1791. He did not have children and bequeathed his several houses to his nephews.

36 Kemble Stout, *Genealogy of the Kemble (Kimble) Family in America,* Pullman, K. Stout, 1992, p. 351.

37 W. Nelson 'Collections of the New Jersey Historical Society, Volume IX', *Biographical and Genealogical Notes. From the Volumes of the New Jersey Archives*, Newark, Published by the Society, 1916, p. 150.

38 Nelson, Collections of the New Jersey Historical Society, p. 150.

39 K. Stout, *Genealogy of the Kemble (Kimble) Family in America*, New York, New York Public Library, 2009, p. 351.

40 Nelson, Collections of the New Jersey Historical Society, p. 150.

He remained a loyalist during the revolution. Kemble, Sr., married Elizabeth Tuite of Trenton, New Jersey, after Gertrude's death in 1749. He had nine children with Gertrude and three with Elizabeth. He died on February 23, 1789, and was buried in the family plot of Mount Kemble, the family's estate.[41] Peter Kemble, Jr., was the third son of Peter Kemble and Gertrude Bayard, born on 17 August 1739. He was educated at the College in Philadelphia (now University of Pennsylvania) before he entered the counting house of Archibald McGall, a leading merchant of New York City who was married to Judith Kemble, Peter's sister. After the revolution Peter Kemble, Jr., married Gertrude Gouverneur. With his brothers in law he founded the firm Gouverneur & Kemble in 1788. He died on 6 July 1823. He had six children.[42]

Samuel Ferguson

was born in 1769 in Halifax, England. After the early deaths of his parents he was raised by his aunt Elisabeth Rawson. When he was 19 years old he went to work for the firm of his cousin Robert Griffith, a wealthy Liverpool merchant who also had an office in Philadelphia. The company traded with the East and West Indies and Europe and in his early years, Ferguson was sent on many voyages. In 1800, Ferguson opened his own business with John Day in the dry goods business in New York City. The original plan called for Ferguson to stay in London to direct business there and for Day to organize business in New York, but by 1802 they both settled permanently in New York. That same year, Ferguson married Day's sister Elizabeth who immigrated with him to the city.[43] After their move, the Fergusons were quickly integrated into New York City's society; they were very well connected to the merchants Edmund Morewood and Jonathan Odgen. The company Ferguson & Day flourished, profiting especially from carrying West Indies products to Europe during the European Wars. Ferguson died on 2 August 1816, when he had a stroke and fell down the stairs at the corner of Wall and Pearl Streets. He left a wife and six children.[44]

---

41 Kemble Stout, *Genealogy of the Kemble Family*, p. 351.

42 Kemble Stout, *Genealogy of the Kemble Family*, p. 354. Kemble's son Gouverneur Kemble was a close friend of Washington Irving and they often assembled at the Kemble mansion in Passaic, NJ.

43 A large part of the correspondence between Samuel and Elizabeth is still preserved at the New York Public Library and provides insight into life in New York City during that time. Ferguson, who had already made plans to relocate to the United States, tried to convince his fiancée Elizabeth Day to come with him. In the letters he describes life in the early republic. Samuel Ferguson to Elizabeth Day, *Ferguson Correspondence,* Ferguson family papers. Manuscripts and Archives. The New York Public Library. Astor, Lenox, and Tilden Foundations.

44 Biographical Note, Finding Aid, Ferguson family papers, New York Public Library.

Little information exists on *William Bell's* biography. Born in Scotland,[45] it is unclear when he came to the United States. He started his career as a clerk at Constable & Rucker. The firm's search for a clerk had not been easy. At first, Constable had considered hiring George Washington's nephew Bushrod Washington as clerk or apprentice[46] but Constable hired Bell instead, who was referred to him by John Porteous, a merchant at Little Falls.[47] Constable sent Bell as supercargo on the *Empress of China's* second voyage to China. Bell remained in the position for many years and frequently sailed as the firm's supercargo on various voyages to Asia. There he maintained the company's contacts and successfully negotiated its concerns. According to Barrett, later in his life Bell was often seen on the stoops of McCormick's house at 57 Wall Street or in the company of Captain Frederick Phillips, whose daughter, Mary Phillips, was married to Samuel Gouverneur.[48]

Isaac Bell, Jr.
was born in Stamford, Connecticut on 16 February 1768. His father's ancestor had come from Edinburgh, Scotland in 1640 and bought land of eight square miles for 36 Pounds sterling. Bell's father Isaac Bell Sr. was a successful merchant who was active mainly in the West Indies trade in New York. Bell Sr. also owned several mills in Stamford, whose flour was sold to Newfoundland. Bell senior married Susannah Smith, daughter of the fur merchant Ephraim Smith of Stamford. Being a Tory, he moved his family to New York during the revolution and during their absence the house and property in Stamford were confiscated.[49] According to legend, thirteen-year-old Isaac Bell Jr. taught Prince William, later William IV how to skate on a pond at St. John's Park in the winter of 1781.[50] After the revolution, the Bells moved to St. Johns, New Brunswick, in Canada, where Isaac Bell, Sr. continued his mercantile business. It was there, that Bell, Jr. was introduced to business and after accumulating enough money, moved back to New York in 1792. In 1793 he went on his first trading voyage to Malaga, Spain, where he traded flour for wine, raisins, and currants.[51] In New York he associated with Moses and Nehemiah Rogers and Archibald Gracie.

45 Barret, *The Old Merchants of New York*, p. 248.

46 Tailby, *Chapters*, p. 179.

47 Porteous was a merchant at Little Falls. Tailby, *Chapters*, p. 182.

48 Barret, *The old Merchants of New York*, p. 248. McCormick was president of the Society of Friendly Sons of Saint Patrick and a close friend of William Constable.

49 Isaac Bell interviewed by Mary E. Farnum, 1856, p. 1. Isaac Bell Papers 1787–1940, Rare Book & Manuscript Library, Columbia University in the City of New York.

50 Bell, interviewed by Mary E. Farnum, 1856, p. 2.

51 Bell, interviewed by Mary E. Farnum, 1856, p. 2.

In 1798 he went to China for the first time as supercargo on the ship *Industry*, along with Captain Rudd where he made valuable contacts. After three voyages to China as supercargo he had acquired a large fortune and settled in New York at 4 Greenwich St. There he lived as one of the city's most notorious bachelors. Later he sold the house to his brother-in-law Nehemiah Rogers and moved to 14 Greenwich Street. On 16 April 1810, he married Mary Ellis, daughter of John Ellis and Marie Faugeres.[52] Bell was rich and popular and socialized with New York City's best circles. He was an intimate friend of Alexander Hamilton who frequently dined at his home.[53] Bell Jr., died in 1860; he had five children.

52 Bell, interviewed by Mary E. Farnum, 1856, p. 4.

53 E.Y. Smith, 'The Gold Coast of New York', Isaac Bell Papers, Butler Library, Columbia University in the City of New York, 1944, p. 9.

Introduction

In December 1787, only a few years after his country had gone through a war, New York City merchant William Constable wrote to his business partner John Inglis in London:

> If fortune would favour us so far as to give us a European War, I have No doubt You and I coud [sic] do something advantageous.—Your Paris friends might make a Contract for Provisions for their Islands they are more abundant and cheaper than ever they were known. The American Flag might do great things in India—in short a War woud [sic] open an extensive field to Enterprize if We had some support.[1,2]

The lines poignantly capture the merchant's speculation with global events. At first glance, it seems an unusual wish, especially from someone whose own country still felt the effects of its recent war-torn history. Upon closer look, the quote is a great example of the complexity of the global economy at the time. It reveals a clear awareness of a rising global interdependence, which Constable aimed to utilize for his benefits.

How eighteenth-century merchants dealt with and managed to profit from a changing global world is the question that will be explored in this study. In particular, it details a group of New York merchants engaged in global trade from 1784 to 1812. I regard these merchants as profiteers and contributors of an early form of globalization: they profited from the fact that large parts of their businesses were only made possible by changing global patterns and their coordination of people, commodities, and capital sent around the world contributed to new forms of global interaction. Their constant search for new business activities, their accommodation to a variety of business fields and their flexibility in responding to changing conditions shows that they were skilled business managers who were able to respond to and interact with larger global economic processes. They speculated on and profited off of wars, food

1 William Constable to his business partner John Inglis, December 1787, William Constable Correspondence, Constable Papers, Constable-Pierrepont papers. Manuscripts and Archives. The New York Public Library. Astor, Lenox, and Tilden Foundations.

2 Archival sources are cited in their original language. Please note that the differences in capitalization represent the conventions of the time and are not mistakes of the transcriptions. The writing within the archival references can vary e.g. letter books and letterbooks.

 | DOI 10.1163/9789004356412_002

crises, trade embargoes, and slave revolts. The more upheaval in Europe and elsewhere in the world, the more excited these merchants became.

I argue that eighteenth-century globalization gave rise to this merchant group that was part of an upcoming social class—the middling ranks—and that consisted to a large extent of self-made businessmen who showed a high degree of vertical and horizontal mobility compared to the elitist merchant classes of colonial times. Global circumstances helped these merchants to establish themselves as entrepreneurs and their global activities in turn, created an intensive economic interdependence of the United States with the rest of the world ultimately promoting social and political change.

The book suggests that the late eighteenth century be viewed as a phase of early globalization. It was a period of wars and revolutions spreading and affecting societies across multiple continents. My argument continues recent research that regards the time as global crisis that allowed quantitative and qualitative forms of globalization to manifest themselves in (1) the increased exchange of commodities, people and ideas, (2) the expansion of free trade and with it the transformation of production processes, and (3) in the emergence of diplomatic and economic institutions. I propose looking into the merchants' life and work in light of that early global phase.

The argument is laid out in three sections: The first chapter highlights how political reforms and global circumstances in the late eighteenth century allowed more men to become self-made businessmen. American Independence and the following period of state building were surrounded by a European power struggle for global dominance that was to a large degree fought out in the Atlantic. Politics of the new republic were consequently influenced by these circumstances—in fact, it was probably the only time before the twentieth century when global events have had such a strong effect on domestic politics. George Washington's presidential administration decided on a number of policies that were beneficial for American merchants and helped them to compete in international commerce. Thereto belong Alexander Hamilton's fiscal and financial reforms as well as Washington's decision to stay neutral during the wars in Europe. Both were equally beneficial for the rise of self-made businessmen: the former because it created a modern financial system that financed entrepreneurship, the latter because it brought with it economic opportunities for those entrepreneurs to succeed. The analysis investigates how the merchants established themselves as businessmen and formed networks of international business associates; it details their high degree of mobility, which enabled them to quickly expand their enterprises and ascend socially.

The second chapter shows how the merchants proved to be skilled entrepreneurs eager to step into new commercial opportunities. Adaptability and flexibility distinguished their work and helped them to quickly expand into new fields of business wherever an opportunity arose. Global crises played into their hands as they created a plethora of new business opportunities: American Independence and the dissolution of Britain's monopoly on large parts of the trade allowed, for the first time, direct commercial relations between the United States and different world regions. The increasing demand for Asian goods such as tea, textiles, china, and indigo had transformed the East Indies[3] trade into a lucrative business that American[4] merchants were now able to pursue independently. Equally important, the wars in Europe that followed the French Revolution and extended to the Caribbean brought along great commercial opportunities. It was a period of global crisis and transition, which opened up new spaces for agency, and American merchants quickly became important players in this global arena. This section illustrates that private actors played a large role in the advancement of global integration.

The third chapter analyzes how global processes bounced back to the local level. The merchants of this study were not only global players, they also actively pursued local improvements. As powerful businessmen they had a strong interest in changing domestic economic, political, and social life and creating a better infrastructure for their trade and business. They contributed to commercialization of society and the implementation of new forms of consumer desire. To leave out a discussion regarding these merchants' local activities, including land development, stock trading, and manufacturing where the profits from international shipping were reinvested, would only portray half the picture of their achievements. This section makes clear how eighteenth-century globalization had an effect on the local, arguing against the notion that globalization did not have qualitative effects on societies before the mid-nineteenth century. There was a tremendous increase of global connections by the late eighteenth century which manifested social and institutional change.

Globalization in History

Scholarly debates of the last decades have centered around the onset of globalization. Many historians argue that globalization does not only describe a

3 The term 'East Indies' encompasses the territories of the Indian Ocean and China. I use 'East Indies' as by then it was the common term to describe the area. To avoid repetition it will be used interchangeably with Asia trade and Indian Ocean trade, although I am aware of the geographical distinctions of the region.

4 'United States' and 'America' are used interchangeably in the text to avoid repetition. If the term 'America' is related to parts of the American hemisphere other than the United States, I will specify accordingly.

modern phenomenon but an affair that goes back centuries, and, though different in scope and manifestation, has had similar effects on societies through time. They point out that the intensity by which the global impacted human life was comparable in strength and effect between modern and earlier times.[5]

If globalization is defined as networks of interdependence on a global level then it can be traced back quite far in history.[6] Worldwide interdependence, not only economically but also environmentally and culturally, was at a new degree after the fifteenth century at which time all of the continents were linked through trade and exchange and contemporaries started to perceive the world as a globe.[7] The development of the Spanish and Portuguese colonial empires

---

5 Good overviews on the topic are: D. Armitage, 'Is there a Pre-History of Globalization.' in Deborah Cohen and Maura O'Connor (eds.), *Comparison and History, Europe in Cross-National Perspective*, London, Routledge 2004, pp. 165–175; M. Lang, 'Globalization and its History', in *The Journal of Modern History,* vol. 78, December 2006, pp. 899–931; A. McKeown, 'Periodizing Globalization', *History Workshop Journal* vol. 63, 2007, pp. 218–230.

6 Jürgen Osterhammel and Niels P. Petersson, for instance, understand globalization as the consolidation of worldwide networks and entanglements, creating spaces of interactions that not only linked together different regions all over the globe, but also entire continents and oceans. J. Osterhammel and N. Petersson, *Geschichte der Globalisierung: Dimensionen, Prozesse, Epochen*, München, Beck, 2003; J. Osterhammel and N. Petersson, trans. D. Geyer, *Globalization: A Short History*, Princeton, Princeton University Press, 2003.

The inception of a World System is often equated with the beginning of a global economic interdependence. Immanuel Wallerstein outlines the expansion, concentration, and acceleration of worldwide relations, accompanied by stable and regular trade connections spanning large parts of the world in his three-volume work which dates the emergence of a European world-economy to the fifteenth century. I. Wallerstein, *The Modern World-System I. Capitalist Agriculture and the Origins of the European World-Economy in the Sixteenth Century*, New York, Academic Press, 1974. Andre Gunder Frank and Barry Gills date the beginning of the world system back 5000 years starting in the geographic zone of eastern Asia to western Europe, including south Asia, southwest Asia and northern Africa. The authors emphasize that—contra Wallerstein's argumentation—the world system had existed before the fifteenth century and that Wallerstein's capitalistic world system must be seen as a particular form of the 'one' world system. They present Wallerstein's approach as being too Eurocentric. A. Frank, B. Gills, 'The 5,000-Year World System', in A. Frank, B. Gills (ed.), *The World System: Five hundred years or five thousand,* London: Routledge 1993, pp. 3–59. Janet Abu-Lughad argues for the existence of a pre-modern world system throughout Eurasia, from northwest Europe to China, which she dates from 1250 to 1350 and which laid the ground for the European world economy in the sixteenth century. J. Abu-Lughad, *Before European Hegemony: The World System A.D. 1250–1350*, New York, Oxford University Press, 1991.

7 Christopher A. Bayly describes an 'archaic globalization' characterized by common ideologies that inflected the activities of consumers and producers: cosmic kingship, universal

in the fifteenth and sixteenth century signified the beginning of an irreversible worldwide interconnection. Expeditions, as well as the establishment of new trade connections, led to increasing contact between Europe, Africa, Asia, and America that solidified into stable, multilateral interdependencies until the mid-eighteenth century. American silver became a global commodity channeled through a trade system that not only transported goods globally but also produced price convergences, which were often considered indicators for economic globalization.[8] The quantitative increase of worldwide economic relations that resulted from the integration of the Americas into the world economy led to a new level of economic integration.

Historian Christopher A. Bayly describes the time between 1720—especially after 1780—and 1820 as 'World Crisis' a crucial period of increasing global interactivity leading to political, social, and economic disruptions.[9] According to him, global integration until the 1750s had been rather moderate, linking various regions around the world, with many economic centers. Europeans had not yet established dominance over the world economy, although its ascendance could already be observed in some areas, especially in the Atlantic region. The dynamism of European colonialism and state-building processes in the eighteenth century propelled forward a new phase of global integration. This period of global conflicts was closely linked to the commercial competition between France and England as well as the fall of various ancient regimes around the world. The Treaty of Utrecht heralded a new era of geopolitics carried out by the European states for which the expansion of trade had become a prime incentive. Europeans enlarged their global dominance to new world regions, regulating flows of commodities and resources of an expanding global market. These states competed for commercial success, which strengthened the interrelationship between politics and economy. Dynastic wars were superseded by commercial wars aimed to extend mercantile influence. In short, the European system was reconstituted by politics driven by interests of trade expansion and

religion, and humoral understandings of the body and the land and flows of plants, spices, and medicines. C.A. Bayly, *The Birth of the Modern World, 1780–1914: Global Connections and Comparisons*, Malden, Blackwell, 2004. Geoffrey Gunn sees a first form of globalization in the cultural exchange that resulted from Euro-Asian trade relationships and travel between 1500 to 1800. G.C. Gunn, *First Globalization: The Eurasian Exchange, 1500 to 1800*, Lanham, Rowman & Litfield, 2003.

8 D.O. Flynn and A. Giraldez, 'Born With a "Silver Spoon": The Origin of World Trade in 1571', *Journal of World History*, vol. 6, no.2, 1995, pp. 201–221.

9 C.A. Bayly, *The Birth of the Modern World, 1780–1914: Global Connections and Comparisons*, Malden, Blackwell, 2004.

market access.[10] The international market rivalry between France and Great Britain brought about changes in Europe as well as overseas. The Americas, the center of the Atlantic economy, were theaters of wars and private violence, often tolerated by the European states. Pirates and privateers were political and economic consequences of a world in which sea trade had become an important constituent of wealth.[11] The American plantation economy was also the scene of European commercial expansion, creating a system that linked the world in unprecedented global flows of commodities, capital and labor.[12]

At the same time, Europeans managed to expand their influence in the Indian Ocean and discover the Pacific Ocean. The Mughal Empire disintegrated in the late eighteenth century allowing the British East India Company to take control of the Indian subcontinent. The Dutch manifested their power in Indonesia and the British in Malaysia, integrating more regions into the world economy under direct European influence. Asian empires were affected by socio-political turmoil at the same time. With the exception of China and Japan, which remained unaffected from outside influences, most parts of the world were shaken by crisis and political upheaval during the eighteenth century. Bayly notes that this period of global crisis, where new spatial patterns were negotiated and fought out, resulted in an irreversible change of world constellations.[13]

Social and cultural change accompanied economic expansion. With the rise of shipping, more people working as merchants, artisans, farmers, and other occupations became directly and indirectly dependent on the world market. New and exotic goods flooded the stores, especially in port cities, bringing changes in consumption habits and with it adjustments in home production and home organization. New spaces of sociability, like coffee houses and tea salons, altered the old order of private and public spheres. Simultaneously,

---

10 Very interesting reads on the intensifying battle between Europeans over overseas commerce are J.E. Thomson, *Mercenaries, Pirates and Sovereigns: State-Building and Extraterritorial Violence in Early Modern Europe*, Princeton: Princeton University Press, 1994; P. Cheney, *Revolutionary Commerce: Globalization and the French Monarchy*, Cambridge, Mass, Harvard University Press, 2010; and I. Hont, *Jealousy of Trade: International Competition and the Nat*ion State, Cambridge, MA, Belknap Press, 2005.

11 A. Colás and B. Mabee, 'The Flow and Ebb of Private Seaborne Violence in Global Politics Lesson From the Atlantic World, 1689–1815' in A. Colás and B. Mabee (eds.), *Mercenaries, Pirates, Bandits, and Empires: Private Violence in Historical Context*, New York: Columbia University Press, 2010, pp. 83–106.

12 On sugar and its effects on slavery, capitalist production, and industrialization read S. Mintz, *Sweetness and Power*, New York, Penguin Books, 1985.

13 Bayly, *The Birth of the Modern World*, pp. 86.

the sciences became more popular and expanded into more realms of society, resulting in new technological discoveries and geographical explorations. People's world knowledge was broadened by epoch-making intellectual debates and the advancement of printing.[14]

By the late eighteenth century the world had become integrated to a degree that went far beyond the transnational relationships of the past. The complexity and the sheer amount of trans-regional and trans-continental exchanges invites the applications of concepts of globalization to study the flows and interactions of people, goods, and money. Adam McKeown addresses this approach as the *quantitative branch* of globalization studies.[15]

Countering this view of globalization is the *qualitative branch*, which argues that globalization is defined differently through its qualitative changes on life and in societies. Most proponents of the latter branch consider the second quarter of the nineteenth century as the beginning of globalization. In their reading, new transportation and communication technologies, the spread of industrial production, free market economies, price convergence and the beginning of new streams of mass immigrations are listed as benchmarks of globalization.[16]

But although qualitative change was less obvious than in later epochs, in the late eighteenth century it was perceptible in the advancement of free trade, the commercialization of societies, political upheavals, as well as in legal, political and commercial institutional changes.[17] It thus raises the question as to whether globalization should be approached as a phenomenon that happened

14 For the perception of the global in eighteenth century writings see S. Muthu, *Enlightenment Against Empire*, Princeton, Princeton University Press, 2003; and S. Muthu, 'Adam Smith's Critique of International Trading Companies: Theorizing Globalization in the Age of Enlightenment', *Political Theory*, vol.36, no.2, April 2008, pp. 185–212.

15 For a summary of the quantitative and qualitative branches in globalization studies, see A. McKeown, 'Periodizing Globalization', *History Workshop Journal*, vol. 63, Spring 2007, pp. 218–230.

16 See M.D. Bordo, A.M. Taylor and J.G. Williamson, (eds.), *Globalization in Historical Perspective*, Chicago, University of Chicago Press, 2003; K. O'Rourke and J. Williamson, 'When did Globalization begin?', *National Bureau of Economic Research Working Paper Series*, no. 7632, April 2003.

17 Good overviews of the global relations of the eighteenth century are editorials by F. Nussbaum (ed.), *The Global Eighteenth Century*, Baltimore, John Hopkins University Press, 2003; M. Grandner and A. Komlosy (eds.), *Vom Weltgeist beseelt: Globalgeschichte 1700–1815*, Wien, Promedia, 2004; and B. Hausberger and J. Lehners (eds.), *Die Welt im 18. Jahrhundert*, Wien, Mandelbaum, 2011. For early modern connections and parallels see also Joseph Fletcher, 'Integrative History: Parallels and Interconnections in "the Early Modern Periods, 1500–1800,"' *Journal of Turkish Studies*, vol. 9, 1985, pp. 37–57.

at different, unrelated times in history. The idea that there are phases of globalization that are uncorrelated but still exhibit a similar increase of network density allows us to question the assumption that there is only one globalization process in the early modern epoch. This approach also helps to capture the intensity of global connectedness at different times in history and their effects on economy, politics and culture.[18]

Matthias Middell, Katja Naumann, and Ulf Engel suggest employing the concept of 'critical junctures of globalization' to research globalization processes. Critical junctures are moments in which new spatial relationships are established as a reaction to the effects of globalization and are shaped by constant processes of re- and de-territorialization. They are signs of clear qualitative change and are the result of 'global crises' or moments of high degrees of synchrony of conflicts and wars, which lead to new spatial relationships. The authors suggest looking into so-called 'portals of globalization' in order to determine how stable territory orders are challenged by periods of higher global connectedness. 'Portals of globalization' are understood as places and moments that experience high degrees of global connection like port cities, international trade, or immigration flows. It is in these portals that new spatial patterns are negotiated by a variety of actors. The synchrony of crises between 1780 and 1820 characterizes this period as a 'global crisis.' Although it did not result in the breakthrough of a 'new regime of territorialization,' Middell et al. interpret it as a period of 'global transition.'[19]

---

18 Joseph S. Nye and Robert O. Keohane suggest viewing globalization as an increase of globalism. They claim that globalism, which they see as a type of interdependence is characterized by networks of interconnections spread over multi-continental distances, not simply single linkages. Differentiating between economic, military, environmental, and social/cultural globalism, Nye and Keohane argue that if globalism is considered a unit of analysis for globalization different phases of globalization can be distinguished. These phases are periods of increased globalism, different to each other and not part of one single unifying globalization process. The authors mention the period between 1850 and 1915 as an example of increased globalism. It was defined by imperialism and intensified labor and capital flows that could be described as economic globalization. That economic globalism decreased again between 1914 and 1945 while military globalism rose. J.S. Nye and R.O. Keohane, 'Globalization: What's New? What's Not (And So What?)', in Nye, J.S. (ed.), *Power in the Global Information Age: From Realism to Globalization*, London, Routledge, 2004, pp. 191–200.

19 M. Middell and K. Naumann, 'Global History and the Spatial Turn: From the Impact of Area Studies to the Study of Critical Junctures of Globalization', *Journal of Global History*, vol. 5, 2010, pp. 149–170; U. Engel and M. Middell, 'Bruchzonen der Globalisierung' *Comparativ*, vol. 15, no. 5/6, 2005, pp. 5–38.

Some of the actors who brought forward global integration were, of course, merchants: they developed practices for global connectedness and expanded their spheres of influence by penetrating new economic spaces. It is thus interesting to study their networks and economic expansions to have a better scope of the degree of global economic density. Economic history of the early modern period has often focused on state interactions and state-sponsored trading companies in the analysis of long-distance trade. Institutional as well as political and military actions played a major role in explaining the success of a country's global commerce and the actions and interactions of non-state actors have been ignored. In recent years, historians have begun to study the complex transoceanic interactions of merchants and their networks. They highlight that especially along the Atlantic and Indian Ocean, different agents and their networks have played a decisive role for economic integration.[20]

Merchants in long-distance trade based their commerce on informal networks.[21] Success depended on the size, strength, and geographical reach of

20 On the British Atlantic see D. Hancock, 'The British Atlantic World: Coordination, Complexity, and the Emergence of an Atlantic Market Economy, 1651–1815,' *Itinerario* vol. 23, no. 2. 1999, pp. 107–127; and D. Hancock, 'Commerce and Conversation in the Eighteenth-Century Atlantic: The Invention of Madeira Wine,' *The Journal of Interdisciplinary History* vol. 29, no. 2, 1998, pp. 197–219; D. Hancock, *Citizens of the World: London Merchants and the Integration of the British Atlantic Community, 1735–1785*, Cambridge, Cambridge University Press, 1995; K. Morgan, 'Business Networks in the British Export Trade to North America 1750–1800' in J. McCusker, and K. Morgan (eds.), *The Early Modern Atlantic Economy*, Cambridge, Cambridge University Press, 2000, pp. 36–64; J.M. Price, 'What Did Merchants Do? Reflections on British Overseas Trade, 1660–1790', *The Journal of Economic History* vol. 49, 1989, pp. 267–284. A good read on Spanish merchant networks in the Atlantic world is X. Lamikiz, *Trade and Trust in the Eighteenth-Century Atlantic World: Spanish Merchants and their Oversea Networks*, Woodbridge, Suffolk, Boydell Press, 2010. On German networks read: K. Weber, *Deutsche Kaufleute im Atlantikhandel, 1680–1830: Unternehmen und Familien in Hamburg, Cádiz und Bordeaux*, München, Beck, 2004; M Schulte-Beerbühl, *Deutsche Kaufleute in London: Welthandel und Einbürgerung 1660–1818*, München, Oldenbourg Verlag, 2007; and M. Schulte-Beerbühl and K. Weber, 'From Westphalia to the Caribbean: Networks of German Textile Merchants in the Eighteenth Century', in A. Gestrich and M. Schulte-Beerbühl (eds.) *GHI Bulletin*, London, German Historical Institute, 2011. On the Indian Ocean trade see: C. Markovits, *The Global World of Indian Merchants 1750 to 1947, Traders of Sind from Bukhara to Panama*, Cambridge, Cambridge University Press, 2000. M. Aghassian and K. Kévonian, 'Armenian Trade in the Indian Ocean in the Seventeenth and Eighteenth Centuries, in D. Lombard and j. Aubin (eds.), *Asian Merchants and Businessmen in the Indian Ocean and Chinese Sea*, Oxford, Oxford University Press, 2000, pp. 154–177.

21 One outstanding work on the importance of kinship networks for early modern long-distance trade is Sebouh Aslanian's analysis of Julfan Armenians. Aslanian analyzes the

those networks which did not follow formally regulated orders, but despite their informal character functioned through distinct rules and mechanisms.[22] Studies of networks reveal the different forms of interactions and interrelations that constituted the basis for commercial relationships and highlight how trust and cooperation played a distinctive role in overseas trade. To explain these networks and the agency within them, it is helpful to include biographic and socio-cultural information on its associates.[23]

---

features of the large overseas trade networks that Julfan Armenians established around the globe in the seventeenth and eighteenth century. S. Aslanian, *From the Indian Ocean to the Mediterranean: The Global Trade Networks of Armenian Merchants from New Julfa*, Berkeley, University of California Press, 2011.

22 On the importance of networks throughout war and crises see S. Marzagalli, 'Establishing Transatlantic Trade Networks in Time of War: Bordeaux and the United States, 1793–1815', *The Business History Review* vol. 79, no. 4, 2005, pp. 811–844; P. Mathias, 'Risk, Credit and Kinship in Early Modern Enterprise', in: J. McCusker, and K. Morgan (eds.), *The Early Modern Atlantic Economy*, Cambridge, Cambridge University Press, 2000, pp. 15–35; P. O'Brien, 'Merchants and Bankers as Patriots or Speculators?: Foreign Commerce and Monetary Policy in Wartime, 1793–1815', in J. McCusker, and K. Morgan (eds.), *The Early Modern Atlantic Economy*, Cambridge, Cambridge University Press, 2000, pp. 250–277. See also the 2005 edition of *The William & Mary Quarterly* on the Atlantic Economy in the Age of Revolutions. C. Matson, 'The Atlantic Economy in an Era of Revolutions: An Introduction', *The William & Mary Quarterly*, vol. 62, no.3, 2005, pp. 357–364. J. McCusker, 'Worth a War? The Importance of the Trade Between British America and the Mediterranean,' in S. Marzagalli, J.R. Sofka and J.J. McCusker (eds.), *Rough Waters: American Involvement with the Mediterranean in the Eighteenth and Nineteenth Centuries, Research in Maritime History*, no. 44, 2010, pp. 7–24.

23 In-depth examples of genuine accounts of merchant groups that stress intentionality and motivation as well as economic and social backgrounds are reflected in the works of Doerflinger and Hancock. Both authors approach their subjects from multiple directions and disciplines to comprehend the diversity of their actions. By reconstructing the merchants' mentality, Doerflinger and Hancock shed light on their political and economic motivations. Both authors argue that the comprehension of social structures, attitudes, and mindsets of merchant groups is a crucial prerequisite for understanding their operations. Accordingly, they include descriptions of the social foundations of the merchant communities; the recruitment of commercial talent; motivations and risk behaviors; attitudes towards politics; family and community ties; and housing and estate building. With this method, the reactions and interactions of merchant groups to global forces become very obvious. T.M. Doerflinger, *A Vigorous Spirit of Enterprise: Merchants and Economic Development in Revolutionary Philadelphia*, Chapel Hill, North Carolina Press, 1986; D. Hancock, *Citizens of the World: London Merchants and the Integration of the British Atlantic Community, 1735–1785*, Cambridge, Cambridge University Press, 1995.

The Merchants of the Study

Eight merchants and two supercargoes are portrayed in detail in the study. The merchants featured are: William Constable, William Edgar, Hezekiah Pierrepont, Samuel Gouverneur, Peter Kemble, Herman Le Roy, William Bayard and Samuel Ferguson. A focus will also be on their acquaintances and close business partners who often invested in the same enterprises and whose activities paralleled theirs. Supercargoes, such as William and Isaac Bell, were agents of ship-owners who sailed with the ship and organized trade along the routes, usually conducting some business for their own interests as well. In the following text this group of merchants and supercargoes will be distinguished in italics as *the merchants*.

The selection of merchants was based on various requirements: first, the merchants had to be involved in global trade extending their business beyond the Atlantic Ocean. Although large numbers of New York merchants participated in the Atlantic trade, only a small group of traders had business relationships with trade in the Indian and Pacific Ocean regions. A second criteria was based on the body of source material. There are few resources left to study on New York merchants trading with Asia. The supercargoes Isaac Bell and William Bell, for instance, mainly participated in the Indian Ocean trade. Hezekiah Pierrepont and Samuel Ferguson, on the other hand, went on few Asian voyages and concentrated more on the Atlantic trade. The remaining sources offer good insights into the impressions and thoughts collected during their voyages despite the range of their global businesses being smaller than the other merchant firms in the study. Due to its high costs, primarily affluent and upper-class merchants carried out trade with Asia. To provide a broader picture of the effects of global trade, a few smaller merchants are depicted in the study. The company Ferguson & Day, for instance, is a remarkable example of how the global crises allowed smaller merchants to join in international trade and grow their businesses.

The remaining records of *the merchants* were studied using archival research that delved into their private and business correspondences. Other sources included business papers and account books, private records, wills, and legacies. Research was conducted at the New York Public Library, the New York Historical Society, the Brooklyn Historical Society and the Special Collections at Butler Library at Columbia University. The archival findings were supplemented with secondary material drawing from publications in economic, political, social, and cultural history to provide a comprehensive picture of the *merchants*' lifetimes.

The time period between 1784 and 1812 was vital to this study: the period starts with the onset of independent trade after the American Revolution and ends at the War of 1812. It was also a time of accelerated global events that greatly affected the organization of trade such as the aftermath of the American Revolution and the French and Haitian Revolutions, as well as the consequent Napoleonic Wars. Those events opened up new spaces for agency, which *the merchants* were eager to pursue. Although they were not among the 'grand' actors, like statesmen or state-controlled commercial companies, their actions were equally important for the expansion of world trade and the economic rise of the United States. By making use of economic opportunities that opened up through various global crises, merchants managed to build a commercial network based on the principles of free trade. In bringing their experiences gained from business abroad to the economy at home, these businessmen paved the way for American capitalism and the establishment of a commercial society. By 1812, on the eve of the war against England, the new republic had completely transformed its political, economic, and cultural spheres.[24] This book helps explain how these changes could transpire in only three decades by applying a global history approach that examines the mutual influences of the global and the local.

Global History

Demands for a realignment of historiography towards a more global perspective have dominated scholarly dialogues for the last two decades. A rising number of researchers beckon a new framing of history. There, however, exists a great variety of different understandings and definitions of global history making it sometimes difficult to identify methods and categories of the approach. Some authors focus on the history of globalization while others categorize it as a form of world history committed to bigger, globe-spanning questions.[25] Nonetheless, most global historians agree on the rejection of the nation as *the*

24 For more on the transformation see G. Wood, 'The Significance of the Early Republic' in R.D. Cray and M.A. Morrison (eds.), *New Perspectives of the Early Republic*, Urbana, University of Illinois Press, 1994, pp. 1–22.

25 J.R. McNeill, and W.H. McNeill, *The Human Web: A Bird's Eye View of World History*, New York, W.W. Norton, 2003; J.M. Diamond, *Guns, Germs, and Steel: The Fates of Human Societies*, New York, W.W. Norton & Company, 1998; C. Lloyd, *What on Earth Happened? The Planet, Life and People from the Big Bang to the Present Day*, London, Bloomsbury Paperbacks, 2009; D. Christian, *Maps of Time: An Introduction to Big History*, Berkeley, University of California Press, 2004.

inherent unit of analysis for historical processes. They stress instead that the historical interconnections and interdependencies have influenced the nation thereby rendering any conceptions of it as a self-contained unit obsolete.[26] This reading of global history can also be described as entangled history because it regards the connections and entanglements of all nations with each other as crucial for their historical becoming. These 'entanglements' are not only observable in our contemporary world, where daily life is in almost all dimensions interconnected with the global arena, but also several centuries prior, when the integrations of world regions had a biological, economic, and cultural impact on one another.[27]

The basic theories of global history are embedded in the ideas of the spatial turn that considers space a fundamental category for historical explanation.[28] Including aspects of space into historical analysis is by no means a new idea and has been applied by early modern scholars, but it disappeared from the historical narrative of nineteenth-century historiography and its implied theories of progress.[29] For this reason, many historians have supported a return to

---

26 Good assessments of the different claims and trends of global history are: R. Grew, 'Expanding Worlds of World-History', *The Journal of Modern History* vol. 78, December 2006, pp. 878–898; P. Manning, *Navigating World History. Historians Create a Global Past*, New York, Palgrave 2003; B. Mazlish, 'Comparing Global History to World History,' *Journal of Interdisciplinary History*, vol. 28, no.3, Winter 1998, pp. 385–395. The editorial, 'Global History' by Peer Vries is a great introduction to the different approaches and thoughts on the global history debate. P. Vries (ed.), *Global History, Österreichische Zeitschrift für Geschichtswissenschaften*, 20.jg, Band 2, 2009. On global economic history see P. Vries, ‚Global Economic History: A Survey' in P. Vries (ed.), *Global History, Österreichische Zeitschrift für Geschichtswissenschaften*, 20.jg, Band 2, 2009, pp. 133–169.

27 On the impact of flora and fauna exchange between the New and Old Words see A.W. Crosby, *The Columbian Exchange: Biological and Cultural Consequences of 1492*, Westwood, Greenwood Press, 1972.

28 See J. Osterhammel, 'Die Wiederkehr des Raumes,' *Neue Politische Literatur*, vol. 43, 1998, pp. 274–397; S. Gunn, 'The Spatial Turn: Changing Histories of Space and Place', in S. Gunn and R.J. Morris (eds.), *Identities in Space. Contested Terrains in the Western City Since 1850*, Ashgate, Burlington, 2001; K. Schlögel, *Im Raume lesen wir die Zeit: Über Zivilisationsgeschichte und Geopolitik* München, Carl Hanser, 2003; M. Middell, ‚Die Konstruktivistische Wende: Der Spatial Turn und das Interesse an der Globalisierung in der gegenwärtigen Geschichtswissenschaft' *Geographische Zeitschrift* vol. 93. Jg. no. 1, 2005, pp. 33–44.

29 Alexander von Humboldt, for example, regarded space and geography as determining factors for social and cultural processes. This approach is laid out in his work: A. von Humboldt, *Cosmos: A Sketch of a Physical Description of the Universe, Vol. II*, trans. O. Ette, Baltimore, John Hopkins University Press, 1997; and A. von Humboldt, *Cuba Werk, Studienausgabe in sieben Bänden*, Hanno Beck (ed.), vol. 3, Darmstadt. Wissenschaftliche

a writing of history approached through space. They argue that addressing the history of humankind through spatial interactions rather than narrating it in the form of chronological national histories allows for an integration of various different events and actors and their impact on historical development. By emphasizing coexistence, parallels and interconnections, these scholars prove that outside factors and invisible global forces were responsible for local happenings. They enhance and even contradict many traditional historical writings by drawing attention to external influences—which can be something as simple as a foreign crop—and their role in changing the economic, political, and social development of entire nations.[30]

It is important to not only integrate national history into a global narrative, which would take the character of a totalizing universal history, but to create instead, as the historians Michael Geyer and Charles Bright have argued, 'historiographical space that treats the national and the global as separate processes but reveals, better than established narratives do, the manifold interactions between them and the imbrications of the one with the other.'[31] Only if historians regard the interactions between the global and the local—or the universal and the particular—as reciprocal processes, which have influenced and shaped each other, can they avoid generalization and totalization. The history of the United States is a good example for such an approach.

American history was from its beginning constituted by global events. At the same time, American developments have influenced other world regions by various means ranging from the spread of political and economic models to the spread of ideas. The historic development of the United States can therefore only be fully comprehended when viewed in a global context, just

---

Buchgesellschaft, 1992. Detailed studies on Humboldt and his concept of space are: O. Ette, *Alexander von Humboldt und die Globalisierung. Das Mobile des Wissens*, Frankfurt am Main, Insel Verlag, 2009; A. Daum,'Alexander von Humboldt, die Natur als „Kosmos" und die Suche nach Einheit. Zur Geschichte von Wissen und seiner Wirkung als Raumgeschichte', *Berichte zur Wissenschaftsgeschichte 23*, 2000, pp. 243–268.

30 An example is the study on the political and economic impact of sugar in the early modern period Sidney Mintz, *Sweetness and Power*, New York, Penguin Books, 1985. On tea read P. Vries, *Zur politischen Ökonomie des Tees: Was uns Tee über die englische und chinesische Wirtschaft der Frühen Neuzeit sagen kann*, Wien, Böhlau Verlag, 2009.

31 T. Bender, 'Introduction: Historians, the Nation, and the Plentitude of Narratives' in Thomas Bender (ed.), *Rethinking American History in a Global Age*, Berkley, University of California Press, 2002, p. 13. The article quoted is C. Bright and M. Geyer, 'Where in the world is America?: The History of the United States in the Global Age,' in Thomas Bender (ed.), *Rethinking American History in a Global Age*, Berkley, University of California Press, 2002, pp. 63–100.

as global history cannot be written without America as a decisive component. This bears the challenge to write the history of the United States as a synthesis of its personal and global history, avoiding the exclusive tendencies of Exceptionalism or the inclusive approaches of a universal history. Such an approach to American history has gained momentum since the late 1990s and early 2000s. Thomas Bender's publication on the outcome of a series of conferences from 1997 to 2000 that reframed the narrative of American history in the context of a global perspective gives insights into the thoughts and motivations of the global approach.[32] A variety of publications have since shed new light on the entanglements between America and the world.[33] This book continues research of America's relations to the world and the peculiarity of the late eighteenth and early nineteenth century global epoch.

Synopsis

In particular, the study analyzes how the global situation of the late eighteenth century created a class of globally savvy businessmen. Three global crises were especially important to the formation and success of that merchant group: the American Revolution and the dissolution of the British Navigation Acts, the Napoleonic Wars, and the crises in the Caribbean. These events permitted American merchants to establish new commercial connections and to take over large parts of the re-export and carrying businesses from the European powers.

Chapter 1, 'A New Merchant Class,' illustrates how domestic financial and fiscal reforms as well as global opportunities allowed for the opening of the merchant community to include self-made men. The new merchant class was less elitist and showed a much higher degree of upward mobility than the merchant class of colonial times. This trend was to a large extent caused by the increase of business opportunities that came with the expansion of the global economy during the eighteenth century but the new republic's politics also

32 T. Bender (ed.), *Rethinking American History in a Global Age*, Berkeley, University of California Press, 2002.

33 See C.C. Mann, *1493: Uncovering the New World Columbus Created*, New York, Knopf, 2011; E.H. Gould and P.S. Onuf (eds.), *Empire and Nation: The American Revolution and the Atlantic World*, Baltimore, The Johns Hopkins University Press, 2005; I.R. Tyrrell, *Transnational Nation: United States History in Global Perspective Since 1789*, Basingstoke, Palgrave Macmillan, 2007. T. Bender, *A Nation Among Nations: America's Place in World History*, New York, Hill and Wang, 2006.

played a role. Alexander Hamilton's financial reforms, especially his establishment of financial institutions, helped to finance entrepreneurs and thus allowed the rise of self-made men. The growth of financial institutions during the New Republic was enormous. In 1781 there was only one bank in the entire country—in 1820 more than 300 existed, wildly financed through merchant capital. The history of joint stock companies is comparably astounding: in 1800 more than 300 of the private companies were registered in the United States. Europe in comparison only had a few of them.[34] These institutions played a tremendous role in economic development as they eased capital acquisition for less affluent people, resulting in an increase in social mobility and more opportunity for self-made men. Along with a change in elites after the revolution, the social changes perpetuated fragmentation of the social order. While colonial society was divided into *upper ranks* and *common ranks*, a new group within the common ranks started to differentiate itself. This group—often described as the *middling ranks, middling sorts,* or *middling class*—had formed itself by the late eighteenth century. Most of *the merchants* were self-made men and part of this middling class. How they established themselves as businessmen is explored in Chapter 1. By detailing their vertical and horizontal mobility, the section also explains how *the merchants* managed to quickly form a global network of business associates. That these networks played a decisive role in their mercantile success will then be scrutinized further in the second chapter.

Chapter 2, 'Global Entrepreneurs,' identifies how three global events helped *the merchants* expand their businesses around the globe. Special emphasis is given to their Indian Ocean trade. The chapter shows that they developed a great amount of knowledge on global interrelationships and an ability to react quickly and flexibly to worldwide political and economic changes. Because they also contributed to an increase of global interdependence, I suggest calling *the merchants* 'actors of globalization'. Their way of 'playing the global' is similar to mannerisms of globalized corporations today. Surviving business records illustrate their network of contacts around the world, which supplied a steady flow of information on markets, supply and demand, and political changes. The exchanged letters disclose a clear image of how the merchants made speculations and calculations with changing economic and political conditions. The letters also importantly reveal that *the merchants* were expanding global interconnections and tightening the world around them.

34 T.C. Cochran, 'The Business Revolution.' *The American Historical Review*, vol. 79, no.5 December 1974, p. 1458.

The merchants' commercial success was based on their communication with others, creating a global network of business partners that remained strong through war and crises and did not stop at national borders. The networks were loosely formed through acquaintances, family, and business ties and were based on mutual trust rather than a legal framework. It was this informal character that allowed those business connections to survive war and crises. Especially throughout the Atlantic Ocean, merchants built the foundation for a commercial system that was self-regulated by private rather than state actors. It was with the help of these networks that merchants managed to quickly penetrate new markets and explore new business areas. But it was also the diplomatic politics of the early administrations that helped them expand their global businesses and practice free, unhindered trade, such as the decision to stay neutral during the European wars or the extension of consular services.

Chapter 3, 'Local Spaces,' focuses on domestic changes resulting from the expansion of *the merchants'* oversea trade. In New York City, the effects of new global businesses were directly observable. While in 1784 only 12,000 people lived in the city, by 1820 the population grew tenfold. The expanding trade fostered new businesses and economic institutions, connecting more people to the world market and especially to profitable industries related to shipping. Though New York had not been an important shipbuilding center before the revolution, by 1792 thirty shipbuilders already lived in the city and by 1805 close to one hundred of these tradesmen had settled in New York.[35] Merchants influenced commercial growth beyond mere trade activities. By making new global goods available on the market, they contributed to a rising consumer society that was largely made of the new *middling class.* The advertisements that were published in all the New York papers and commercial gazettes spoke to the idea of a genteel way of life and were thus part of the forming group identity of this class.

The rise of shipping and trading secured the expansion of new markets abroad as much as at home. Many of *the merchants* were active in the development of America's 'wild land,' purchasing acres of land mostly in upstate New York to develop settlements, roads, and turnpikes. They aquired the land to either re-invest money from the expanding shipping trade or to connect the world market to America's hinterland, which supplied the exported American goods: foodstuffs and ginseng. William Constable's estate, for instance, lists more than 600,000 acres of land in New York, Ohio, and Georgia: some of the towns that still exist today are named after his children. The building of turnpikes was central to the integration of new markets. By the early nineteenth

35 J.H. Morrison, *History of New York Ship Yards*, New York, W.F. Sametz, 1909, p. 21 and 23.

century all turnpike travel was possible throughout the northeastern parts of the country. The infrastructural development of the New Republic was enormous and has been described by some historians as a 'transport revolution.'[36] As turnpike companies were organized as joint stock companies they also constituted an investment opportunity for smaller and less affluent people.

Urban development spurred the increase of shipping and trading and the New York City harbor was a magnet, pulling more people to the city from abroad or from within the United States, changing the socio-economic order tremendously. The increase of migrants brought more workers to the city. Land in Manhattan and Brooklyn was developed and mapped out and neighborhoods completely transformed. Being large landholders in Manhattan, some New York merchants not only profited from these changes but were also among the driving forces behind urban growth.

The following study draws from interdisciplinary approaches that combine economic and cultural history to portray the plurality of forces that caused human behavior and served as motivator for actions. It is divided into 'global' and 'local' sections, to analyze *the merchants'* effects on the two and to highlight the deep entanglements between them.

---

36 P.A. Gilje, 'The Rise of Capitalism in the Early Republic', *Journal of the Early Republic* vol.16, no.2, Special Issue on Capitalism in the Early Republic, 1996, p. 165.

CHAPTER 1

A New Merchant Class

Self-Made Businessmen

From America's Independence to about 1840, the United States experienced a period of substantial economic growth. Economic historian Richard Sylla has called it the beginning of 'modern economic growth'.[1] He argues that from 1650 to 1900, the United States had a relatively sustained total product growth of three to four percent per year. Before 1776 the rate was often the result of population increases, which were around three percent per year with a growth of 0.3 to 0.5 percent in product per person. After 1840, population growth was at two percent with a 1.5 to 1.6 percent product growth per person per year.[2] By 1840, the gross national product per capita in the United States was 40 to 65 percent larger than that of European countries such as France and approaching that of Great Britain.[3] Between 1776 and 1840 changes happened that radically transformed the economic landscape of the country. Old colonial institutions were replaced with new ones, paving the way to as Sylla calls it, a 'modernized financial system.'[4]

Historian Robert E. Wright considers the economic changes happening between 1787 and 1800 a 'financial revolution'.[5] Much of the development was a result of Alexander Hamilton's fiscal and financial policies that were optimized to support America's business community. According to Wright, entrepreneurs found themselves struggling with a variety of obstacles during colonial times. A high fluctuation of money supply, a shortage of specie and volatile interest rates, as well as information asymmetries made it difficult for merchants to pursue stable business enterprises. As there were almost no formal financial intermediaries, it was close to impossible for smaller merchants, who could not

1 R. Sylla, 'The United States: Financial Innovation and Adaptation' in M.D. Bordo and R. Cortes-Condo (eds.), *Transferring Wealth and Power from the Old World to the New World. Monetary and Fiscal Institutions in the 17th through the 19th Centuries*, Cambridge, Cambridge University Press, 2001, p. 231.

2 Sylla, 'Financial Innovation and Adaptation', p. 231.

3 T.C. Cochran, 'The Business Revolution.' in *The American Historical Review*, vol. 79, no.5 (December 1974), p. 1451.

4 Sylla, 'Financial Innovation and Adaptation', p. 232.

5 R.E. Wright, *Hamilton Unbound. Finance and the Creation of the American Republic*, Westport, CT, Greenwood Press, 2002, p. 97.

 | DOI 10.1163/9789004356412_003

rely on extensive kin-based networks, to obtain credit.[6] As Secretary of Treasury, Hamilton pursued financial and fiscal reforms in the 1790s that helped to create economic stability. These reforms were the fixing of the national debt, the establishment of a national bank, and the diversification of the economy. Hamilton, whose background had acquainted him with international trade, regarded the stimulation of commerce as a prime motor for the nation's well-being. He favored a diversified economy that was not only based on agriculture but also to a large extent based on manufacturing and global trade.[7]

Hamilton made three reports to Congress in the 1790s, which illustrate that the stimulation of commerce was his prime objective to achieve economic prosperity. In the First Report on Public Credit of 1790, he detailed his plan to restructure the nation's debt by issuing long-term, interest paying, and negotiable government bonds. The bonds, thought Hamilton, would create an atmosphere of security and reliability for the country's business community, which was in desperate need of a steady capital supply. The establishment of the national bank, expressed in the Second Report on Public Credit in 1790, helped consolidate the debt plan by facilitating the circulation of government funds. It introduced a financial service sector to the public replacing the dependence on informal intermediaries for credit supply and served as a source for the government to obtain money in case of emergencies. After convincing President Washington of the constitutionality of such a bank, Hamilton saw the First Bank of the United States chartered in 1791. In his third report in 1791, Hamilton laid out his vision of a diversified economy based on agriculture and manufacturing in opposition to Thomas Jefferson's agrarian economy. The report lists the benefits that manufacturing provided society by way of increasing employment and stimulating commodity exchange. The advancement of manufacturing, Hamilton argued, should be achieved through government encouragement like bounties to industry and moderate tariffs. Hamilton favored a strong national government whose policies could encourage and facilitate national commerce. In his understanding, economic prosperity and political stability were dependent on each other. Hamilton's plans were successful; by 1800 the United States had a single national money supply that was based on a specie standard. A broad class of people invested in joint stock companies that

6 Wright, *Hamilton Unbound*, p. 36.

7 M.P. Federici, *The Political Philosophy of Alexander Hamilton*, Baltimore, John Hopkins University Press, 2012, p. 190.

were often geographically distant to their homes and by 1825 the United States had about 2.4 times more banking capital than England and Wales.[8]

Wright regards the ability to finance entrepreneurs resulting from Hamilton's reforms as the main reason for U.S. economic wealth, playing a much larger part than the country's natural and human resources. The funding of business enterprises helped create new economic prosperity, which increased political stability and brought additional incentives for business expansion. For smaller and less affluent businessmen, the capacity to finance their businesses and the ability to invest money in public securities meant a fundamental difference compared to colonial times. The rise of formal intermediaries like banks and joint stock companies especially, allowed for broader access to business financing and money investment, and helped less affluent entrepreneurs sponsor their enterprises. Networks were still important for business but their values shifted more towards the supply of information than the providing of funding.[9]

Increase of maritime commerce was another prime motor for economic growth, resulting in an expansion of American foreign trade after the country's independence.[10] The number of ships involved in coastal or overseas trade increased immensely after 1793, such that the years between 1793 and 1807 have been described as the 'golden age of American shipping.'[11] Curtis Nettels states that American ship owners obtained twice as much shipping during this time as they owned in 1790: an increase from 355,000 tons to 1,089,000 tons total.[12] Combined imports and exports rose from $43 million in 1790 to $246 million in 1807.[13]

Several global factors contributed to this shipping boom. The political instability of European powers during the European Wars and president Washington's decision to stay neutral enabled American merchants to take over large parts of the carrying trade between Europe and the West Indies. Their share in the carrying trade rose from less than 50 percent in 1790 to 95 percent in 1800.[14] Furthermore, Americans were able to conduct large parts of the carrying trade

8 Federici, *Political Philosophy of Alexander Hamilton*, pp. 99–119.

9 Wright, *Hamilton Unbound*, p. 4.

10 Wright, *Hamilton Unbound*, p. 4.

11 C.P. Nettels, *The Emergence of a National Economy, 1775–1815*, Armonk, M.E. Sharpe, 1989, p. 232. Douglas C. North describes the period from 1793 to 1808 as 'years of unparalleled prosperity.' D.C. North, *The Economic Growth of the United States, 1790–1860*, Englewood-Cliffs, Prentice Hall, 1961, p. 53.

12 Nettels, *The Emergence of a National Economy*, p. 232.

13 Nettels, *The Emergence of a National Economy*, p. 232.

14 Nettels, *The Emergence of a National Economy*, p. 234.

within Europe, as well as from the Indian Ocean ports and China. The rise of foreign trade was also facilitated by local conditions such as the low costs of ship production, which was attributed to rich timber resources and shipwright skills, lower operation costs,[15] and federal legislation banning foreigners from holding shares in American vessels in 1790.[16] Shipping was stimulated by new laws such as the Navigation Act of 1789, which imposed duties on foreign vessels, as well as the Tariff Act of 1789, which significantly increased the costs of importing goods from the East Indies by foreign vessels.

In the decades after independence, the economic development of the United States was 'tied to international trade and shipping,' with most of its expansion stemming from the Northeastern and Mid-Atlantic states and unrelated to the expansion of the cotton trade.[17] New York, for example, underwent substantial changes during that time. After the revolution the city had been at a standstill: no other city in the United States had endured such a long occupation during the Revolutionary War. New York lost about two-thirds of its population and was reduced to 12,000 inhabitants. Two fires destroyed half of the buildings in the city and commerce and shipping were disrupted when major trade markets in the Caribbean closed after Britain prohibited trade with its islands for American merchants. The city, however, recovered rapidly: within six years, the population had once again reached 30,000 and commerce had returned to its former rate.[18] From 1789 to 1801 the city rose to become America's most important port, with duties increasing from less than $150,000 to $500,000 and exports increasing from $2.5 million to almost $20 million.[19]

The availability of business funding and the increase of global trade allowed more men to establish themselves as businessmen. New York's merchants became a fairly heterogeneous group with an array of different geographic and

15 Nettels states that the operating expenses for an American vessel of 250 tons roundtrip from Britain to the United States were assessed at £513 whereas the same journey performed by the British demanded twice as much. Nettels, *The Emergence of a National Economy*, p. 235.

16 While it is estimated that French shipbuilders produced at a rate of $55 to $60 a ton, Americans fabricated for $33 to $35 a ton. Nettels, *The Emergence of a National Economy*, p. 234.

17 North, *Economic Growth*, p. 46.

18 The population of New York increased from 33,131 in 1790 to 60,489 in 1800, and 96,373 in 1810. By 1810 New York had surpassed Philadelphia as the biggest northeastern port city. North, *Economic Growth*, p. 49.

19 In 1806 revenue from the port of New York constituted one-quarter of the national revenue, see Ships and Shipping of Old New York, p. 33.

cosmopolitan origins and experiences. Before the revolution, merchants and large landholders dominated the city's upper class. New York's land gentry were a politically and economically well-connected group. Associated with the mercantile elites through marriage and family ties, the two groups formed a powerful upper class.[20]

Jackson Main's study on social mobility in colonial America illustrates the social changes in New York City. He reveals, through an analysis of city directories and tax returns that the proportion of self-made men in New York's merchant class grew considerably after independence. From 1768 to 1769, the majority of the members of the New York Chamber of Commerce were large property owners, including most of New York's commercial upper class. Two-thirds of the members were born in the colonies, principally in New York where they usually descended from the colony's elite families. Main concludes that only one-third to two-fifths of the merchants in pre-revolutionary New York were self-made men who did not come from well-off families. In 1786, New York's city directory shows already a much higher proportion of self-made merchants; only one-fourth descended from wealthy landowners or merchants and at most another tenth came from well-to-do families. Roughly two-thirds were native to the state, coming from artisan and farmer families, and about one-fourth were immigrants. Main summarizes that the majority of New York's merchant class, at least 60 percent, were self-made men in 1786. An analysis of a 1791 tax list of the city's East Ward, the neighborhood of New York's wealthier merchants, also shows a relative high degree of social mobility. Although, when compared to New York's merchants in general, the list of self-made men in the East Ward is shorter, half of them still came from modest origins.[21] Commercial growth fostered a considerable increase of self-made merchants, which resulted in a plurality of occupation entries and paths.

20 See Frederic Jaher's comprehensive study of the upper classes in the United States. F.C. Jaher, *The Urban Establishment: Upper Strata in Boston, New York, Charleston, Chicago, and Los Angeles*, Urbana, University of Illinois Press, 1982, p. 60ff.

21 J. Main, *The Social Structure of Revolutionary America*. Princeton, Princeton University Press, 1965. The most famous example for New York's upward mobility and the possibility of entering the city's merchant class without family ties or personal capital is the story of the eminent New York merchant John Jacob Astor. Astor, who was born in 1763 as son of a butcher in Waldorf, Germany, managed to become one of America's first merchant millionaires, although he had embarked to the United States in November 1783 with nothing more than 'twenty-five dollars in money, a merchandise stock of seven flutes, and a passage paper entitling him to a berth in the steerage with sailor's fare of salt beef and biscuit.' Within two years, Astor owned his own place of business at Water Street and was

This can also be noticed in the different ways *the merchants*' entered business:

William Constable started his business career in 1771 as apprentice for Phyn, Ellice & Company, which was active in the fur trade. Family ties helped him obtain the position—James Phyn was his brother in law—which allowed him to gain business insight and make valuable contacts. William Constable, William Duer, Alexander Macomb, and William Edgar had known each other in the Northwest posts of the Great Lakes area of Detroit and Michillimackinac, where the British fur business was posted. In 1774, Phyn, Ellice & Company, which at that time was still a 'small commercial middleman prominent in the fur trade of the period,'[22] had relocated to London as the fur trade became more disorganized with the prospect of political upheaval.[23] In London they stabilized their business within a decade, joining the firm of John Inglis who had good business contacts to the West Indies, in 1787.[24] The firm became known as Phyn, Ellice & Inglis. Constable benefitted not only from their important trade network but also their financial success, which gave him many of his early contacts and financed many of his enterprises.

William Edgar had established himself in the fur business after coming to Detroit as a financial agent of the British Army. He was active in the fur trade between New York, Detroit, and Montreal and in 1779 joined the firm of Alexander Macomb. The firm accumulated a fortune in military contracting.

---

engaged in the fur trade. By 1800 he had already accumulated half a million dollars in wealth and was known as the leading merchant in the fur trade as well as a prosperous China merchant. His career was marked by lucky encounters; on his journey to America he met a successful businessman who told him about the fur business and on one of his trips to London, an East India House official granted him a license to trade freely in any port monopolized by the East India Company. His wife, Sarah Todd, who was said to have a good sense for furs, also helped his business. Among others, Astor became owner of the American fur company, erected a large trading network penetrating deep into the American West and bought large parts of Manhattan's real estate. Although his grand idea of establishing a large trading network in the Pacific Northwest, known as Astoria, from where furs could be directly shipped to China, failed, he nevertheless remained New York's most affluent merchant. Upon his death on March 29, 1848, Astor was by far the richest man in America, leaving behind a fortune of $20 million. *Dictionary of American Biography*, edited by Allen Johnson, vol. 1, New York: Charles Scribner's Sons, 1928, p. 397f.

22 Fleming, *Phyn, Ellice and Company*, p. 11.

23 James Phynn had embarked with his family to London on 10 November 1774. In London, his first business address was the New York Coffee-house. Fleming, *Phyn, Ellice and Company*, p. 23.

24 Fleming, *Phyn, Ellice and Company*, p. 38.

In 1783 Edgar left the company taking a share of £48,000 New York currency[25] and afterwards engaged in a variety of business activities.[26]

Hezekiah Pierrepont was familiarized with business through his uncle Isaac Beers in New Haven and during his time as a clerk at the Custom House in New York in 1790. While in Philadelphia between 1791 and 1794, he made a small fortune in the speculation of national debt. Back in New York, the money enabled him to establish the firm Leffingwell & Pierrepont.[27]

For William Bayard, becoming a merchant ran in the family: his father, Colonel William Bayard, had been a successful merchant before the revolution. In 1786 William Bayard Jr. decided to launch into the international shipping business. With some money to invest and with his partner Herman Le Roy, he founded the firm Le Roy, Bayard & Co. in December 1786.[28] According to Walter Barrett, Bayard raised resources by selling his 150-acres farm located on the western side of Broadway. He divided the land into lots, for which he asked up to $20,000 per lot.[29] Similar to the Leffingwell & Pierrepont, Constable & Ruckers, and Gouvereneur & Kemble firms, the firm Le Roy, Bayard & Co. started trading in the Atlantic, which achieved enough profit to fund further enterprises. Herman Le Roy, Bayard's business partner, was also the son of a well-known New York merchant, who owned Jacob Le Roy & Sons. While his brothers continued their father's legacy, Herman Le Roy joined William Bayard in business.

Very little is known about the Gouverneur brothers' introduction to business. In *Ships and Shipping of Old New York*, it is mentioned that the family had been involved in trade with the West Indies during colonial times,[30] assumedly through family ties. Peter Kemble, the business partner of Samuel Gouverneur, was the son of Peter Kemble Sr., a prominent merchant and political figure of New Jersey. Growing up in a business environment, Kemble must have been well informed on mercantile practices when he started his career at the counting house of Archibald McGall. During his early business years he was mostly engaged in mercantile relations with the West Indies and resided several years

---

25 Until 1785 each state had its own monetary system. In New York the common unit was the New York pound.

26 D. Dill Jr., 'Portrait of an Opportunist: The Life of Alexander Macomb.' *Watertown Daily Times*, 9 September 1990, accessed at http://mlloyd.org/gen/macomb/text/amsr/wt.htm, 13 December 2012.

27 Photocopy of Pierrepont Family History prepared by John Jay Pierrepont for nephew J. Jay Pierrepont II. 1904, *Pierrepont Collection, Series II*, Pierrepont family papers, ARC.263, Brooklyn Historical Society.

28 Steward, *Le Roy Family*, p. 22.

29 Barett, *Old Merchants of New York*, p. 188.

30 *Ships and Shipping of Old New York*, p. 31.

in St. Kitts and St. Eustatia in the Lesser Antilles. There he became well acquainted with the Atlantic trade system, which proved of great importance for the company he later founded.

Samuel Ferguson was acquainted with business in his uncle Robert Griffith's Philadelphia office. During his time as an apprentice, Ferguson traveled extensively, accustoming himself with foreign business practices that then enabled him to open his own company with John Day.

Supercargo Isaac Bell was also introduced to business through family. Bell's father was a New York merchant active in the Atlantic trade, mostly the West Indies trade with strong personal ties to the fur business. William Bell started as clerk in the firm of Constable & Rucker who then sent him as supercargo on various voyages.[31]

Thomas Doerflinger distinguishes four typical career paths for young Philadelphia merchants in revolutionary Philadelphia. A first and easy way to become a merchant was through family wealth. The men entered the firm of their fathers or other family members or had enough capital to fund and operate at least a third of a ship. A second possibility was through good connections, which helped merchants who came from well-connected families but had meager capital. Their contacts helped them to establish a network of associates or allowed them to begin their career as clerks, apprentices, or supercargoes in well-established firms. They could thus collect knowledge and business contacts through which they would later be able to obtain local credits and patronage. Third, the dry goods business with England was a favorable entrance for merchants with limited means.[32] Doerflinger's analysis, which draws from business directories and tax information, reveals that it was mainly in this sector that minor middling classes like mariners, artisans, grocers and shopkeepers managed to ascend their social position and become merchants and wholesalers. Captains also often took this path as they either owned shares on ships or were allowed to take some freight space for their own business, which enabled them to make additional profit. Similarly, artisans were able to make more money by trading their products to larger markets. This was particularly common during years of war and crises, which created scarcity of certain products. The 'occupationally mobile merchants' constituted about one-third of Philadelphia's merchant class in the years from 1774 to 1799.[33]

31 Tailby, *Chapters*, p. 182.

32 Doerflinger, *Vigorous Spirit of Enterprise*, pp. 47–48.

33 Doerflinger, *Vigorous Spirit of Enterprise*, p. 50. Doerflinger states that of the sixty-six people who were merchants in Philadelphia in 1774, twenty-two had been retailers, mariners, artisans or of other occupation in 1756. Of the 140 merchants in 1785, 51 had been in

A fourth career path was achieved through contacts and experience abroad. The Atlantic trade offered a variety of trading possibilities and some merchants managed to establish valuable business connections sailing around the Atlantic world. Likewise, many immigrants who became merchants used their connections at home to gain information, establish trade channels, or obtain credit. A large part of the trading enterprises by American merchants were at least in some part financed through outside credits. In particular the dry good houses of London, Bristol, and Manchester guaranteed a steady flow of credit to American merchant houses, which enabled a successful minor merchant to operate a considerable amount of capital.[34]

Doerflinger's conclusion that entering Philadelphia's merchant circle was not difficult when one had contacts, capital, or experience, can also be extended to the merchants of New York. One finds at least one of *the merchants* for each of the four paths mentioned above. A few came from merchant families. William Bayard and Peter Kemble were fortunate sons who could draw from family assets and an early business education. But it was possible to ascend social status relatively fast even when coming from a less affluent family background, exemplified by William Constable, Hezekiah Pierrepont, and Isaac Bell. Their successful careers prove that business connections and local patronage were just as valuable to enter the merchant circle as family ties, even though most of them secured their business connections through intermarriages. The supercargoes William Bell and Isaac Bell, as well as Pierrepont who started his career as clerk, are great examples of how experience in minor positions helped entry into the business world. All *the merchants* had strong affiliations with local and international business partners and often obtained funds through creditors abroad. In this case it was of great advantage to work with a European-based agent, as in the case of Constable & Rucker or Ferguson & Day, or to maintain good relationships with business partners in shipping houses in Europe. Most of *the merchants* could draw on business experience collected during their adolescence, whereas the fur trade and the West Indies trade were helpful career entries. What is striking about *the merchants* is their relatively high horizontal and vertical mobility. They frequently moved to other cities and even continents. Almost all of them were either born outside New York, had migrated to the United States, or had at least spent some time in Europe or the West Indies.

other occupation in 1774, and of the 256 merchants in 1799, 35 percent had been affiliated with other occupations in 1791. These numbers also identify a remarkable increase of merchants in general—a result of the trade boom after independence.

34 Doerflinger, *Vigorous Spirit of Enterprise* pp. 47–57.

Main as well as Doerflinger's study show that changes in the merchant community already started happening during revolutionary times suggesting that the increase of global economic opportunities during the eighteenth century opened up room for social change. After independence, that trend accelerated. During the revolution, many of New York's elite families left, leaving room for new people. Their exodus, along with the city's commercial expansion after independence allowed for a relatively easy entry into the city's merchant class, a trend similarly observed in Boston and Philadelphia, which were also major ports in the global trade. In the southern planting aristocracies of South Carolina and Virginia, upward mobility remained more restricted.[35]

According to historian Burton Bledstein, that social change is also observable in the semantic popularization of the concept of 'middling sorts'. The usage of 'middling' as in 'middling ranks', 'middling sorts', and 'middling station' has appeared since the seventeenth century and was usually meant to distinguish a social group within the category of the 'common ranks'.[36] Ranks were rigid, inflexible social categories that stood for the social organization given at birth in a time when society was classified into 'gentry' and 'common ranks'. During the eighteenth century the term 'middling' began appearing more regularly, pointing 'to a development within the dual classification of rank.' Certain groups felt the need to distinguish and separate themselves from the lower bottom of the common ranks. These groups consisted of artisans, merchants, professionals, and farmers, who were described by contemporaries as 'the middle sorts who live well', 'honest sober men who mind their own business', 'the better kind of people', 'orderly and industrious'.[37] Bledstein points out that the usage of 'classes' instead of 'ranks' exemplifies another semantic change. The rigid classification of social ranks began to soften and transition towards a more neutral grouping less determined by birth and wealth. 'Ranks differed in absolute kind, not in degrees' and could thus not capture the changing realities of late eighteenth and early nineteenth century. With the increasing market economy, social status became linked to talent rather than birth and a popular understanding that social classes that were made by men—not universally given—began to take shape.[38]

---

35 Jaher, *The Urban Establishment*, p. 157.

36 B.J. Bledstein, 'Introduction: Storytellers to the Middle Class,' in B.J. Bledstein and R.D. Johnson (eds.), *The Middling Sorts: Explorations in the History of the American Middle Class*, New York, Routledge, 2001, p. 3.

37 Bledstein, *Storytellers*, p. 3.

38 Bledstein, *Storytellers*, pp. 3–5.

In 1830, the Boston printer Joseph T. Buckingham talked about the 'middling classes' as those, 'who in contrast to the unproductive poor and the unprofitable rich worked for a living and whose inextinguishable desire for more gave birth to invention and imparted vigor to enterprise. [...] the farmers, the mechanics, the manufacturers, the traders, who carry on professionally the ordinary operations of buying, selling and exchanging merchandize.'[39] Traveler John Lambert also divided American society into different classes. In 1810, he writes: 'The higher and middling classes of the Americans who reside chiefly in the great towns, or their neighborhoods, live generally speaking, in a more luxurious manner than the same description of people in England.'[40]

However, these middling ranks differed from the later middling classes of the industrialized society. Industrialization brought about an increased awareness of class identity and need to further distinguish among groups. Laboring and working people felt a need to separate themselves from the middling class. They labeled themselves the 'producing class' as compared to the middle class of vendors, distributors or entrepreneurs.[41] The bourgeoisie of rich merchants and manufactures also shaped an awareness of itself as a distinct class differing from the middle class or petite bourgeois of artisans, shop owners.

The boundaries and established structures of social status and career lines were mitigated during the eighteenth century. Global economic integration and political changes were decisive factors to their fading.[42] The American

39 G.S. Wood, 'Was America Born Capitalist?' *The Wilson Quarterly* vol. 23, no.1, (Spring 1999), p. 44.

40 Lambert, *Travels*, p. 187.

41 Bledstein, *Storytellers*, p. 9.

42 The biographies of London merchants trading in the Atlantic world from 1735 to 1785, analyzed in Hancock's study *Citizens of the World,* show a similar social heritage. These merchants came from middling families with little to no material possessions. Many of them were born overseas or in Scotland and left their homes early on to move to the mercantile centers of Glasgow, London, or abroad where they worked and became shippers and traders. After they had established themselves as merchants in London, they used their experience from abroad for their first trading ventures. Most of them were engaged in the private trade of African slaves, purchased American lands, and built plantations in the new colonies. Hancock points to the effects of the Seven Years War on the growth of business opportunities for English merchants. Interestingly enough, all of Hancock's merchants, although they were neither from London nor from aristocratic families still managed to become leaders of London's mercantile community. Their biographies draw a different picture than that often outlined by historians on British history, which usually assumed that merchants were either taking on family businesses or were part of elite circles, where formal apprenticeship and financial help of one's family were the common career paths for successful merchants. Hancock, *Citizens of the World*, pp. 41–44.

Revolution and the subsequent financial and commercial changes influenced the social structure of America's merchant community. Its relatively low stratification remained, however, a distinct characteristic of the period from 1780 to 1830. By the mid-nineteenth century America's merchant class had already become less open to upward mobility and trade was in the control of few merchant houses.[43]

Merchant Networks

The opening of New York's society to merchants from lesser-off and immigrant families proved to be very beneficial for the city's commercial expansion. The merchants' diverse origins and geographical mobility helped establish international trade and information networks channeling their mercantile enterprises. These networks constituted a large part of eighteenth century trade infrastructure. They allowed entrepreneurs to enhance and stretch their operations to wider regional, national, and international markets while at the same time reducing the costs of acquiring information. Business partners provided information regarding demand and surplus of distant markets, the availability and quality of goods, and about new opportunities and enterprises. The value of that information cannot be underestimated. Networks obviated the need for market research, the monitoring of competition or the appraisal of cost calculations. Furthermore, networks were important channels of finance. On the one hand, they often provided entry money into business (overseas voyages required an especially high amount of capital), and on the other hand, they helped organize the diffusion of payments, in the form of bills of exchange and local credit providers. Historians of the Atlantic economy have long written on the Atlantic commercial system in light of the competition between the different states and their national organizations of commerce. Recently, however, scholars have started to highlight the importance of an actor-centered scholarship. They emphasize that merchants collaborated for various enterprises, often ignoring national borders. These enterprises, though characterized by a multitude of different relations and interactions, still exhibit specific transregional characteristics that eased the operations of business. As they were

---

43 S. Beckert and J.B. Rosenbaum, *The American Bourgeoisie: Distinction and Identity in the Nineteenth Century*, New York, Palgrave Macmilian, 2010. By 1830 and 1840, leading firms were G.G.& S. Howland, A.A. Low & Brothers, N.L & G. Griswold, and John Jacob Astor. Jaher, *Urban Establishment*, p. 180.

more embedded in social and cultural practices than institutional or national frameworks, a closer look at those trans-Atlantic networks allows for a micro-level approach to Atlantic commerce, emphasizing the interrelation of the local and the global. They also reveal the infrastructure of Atlantic commerce that constituted an unprecedented economic entity by the late eighteenth century, characterized by, as Hancock writes: '[a] surge in commercial correspondence, the growth in the number and intricacy of supplier/consumer relationships, the rise in the availability and flexibility of financial services involving credit and insurance, and the increase in the publication and dissemination of maritime and mercantile information.'[44]

Trust and personal connections were key to international business relationships. Although ethnic and religious affiliations often helped, they were not crucial. Of the analyzed New York merchants, most established their business networks through personal connections. Recommendations were the most common method for finding business partners in new markets. A merchant received a letter of introduction from an affiliated partner or friend, which he then sent to the desired partner. The confidence in these mediations was so high that many times merchants did not even bother to establish contact before and simply sent an introduction letter with their supercargoes. In 1790, for instance, when William Constable dispatched the ship *Washington* to the East Indies, he supplied his supercargo William Bell with a letter to John Forbes, who was recommended to him by his English business partners Phyn, Ellice & Inglis. Bell also carried a letter for Henry Forester in Bombay, India, in which Constable wrote:

> Dear Sir,
> Our mutual friends Mr. Phyn, Ellice and Inglis of London having promised to introduce us to your correspondence. We do ourselves the pleasure of addressing to you. The present will be handed you by Mr. William Bell Supercargo of our ship Washington who will value himself on you, having fully expressed our views and intentions to Mr. Bell. We refer to this Gentlemen for information as to what relates to the Cargo and recommending him at same time to your Civilities and guaranteeing any Engagements which he may make.[45]

---

44 Hancock, *The British Atlantic World*, p. 111.

45 William Constable to John Forbes, 10 December 1790. *William Constable Letterbooks 1790–1791*, Constable-Pierrepont papers. Manuscripts and Archives. The New York Public Library. Astor, Lenox, and Tilden Foundations.

Another way to increase international business connections was to join with an established business partner. When Bayard's cousin James McEvers joined the company of Le Roy, Bayard & Co. his contacts were a valuable supplement to the firm's business.[46] A note in the company's correspondence lists the letters of introductions to European merchant houses that had been furnished to McEvers and which he brought into the firm. The list includes houses in Naples, Leghorn, Genoa, Marseilles, Valencia, Barcelona, Malaga, Cadiz, and Lisbon, and it permitted Le Roy, Bayard & Co. to expand their business into the Mediterranean and Iberian markets.[47] Similarly, William Constable profited from the European network of his partner John Rucker who helped him establish commercial relations with solid European bank houses like Le Couteulx in Paris and Van Staphorst in Amsterdam.[48] Rucker also had contacts to commercial houses in London and Hamburg, as well as to Caribbean sugar plantations. With Rucker's return to Europe in September 1784, the firm secured its international place in business and finances.

Family and kinship connections entailed a different form of assurance and credence than loose business links. Especially for merchants who had not yet established a name for themselves and were not associated with big merchant houses, familial connections were often the only reliable basis for conducting business. The firms of Gouverneur & Kemble, Le Roy, Bayard & Co., and Leffingwell & Pierrepont were all established by partners connected through family. Gouverneur & Kemble could rely on their family's strong connection to Curaçao. Their uncle, Nicholas Gouverneur, was married to Maria Winkler, the daughter of Herman Winkler and Gertrude Van Kinswilder, who was born on Curaçao. Their son, Isaac Gouverneur, opened the business firm Gouverneur & Rutgers in Curaçao with his brother in law, Captain Anthony Rutgers. Le Roy, Bayard & Co. relied heavily on their family connection in London where

---

46 McEvers was also stationed as an agent for the firm in Paris. Jacob Le Roy & Sons Correspondence and Papers 1791–1832, New York Historical Society Mss Collection.

47 Contacts: In Naples: Edmund Noble; in Leghorn: Frans. O'Honore Berte and Porter Huddart & Garland; in Genoa: Wollaston & Fasy; in Marseilles: Collique & Co. and Samadet & Cushing; in Valencia: Melchior Ferrer; in Barcelona: Jerome Facchella and A.B. Gasso & Co.; in Malaga: John Murphy; in Cadiz: James Duff and M. Lopez & Co.; in Lisbon: J.V. Montano; and in St. Sebastian: the Widow de Bermingham & Sons. The letters were furnished to McEvers by four of his business contacts, which were the firms of Joseph Garland & Alex MacKinnon, Ch. Th. Cazenove & Batard, William Ballantyne and Fermin DeTastet & Co. 'Letters of Introduction furnished Mr. M. Evers', Bayard Correspondence 1751–1832, Bayard-Campbell-Pearsall families papers. Manuscripts and Archives. The New York Public Library. Astor, Lenox, and Tilden Foundations.

48 Davis, *William Constable*, p. vii–viii.

William's father Colonel William Bayard was an important mediator for the company's business. Ferguson's contact was his uncle Robert Griffith in Philadelphia. For William Constable, kinship relations had helped to boost his business in several ways. One was the marriage of his sister Eweretta to James Phyn, which not only helped Constable to obtain clerkship at the Phyn, Ellice & Company's New York post, but also proved an important source for Constable's later commercial activities. Another valuable connection was his own nuptial bond connecting him to William Edgar and the marriage of his daughter Ann, who wedded Hezekiah Pierrepont. His other children married into the McVickar, Livingston and Duane families.[49] William Edgar also married strategically; his second marriage was to the daughter of David Van Horne, a prosperous New York merchant. Further relationships were achieved through the marriages of his children: his daughter Maria was wedded to Garner G. Howland, the founder of the merchant firm G.G. and S.S. Howland that was involved in the coffee import; his son Edgar Jr., married Cornelia Le Roy, daughter of Herman Le Roy. His daughter Juliet married Herman Le Roy Jr.[50] The Le Roy family was intermarried with a variety of affluent New York families: Caroline Le Roy was married to Daniel Webster and William Le Roy married Elizabeth Emmet the daughter of Thomas Addis Emmet in 1819. Further family relations were to the Clarksons, Van Hornes, Livingstons, Dyckmans, Gouverneurs, Hoffmans, Crugers, Barnewalls, Rutgers, Beekman, Otis, and Fish families.[51] The Kemble family was related to the Bayard family through the marriage of Peter Kemble Sr., and Gertrude Bayard as well as to the Gouverneur family through the wedding of Peter Kemble Jr., and Gertrude Gouverneur. Connections to mercantile and political elites through kinship were not a prerequisite for becoming a merchant but they certainly helped to ease commercial success. The high number of intermarriages between affluent New York families shows that the merchants themselves attached a great importance to these links.[52]

---

49 Duyckinck and Cornell, *The Duyckinck and Allied Families*, p. 18.

50 Duyckinck and Cornell, *The Duyckinck and Allied Families*, p. 17.

51 Steward, *Le Roy Family*, p. 22ff.

52 The importance of kinship networks for mercantile business is highlighted in Rachel Tamar Van's dissertation on the Perkins, Forbes, and Sturgis families in Boston. Tracing the commercial networks of those merchant families from 1740 to 1840, Van analyzes how family bonds have worked to shape economics and politics in early America as a 'core market institution used for protection from risk and speculation.' Van draws a clear picture of the merchants' networks around the world and their function for the management of business showing that cultural and social capital were just as valuable for the formation of successful enterprises as was financial capital. R.T. Van, 'Free Trade & Family

Local patronage as well as memberships in clubs and societies were further means in establishing reliable business contacts. Merchant companies often helped friends and their children by introducing them to their business partners. Gouverneur & Kemble for instance helped give the firm Rutgers, Seaman & Odgen a jumpstart by referring them to Smith & Atkinson of London. On 1 February 1796, they issued a letter of introduction in favor of Benjamin Seaman of the house Rutgers, Seaman & Ogden as a 'young gentlemen of Respectability & whose Welfare We feel ourselves interested for.' They further helped the young company by giving them a share on their ship *Briscis* loaded with a cargo of sugar and dyewood to Europe. Benjamin Seaman was sent to sail with the ship and seek the best markets for the goods, most likely in Amsterdam or Hamburg. Gouverneur & Kemble also equipped them with letters to the houses of Van Eghen in Amsterdam and DeChapeaurouge in Hamburg.[53]

Clubs and societies, although often formed for different reasons, were a further beneficial source for contacts. For example, the Sub Rosa Dining Club was attended by several of the city's influential merchants such as Nicholas Cruger, Edward Goold, Peter Kemble, Nicholas Gouverneur, Captain Crowninshield, Archibald Gracie and Robert Lenox and although its house rules stated, 'no motion on business of any kind shall be proposed or debated upon, at or after dinner,'[54] it was still an advantageous place to mingle and establish business bonds. *The merchants*' involvement in these establishments as well as their value for local patronage and politics—also important means for establishing commercial bonds—will be further discussed in later sections.

Three purposes of commercial networks were especially relevant for a merchant's mercantile operations: information, finance, and trade operations. The seventeenth and eighteenth centuries had witnessed a rise in information circulation, which also greatly affected commercial correspondence. The spread of information through the development of the postal service and the packet ship had tremendous effects on the integration of the trans-Atlantic region as people were now able to obtain news on a more regular basis. Merchants were anxious promoters of improvements in the communication systems as reliable information had a direct impact on business outcomes and separating information from freight was a great advantage.[55]

Values: Kinship Networks and the Culture of Early American Capitalism', PhD Thesis, Columbia University, 2010.

53 Gouverneur & Kemble to Smith & Atkinson, 1 February 1796, Gouverneur and Kemble, Letter book, 1794 May–1796 June, New York Historical Society Mss Collection.

54 Sub Rosa Club, Records 1795–1800, New York Historical Society Mss Collection.

55 I.K. Steele, *The English Atlantic, 1675–1740: An Exploration of Communication and Community*, Oxford, Oxford University Press, 1986, p. 214.

The communication of commercial and market intelligence constituted a great part of *the merchant's* daily routine and their remaining letterbooks give insight into the magnitude of their epistolary proceedings.[56] The letterbook of Gouverneur & Kemble from May 1794 to June 1796 is 747 pages long and besides business news, the letters also contain information on political and social news as well as news about merchants and their families. Often they also describe local gossip or information on marriages or other life events. In this sense they resembled the common style of business correspondence during that time and highlight the linkage between a person's economic and social reputation.[57]

The receipt and consignment of information in a timely manner was crucial to a successful business operation. Communication with business associates in distant ports provided valuable market information. This allowed merchants to stock their vessels more effectively as they had the assurance that their goods would find an open market. *The merchants*' correspondence bear numerous examples of how market information sent by their business partners were decisive for deciding which goods to ship out. Letters coming from overseas often entailed price currents and memorandums of goods suitable for the markets of the respective ports. Le Roy, Bayard & Co. for instance received regular price currents from their contacts in Europe, most notably from LeHavre, Amsterdam, Leghorn, and Smyrna.[58] Another example of the

56 On the importance of letter writing in the eighteenth century see E.T. Bannet, *Empire of Letters: Letter Manuals and Transatlantic Correspondence, 1688–1820*, Cambridge, Cambridge University Press, 2005; K. Dierks, *In My Power: Letter Writing and Communications in Early America*, Philadelphia, University of Pennsylvania Press, 2009.

57 Francesca Trivellato also points to the importance of merchant letters for the circulation of information and international business. F. Trivellato, 'Merchants' letters across geographical and social boundaries', in F. Bethencourt and F. Egmond (eds.), *Cultural Exchange in Early Modern Europe. Volume III, Correspondence and Cultural Exchange in Europe 1400 to 1700*, Cambridge, Cambridge University Press, 2007, pp. 80–103.

58 See for instance, 'Memorandum of India Goods suitable for the Leghorn Market', *Leghorn Price Current*, 23 September 1816; *LeHavre Price Current*, 31 August 1817; *Smyrna Price Current*, 22 October 1806; *Amsterdam Price Current*, Gebhard & Company, 4 November 1819; Also in the collection are the 'Memorandum of goods suitable for trade'; 'India Goods proper for the Leghorn Market with the actual prices'; and a 'Memorandum of a Cargo suitable for Commerce on the West Indies' Foreign Trade, Bayard Papers, Bayard-Campbell-Pearsall families papers. Manuscripts and Archives. The New York Public Library. Astor, Lenox, and Tilden Foundations. From other collections: 'William Constable: India Manufactured Articles Recommended for the New York Market', December 1788, Constable Papers, Constable-Pierrepont papers. Manuscripts and Archives. The New York Public Library. Astor, Lenox, and Tilden Foundations.'Memorandum for Gouverneur Morris', New York, 23 October 1788, Constable Papers, William Constable Correspondence,

benefits of market intelligence is William Constable's reaction after he found out that a load of Batavia sugar was desirable in Europe. His ship *Washington* had just sailed for Bombay and Canton when he received a letter from Phyn, Ellice & Inglis in London in 1791 who informed him:

> ...[A] Cargo of Sugar from Batavia would be very desirable. The Article is become very dear in Europe, the Consumption increases more than the Cultivation on the Islands—which with the disturbances in the French West Indies must keep up the price this year and the Next.[59]

Constable immediately sent out a letter to Bell, his supercargo on the *Washington*, advising him to bring sugar from Batavia on his return journey. He also thought about sending another vessel to Batavia to buy more sugar.

Similarly, it was with the help of Phyn, Ellice & Inglis that Constable realized his first plans of sending a vessel to the East Indies. Hearing of the promising profits of the *Empress of China*, Constable reified his plans in a joint China enterprise with William Edgar in 1784. International contacts provided by Phyn, Ellice & Inglis and William Morris helped him gather information regarding the trade. He corresponded with Antwerp, Cape Town, Calcutta, Canton and the West Indies. One of his contacts were the Bondfield brothers, two Englishmen who were both actively engaged in the East Indies trade. One as a member of the British East India Company in Calcutta and the other in the European China trade.[60] A letter with more precise instructions came from

---

Constable-Pierrepont papers. Manuscripts and Archives. The New York Public Library. Astor, Lenox, and Tilden Foundations. A list of East India Goods Suitable for the Philadelphia Market, 22 October 1789, Constable Papers, Constable Shipping Papers, Constable-Pierrepont papers. Manuscripts and Archives. The New York Public Library. Astor, Lenox, and Tilden Foundations. 'Estimate of a Cargo of Calcutta Bale Goods suited to the New York market,' Oliver Wolcott to Solomon Ingraham and William Taylor, 12 January 1805, Oliver Wolcott letterbook 1803–1808. Manuscripts and Archives. The New York Public Library. Astor, Lenox, and Tilden Foundations.

59 Davis, *William Constable*, p. 167.

60 Morris sent Constable abstracts from a letter he received from Bondfield who advised him to sail to Isle of France before proceeding to India. He recommended bringing a freight of liquors, irons and specie and in particular: Madeira wine, gin, brandy, rum, port, copper, tin and iron as well as turpentine and spars. He also advised going to L'Orient in France where they could take freight on board belonging to the servants of the different European companies. Attached to the letter is an abstract of a letter sent to Bondfield by a merchant of the Isle of France. Robert Morris to William Constable 12 February 1784, Constable Papers, William Constable Correspondence, Constable-Pierrepont papers. Manuscripts and Archives. The New York Public Library. Astor, Lenox, and Tilden Foundations.

Frederic Molineux who informed him in detail about the best routes, times to sail, and commodities to bring.[61]

During times of war and crises timely information was particularly crucial. The wars in Europe were a great opportunity for American merchants to supply goods to excess-demand markets and the more information they had about those demands, the better. Furthermore, the constantly changing political situation made it necessary to be up to date to avoid the risk of having a vessel seized by the European powers. *The merchants*' correspondence and network with European partners increased enormously during that time. These exchanges did not only fill freight shortages faster, they also helped prevent gluts. Especially in the East Indies trade where large sums were invested, it was crucial to know which goods were in demand in the foreign markets as well as which were in short supply at home and in re-export markets.[62] Markets were subject to swings caused by season and the arrival of ships which is why *the merchants* usually advised their supercargoes to observe how many other American ships were at the ports to judge which goods to load. In 1790, Constable complained several times that with too many ships going to the East Indies too much tea had been imported to the United States, leaving a large supply for several years.

> I do not know what can be done with the Tea which will be imported this Season, if the thirteen Vessels all arrive We shall have full three Years supply & six ships have sailed for the next year.[63]

Regular exchange with business associates also yielded other advantages besides information on market statuses. It enabled merchants to notify their partners in advance about the cargos sent so they could prepare for the delivery by announcing it in local newspapers or writing to their local associates.

---

61 Frederick Molineux to William Constable 19 June 1785, Constable Papers, William Constable Correspondence, Constable-Pierrepont papers. Manuscripts and Archives. The New York Public Library. Astor, Lenox, and Tilden Foundations.

62 On 2 October 1804, the New York merchant Oliver Wolcott informed his trade partners Hope & Co. in Amsterdam that he was expecting a cargo from Canton in early spring 1805. He wanted Hope & Co. to send him timely information on their markets in Amsterdam. Also enclosed in the letter was a price current on provisions, Oliver Wolcott to Hope & Co., New York 2 October 1804, Oliver Wolcott letterbook 1803–1808. Manuscripts and Archives. The New York Public Library. Astor, Lenox, and Tilden Foundations.

63 Constable to Morris, 15 June 1790. William Constable Letterbooks 1790–1791, Volumes, Constable-Pierrepont families papers. Manuscripts and Archives. The New York Public Library. Astor, Lenox, and Tilden Foundations.

It also gave them time to collect and negotiate the return cargo before the ship even arrived. Speed and steadiness of information not only eased business between foreign ports, it also made commerce more efficient, ultimately saving time and expenses, and allowed merchants to pursue more voyages. Additionally, it was a means to communicate about products. Merchants informed themselves about new commodities, how they were stored, shipped, distributed, and consumed and which ones were suitable for which markets. They received samples of textiles, and lists stating availability, quality, prices, and ranges of commodities. Emphasizing the importance of these means of information exchange, John McCusker and Cora Gravesteijn call commodity price currents, exchange rate currents, and money currents the antecedents of financial journalism.[64]

A further purpose of networks was to secure finance and credit proceedings. Credit was not only made available through networks, they were also used to channel payments. Most of *the merchants* used English houses for their overseas transactions. London was still the financial capital for Americans and it was important for merchants to be on good footing with prominent London merchant houses. Phyn, Ellice & Inglis and Smith & Atkinson were two houses working with many of *the merchants*. Samuel Smith, who was a partner of Smith & Atkinson also owned a banking house named Smith, Sons & Co.[65] Another financial heavyweight was the London firm Baring Brothers & Co.[66] It was a common practice of American merchants to create funds in London through shipments of produce to Europe. They could then draw bills of exchange or credit on those houses or transact the payments of other European trade partners through them. Most trade was organized by commercial credit rather than through banks. With the expansion of trade, long credit was crucial and British merchants often allowed American traders up to nine, twelve, or even eighteenth months of credit.[67] According to historian Kenneth Morgan it

64 J.J. McCusker and C. Gravesteijn, *The Beginning of Commercial and Financial Journalism: The Commodity Price Currents, Exchange Rate Currents and Money Currents of Early Modern Europe*, Amsterdam, NEHA-series III, 1991.

65 This association was a great benefit, as they served not only credit givers but also trade partners, especially Gouverneur & Kemble who operated on numerous accounts with both firms. The connection of the two firms is mentioned in E. Christian, *The Origin, Progress and Present Practice of the Bankrupt Law Both in England and Ireland*, London, W. Clarke and Sons, 1814, p. 408.

66 Baring Brothers & Co. Jacob Le Roy & Sons Correspondence and Papers 1791–1832, New York Historical Society Mss Collection.

67 Morgan, Business Networks, p. 52. Long credits were paramount in the East Indies trade where it could take up to two years until returns from a voyage were made.

was because of those lengthy credits, that most American merchants stayed in close commercial partnership with British houses despite their newly obtained capacity as an independent nation to trade with whomever they wanted.[68]

Especially during times of war, it was most important for merchants to work with reliable correspondents. Due to the difficulty in checking credit standing and worthiness from abroad and the few existing legal regulations regarding credit, personal relations were mostly the only guarantee that funds would be remitted. Although merchant networks bore the advantage of great flexibility and the possibility for quick adjustments to changing markets, they were also a risk factor. Unforeseen events like a partner's bankruptcy or death or changing political situations could terminate business relationships, especially since many of these firms were run by their owner and often ended with his death.

By the late eighteenth century trans-Atlantic trade was to a great part managed through a web of interconnected business partners. Silvia Marzagalli points out that, '[j]ust like Adam Smith's invisible hand … recent approaches to Atlantic history postulate a sort of inherent order that actors unknowingly obeyed, or at least suggest that the world they lived in was largely self-regulated.'[69] Hancock has described the Atlantic world of the late eighteenth century as 'a more extensive, intensive and coordinated economic entity than the world had ever known before'.[70] The commercial networks were self-organized coordinating mechanisms that were to a large extent based on loose business partnerships. Despite their informal nature, they still featured common structures and regularities. These networks were perhaps the most crucial advantage of private traders as they allowed them to react in a flexible and timely manner and thus go beyond national borders despite war and crises.

68 Morgan, *Business Networks*, p. 52f.

69 Marzagalli, *Establishing Transatlantic Networks*, p. 814.

70 Hancock, *The British Atlantic World*, p. 111. These studies suggest viewing the Atlantic as a commercial system—not in the sense of a commercial system based on state alliances, but as an open, complex, interconnected network of different, high density economic entities. The editorial, 'Atlantic History: History of the Atlantic System 1580–1830', edited by Horst Pietschmann shows that especially in the last quarter of the eighteenth century such a system became most evident. H. Pietschmann (ed.), *Atlantic History: History of the Atlantic System 1580–1830*, Göttingen, Vandenhoeck & Ruprecht, 2002. Marzagalli also argues that those complex Atlantic interactions brought some methodological implications for the approach to Atlantic trade. Instead of viewing the Atlantic as following a linear logic, it is necessary to see it in a systemic context as each transaction is preceded by a set of previous transactions and relations and would entail following transactions. Marzagalli, *Establishing Transatlantic Networks*, p. 825.

Claude Markowitz characterizes networks as a 'structure through which goods, credit, capital and men circulate regularly across a given space which can vary enormously in terms of both size and accessibility.' It usually 'consists of a centre, a locality or a cluster of localities where capital is raised and where capitalists have their main place of residence, and of dispersed colonies of merchants and commercial employees which keep close links with the network centre.'[71] New York City quickly rose to the center of a multi-continental trade network. From there merchants steered their trade activities across the world's oceans. They relied on commercial employees and network partners residing in different trading stations. I would suggest to regard New York City as a 'portal of globalization' as put forward by Middell and Engel as it was one portal from where a high degree of global activity was diffused. From there, global flows of goods were coordinated and high-information velocity existed. Since it stood in direct exchange with several other portals of globalization—mostly other port cities—it deepened global synchrony and integration.[72] To understand this complex system it is important to follow the activities of its actors, which the next chapter pursues.

71 C. Markovits, *The Global World of Indian Merchants 1750–1947. Traders of Sind from Bukhara to Panama*, Cambridge, Cambridge University Press, 2004, p. 25.

72 Middell and Engel, Bruchzonen der Globalisierung, p. 27.

CHAPTER 2

Global Entrepreneurs

The East Indies Trade

Much literature exists on the trade and mercantile commerce of the United States and the Atlantic world in the late eighteenth and early nineteenth century. Few, but no less important, studies draw attention to the commercial encounters of the young nation in the Indian and Pacific Oceans and the impact of that trade on America's economic growth.[1] In past years, the topic has especially received new attention with foci laid not only on commercial interactions but also on the social and cultural impact of the trade as highlighted in scholarship on material culture and cross-cultural encounters between the United States and Asia.[2] The East Indies trade opened in 1784, shortly after

---

1 One recent publication on American trade with the East Indies after independence is *So Great a Proffit: How the East Indies Trade Transformed Anglo-American Capitalism* by James Fichter (2010), which depicts a concise picture of the scope and importance of the American India trade and its long-term economic consequences. Fichter argues that the trade achieved such great profits that it 'abetted the accumulation of wealth and financial capital in the hands of the wealthiest Americans, creating financiers who would profoundly alter the shape of American business.' America's free trade with the East Indies debilitated the East India Company's monopoly on the British India trade and helped to establish Britain's nineteenth century free trade empire. When Britain noticed that American private merchants were more successful than the East India Company, the British Parliament authorized private British trade with India in order to reduce the Americans' commercial presence and ensure profits went back into British hands, something the Company had been unable to achieve. Fichter concludes that America's commerce with the East shows a strong interaction between the United States and rest of the world since its inception and had impacted Anglo-American capitalism. R. Fichter, *So Great a Proffit: How the East Indies Trade Transformed Anglo-American Capitalism*, Cambridge, MA, Harvard University Press, 2010.

2 See J.S. Islam, 'Contributions of Asian Trade to the Early Transformation of the United States of America', in *Journal of the Asiatic Society of Bangladesh,* (Humanities) vol 54,1 (2009), pp. 1–26; S. Islam, 'Americans in Calcutta Bazaars in the Early Nineteenth Century: Images and Interpretations,' in *Journal of the Asiatic Society of Bangladesh,* (Humanities) vol. 50, 2005, pp. 219–245; J.M. Downs, 'American Merchants and the China Opium Trade, 1800–1840,' in *The Business History Review* vol. 42, no. 4, 1968, pp. 418–442; J.M. Downs, *The Golden Ghetto: American Commercial Community at Canton and the Shaping of American China Policy, 1784–1844*, Bethlehem, PA, Lehigh University Press, 1997; P.E. Fontenoy, 'Ginseng, Otter Skins, and Sandalwood: The Conundrum of the China Trade,' in *The Northern Mariner/ Le Marin du Nord* vol. 7, no. 1, 1997, pp. 1–16; M.A.Y. Gallagher, 'Charting a New Course for the China Trade, the Late Eighteenth Century American Model,' in *The American Neptune, A Quarterly Journal of*

 | DOI 10.1163/9789004356412_004

America gained its independence, and when the first American vessel, the *Empress of China*, set sail to the East. The English Navigation Acts had strictly regulated trade with English colonies using only English ships, but America's Independence had given the merchants more room for agency as they were now freed from trade restrictions with the Indian Ocean world and were able to pursue new trade opportunities.

A long debate in Congress on the Asian trade followed. Opponents of the trade contested it out of the fear that involvement of American merchants could cause conflicts and crises with the already dominant European powers. They saw America's economic future in the pursuit of an agrarian society modeled after China, which was seen as an example of how peace and prosperity could be maintained without foreign trade.[3] One strong supporter of the expansion of mercantile commerce was John Adams, who had studied maritime Europe and its secret for prosperity. He advocated that the United States needed to join the Indian Ocean trade if it wanted to reach economic greatness. Another argument was that many British officials favored America's participation

Maritime History and Arts vol. 57, no. 3, 1997, pp. 201–218; J.R. Gibson, *Otter Skins, Boston Ships, and China Goods: The Maritime Fur Trade of the Northwest Coast, 1785–1841*, Seattle, University of Washington Press, 1992; J. Goldstein, *Philadelphia and the China Trade, 1682–1846: Commercial, Cultural, and Attitudinal Effects*, University Park, Pennsylvania State University Press, 1978; S. Greenbie and M.L. Greenbie, *Gold of Ophir the China Trade in the Making of America*, New York: Wilson Erickson, 1937; D.S. Howard and C.E. Wright, *New York and the China Trade*, New York, New-York Historical Society, 1984; R. Richards, 'United States Trade With China, 1784–1814', in *The American Neptune: A Quarterly Journal of Maritime History and Arts* vol. 54, Special Supplement 1994; D. Van and P. Arthur, *The Canton Trade: Life and Enterprise on the China Coast, 1700–1845*, Hong Kong, Hong Kong University Press, 2005; R. Spindler, *New York und der Amerikanische Indienhandel (1784–1812)*, Stuttgart, Steiner, 1994; G. Bhagat, *Americans in India, 1784–1860*, New York, New York University Press, 1970; H. Furber, 'The Beginnings of American Trade with India, 1784–1812', *The New England Quarterly*, vol XI, 1938, pp. 235–265; J.W. Synder Jr., 'The First American Voyage to India' in *Americana (American Historical Magazine)* vol. XXXII, no. 2, April 1938, pp. 284–304; J.C. Sinha, 'Indo-American Trade, Past and Present,' in *Asiatic Society of Bengal* vol. XXV, 1929, pp. 201–221. A remarkable study on the cultural encounter of Americans with Chinese throughout the nineteenth century is J.K. Wei Tchen, *New York Before Chinatown: Orientalism and the Shaping of American Culture, 1776–1882*, Baltimore, Johns Hopkins University Press, 1999. On the impact of Asian objects on American culture and identity see also S.S. Bean, *Yankee India: American Commercial and Cultural Encounters with India in the Age of Sail 1784–1860*, Salem, MA. Peabody Essex Museum, 2000. For the time before American Independence, see C. Frank, *Objectifying China, Imagining America: Chinese Commodities in Early America*, Chicago, University of Chicago Press, 2011.

3 Good summaries of the debate are found in Islam, *Contributions*, pp. 4–5 and Fichter, *So Great a Proffit*, p. 39.

for a chance to ship their personal funds in American vessels. John Adam's letter to John Jay in November 1785 presents this argument in a clear language:

> There are many persons in the European factories in India particularly the English who have accumulated large property, which they wish to transmit to Europe, but have not been able to do it ... They would be glad to sell us their commodities, and take our bills of exchange upon Europe or America ... Therefore, there is no better advice to be given to the merchants of the United States, than to push their commerce to the East as fast and as far as it will go.[4]

The question of whether to organize foreign trade through state-regulated trading companies was a central matter in the debate over the establishment of an American East Indian Company.[5] Although Congress turned the initial proposal of such a company down in late 1785 (America's sentiments against any kind of monopolies were strong and it was believed that the trade would be more prosperous if carried out by private hands), by 1787 it was one of the central debates at the Constitutional Convention. The commerce clause of the Constitution that gave Congress the authority to regulate commerce left the issue of monopolies open. But several states—Massachusetts, Rhode Island, New York, New Hampshire, and North Carolina—made clear that they would only approve of the Constitution if it was amended with an explicit ban on the right of Congress to create monopolies, keeping the American East Indies trade in the hands of private and individual entrepreneurs.[6]

Robert Morris of Philadelphia and William Duer and Daniel Parker of New York were the first entrepreneurs to outfit a ship and send it to China. The *Empress of China* departed New York's port on 22 February 1784. The first American ship to be copper bottomed, she was a 360ton vessel, outfitted with a crew of 46 men and carried a cargo worth $120,000 including Spanish dollars, ginseng, furs, lead, and wine.[7] Only a few months later, two more ships left for the East

4 John Adams to John Jay, 11 November 1785, The Works of John Adams, vol. 8, pp. 343–344 cited by Islam, *Contributions*, p. 4.

5 This claim was most famously presented by the Englishman John Wingrove who came to New York in 1787 and proposed to form and lead an American East India Company. The claim was supported by John Adams, then American minister in London. Fichter, *So Great a Proffit*, p. 39.

6 See Fichter, *So Great a Proffit*, pp. 39–42.

7 Ships and Shipping of Old New York, p. 32; J.K. Bauer, *A Maritime History of the United States: The Role of America's Seas and Waterways*, Columbia, SC, University of South Carolina Press, 1988, p. 54; On the voyage of the ship see also J.W. Swift, P. Hodgkinson, and S.W. Woodhouse, 'The Voyage of the Empress of China.' In *The Pennsylvania Magazine of History and Biography*, vol.63, no. 1. January 1939, pp. 24–356.

Indies: the *United States* who sailed for Madras and the *Hydra* to Calcutta.[8] *The Empress of China* returned from Canton the following year with a cargo of teas and Chinese goods, yielding a profit of 25 percent ($30,000) and revealing a great commercial potential in the trade.[9] The successful voyages of the early vessels to Asia encouraged other American merchants to send their own ships. There is no reliable data on the total figures of ships leaving to the East Indies but a variety of sources indicate relatively similar numbers. They reveal that in the decade after 1784, American merchants continuously expanded their trade with China, and especially in the 1790s, a China trade boom set in.[10]

Table 1 shows the number of American Ships in Canton as listed in William Milburn's publication on *Oriental Commerce*. He was a servant of the East India Company who published a merchant compendium on the Oriental Trade in 1813.

8 Islam, *Contributions*, p. 10.

9 Ships and Shipping of Old NY, p. 32; Bauer, *Maritime History*, p. 54.

10 Hezekiah Pierrepont recorded in his notes on the East Indies trade the number of foreign ships in China from 1776 to 1795. His observation for American vessels exporting tea from China count 2 ships in 1785, 1 in 1786, 5 in 1787, 2 in 1788, 4 in 1789, 14 in 1790, 3 in 1792, 6 in 1793, 7 in 1794 and 7 in 1795. See H. Pierrepont, Notes on the trade of China made at Canton 1796, Hezekiah Beers Pierrepont Miscellany, Volumes, Constable-Pierrepont papers. Manuscripts and Archives. The New York Public Library. Astor, Lenox, and Tilden Foundations. Pierrepont's observations corresponded with one of his contemporaries who recorded similar numbers and registered one vessel in 1785, 1 in 1786, 5 in 1787, 1 in 1788, and 4 in 1789. 'Statement of the Shipping Employed in the Trade to Canton in China, for the Six Years Last Past, by a Gentleman Well Informed on That Subject', 'The American Museum or, Universal Magazine', vol. 7, no. 3, March 1790, pp. 127–128. Modern historians R. Richards, M. Malloy, and B. Bush provide slightly different numbers compiled in a supplement of the *American Neptune* in 1794 where they state that there were 5 vessels in 1786; 3 in 1787; 6 in 1788; 18 in 1789; 8 in 1790; 9 in 1791 and 1792; 12 in 1793 and 1794; 16 in 1795; 14 in 1796 18 in 1797; 19 in 1798; 26 in 1799; 31 in 1800; 37 in 1801; 45 in 1802; 21 in 1803; 39 in 1804; 40 in 1805; 32 in 1806; 44 in 1807; 15 in 1808; 44 in 1809; 10 in 1810; 31 in 1811; and 22 in 1912. They received their data from the Factory Records of the British East India Company and from records of the Dutch East India Company. R. Richards, 'Introduction: United States Trade with China, 1784–1814', *The American Neptune: A Quarterly Journal of Maritime History & Arts* vol. 54, special supplement, 1994, pp. 8–9. Richards et. al's. numbers almost exactly coincide with Pierrepont's numbers with the exception of one year. While Richards et al. note a rise from six vessels in 1788 to eighteen in 1789, Pierrepont states the same increase from 1789 to 1790. Considering that Pierrepont does not list any ship for the year 1784, although he must have known about the *Empress of China*, it can be assumed that his numbers account for the time the ships were leaving China, which was usually in December or January. With this reading, the two ships he lists in 1785 would be the ships arriving in China in fall 1784 and leaving late in 1784 or early in 1785.

TABLE 1 *American ships in Canton 1784–1812*

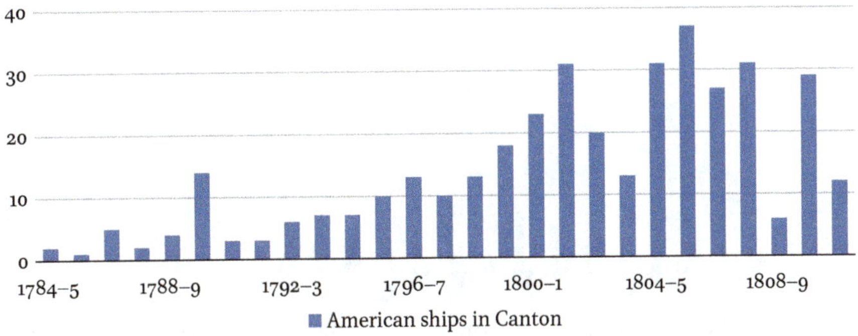

SOURCE: W. MILBURN ORIENTAL COMMERCE, VOLUME II, LONDON, PUBLISHED BY BLACK, PARRY, & COMPANY, 1813.

When viewed in comparison to European ships in Canton at the time, the number of American ships reflects the prominent role American merchants gained in the East Indies within a relatively short time, see Table 2. During the 1790s American ships outnumbered European ships and even managed to exceed the numbers of English ships from 1799 to 1801. Wars and crises in Europe led to a decrease in European commercial enterprises in the East Indies which allowed American merchants, who remained neutral during the wars, to take over a large part of the importation of Asian commodities to Europe.

Reinhard Spindler's study on New York's India trade thoroughly documents the city's role in the trade with India. Through the analysis of shipping records and newspaper articles Spindler was able to list the shipping movements between New York and Indian ports between 1784 and 1812, see Table 3. Spindler's results disprove the assumption that New York only played a minor role in the American India trade compared to New England's ports.[11] Though Spindler focused solely on New York's trade with India, his numbers are still useful for a general analysis of the East Indies trade. At least in the early years of the trade, trips exclusively to India were rare and voyages usually included numerous Asian destinations.

New York took a leading role in the American East Indies trade from the beginning. Several other vessels immediately followed the *Empress of China*, and in 1787, three of five American vessels at Canton were from New York.[12] The ships usually took the same routes as European ships and sailed across

11 Spindler, *Amerikanischer Indienhandel*, p. 441.

12 *Ships and Shipping of old New York*, p. 32f.

TABLE 2 *Total ships in Canton 1784–1812*

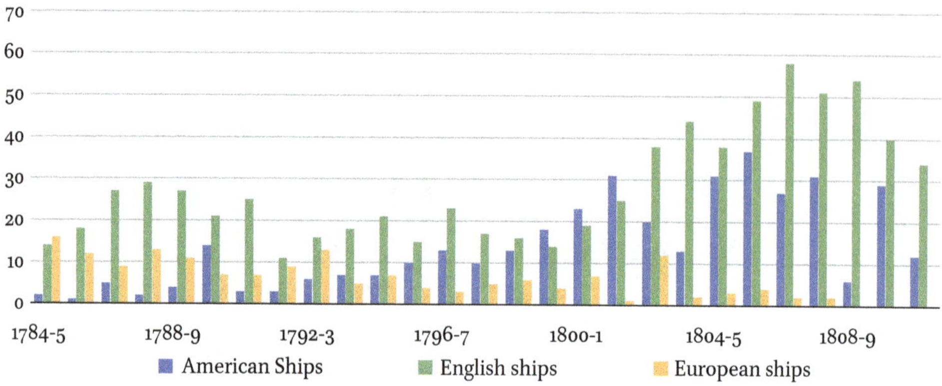

SOURCE: W. MILBURN ORIENTAL COMMERCE, VOLUME II, LONDON, PUBLISHED BY BLACK, PARRY, & COMPANY, 1813.

TABLE 3 *Departures New York–India*

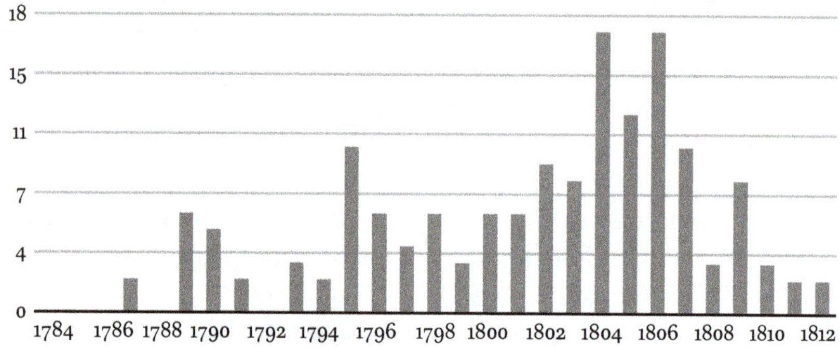

SOURCE: R. SPINDLER NEW YORK UND DER AMERIKANISCHE INDIENHANDEL, STUTTGART: STEINER, PP. 447–461.

the Atlantic and along Africa's Cape of Good Hope to the Indian Ocean where they would usually stop at the Isle of France before they proceeded to Bombay and/or Calcutta. From India the ships generally followed the Straits of Malacca to the Chinese Sea where they stopped at Canton and/or Batavia. Leaving New York in February they arrived in China with the South West Monsoon winds during August and October. The route from New York to Canton took 120 to 140 days. Trading season in Canton usually started in fall and lasted until late November and December, when most ships returned to New York or went straight to Europe. The passage from Canton back to New York lasted 110 to 140 days; a passage back to Europe took 140 to 170 days, which meant that East Indies voyages lasted well over a year.[13] By 1795 New York's harbor had become America's major port and commercial hub for the Asian trade and often ships from Philadelphia, Boston and Salem put in at New York to drop their cargo. The New York commission merchants would then further distribute the commodities.[14]

William Constable was one of New York's early East India merchants. In 1784, only a few weeks after the *Empress of China* had set sail, he and William Edgar sent the schooner *Betsy* to Canton in a joint enterprise. Constable had used his various international contacts to gather information regarding the trade and received answers from around the world including Antwerp, Cape Town, Calcutta, Canton, and the West Indies. The *Betsy* was outfitted with ginseng, furs, and specie and was bound for Bombay, Madras, Batavia, and Canton. She brought home a cargo of teas, textiles, chinaware, and silk, which was readily sold in New York and yielded $90,000, a profit rate of 25 percent.[15] In the 1785–86 season, Constable sent two ships, the *Empress of China* and *Hope,* to the East Indies which returned to New York in 1787 bringing a great variety of teas and textiles. The following year Constable had the *America* built. She was a vessel of 600 tons and property of William Edgar and Alexander Macomb who invested £30,000 pounds New York currency.[16] The vessel was dispatched to the East Indies on 20 February 1789, with a cargo worth $106,520 (£42,669) and almost $84,000 of which was in specie with only $22,000 in commodities.[17] William Bell went as supercargo. The *America* sailed to Bombay and Canton where she obtained a large cargo of teas and nankeens, which were disposed

---

13 H. Pierrepont, Notes on the trade of China made at Canton 1796, Hezekiah Beers Pierrepont Miscellany, Volumes, Constable-Pierrepont papers. Manuscripts and Archives. The New York Public Library. Astor, Lenox, and Tilden Foundations.

14 Spindler lists Edward Goold, Bailey & Bogert, Green & Lovett, and Peter Remsen as a few of these commission merchants. Edward Goold and Bailey & Bogert were mainly connected to Crowninshield in Salem, MA, and Peter Remsen was affiliated with Jackson & Lee in Boston. Spindler, *Amerikanischer Indienhandel*, p. 436.

15 Tailby, *Chapters*, p. 251; W. Constable Shipping Papers, Constable Papers, Constable-Pierrepont papers. Manuscripts and Archives. The New York Public Library. Astor, Lenox, and Tilden Foundations.

16 Tailby, *Chapters*, p. 251; W. Constable Shipping Papers, Constable Papers, Constable-Pierrepont papers. Manuscripts and Archives. The New York Public Library. Astor, Lenox, and Tilden Foundations.

17 Taillby, *Chapters*, p. 258.

of quickly in New York upon her return netting Constable and his partners a fortune. The Bohea, Souchong, and Hyson teas yielded returns of $69,519.59 and the nankeens $99,065.17.[18] Within five years, Constable's East Indies business brought him great success, making him one of America's most influential East Indies merchants.

Indian Ocean Trade Networks

The important role the East Indies trade played commercially and politically after its first decade can be understood in the newspaper debates regarding the implementation of the Jay Treaty of 1795. The treaty, officially known as *The Treaty of Amity, Commerce and Navigation, Between His Britannic Majesty and the United States of America* was signed in 1794 between the United States and Great Britain. After the outbreak of war between France and Great Britain, Americans were divided between supporting the French or British. Alexander Hamilton, who feared that the United States was too weak militarily, argued for the reliance on British protection even if it meant complying with Britain's trade restrictions.[19] Fearing a new war with Great Britain, George Washington sided with Hamilton and sent John Jay to negotiate with the British Government. The treaty was a success for Great Britain, attending to only few American interests. It addressed some remaining issues of the Treaty of Paris such as the withdrawal of British Army forces in the Northwest Territory, disputes over wartime debts, and the American-Canadian boundaries. It also granted rights for Americans to trade with British possessions in the West and East Indies. These trading rights were, however, constrained to direct journeys of ships with seventy tons or less, prohibiting any participation of Americans in the Indian country trade. It was signed on 19 November 1794, and approved by the Senate on 24 June 1795. As it failed to address important American issues such as impressments and compensations, the treaty was received by an outraged public who considered it a capitulation to Great Britain.[20] A highly

18 Davis, *William Constable*, p. 140.

19 J.R. Sofka, 'The Jeffersonian Idea of National Security Revisited' in S. Marzagalli, J.R. Sofka and J.J. McCusker (eds.), *Rough Waters: American Involvement with the Mediterranean in the Eighteenth and Nineteenth Centuries, Research in Maritime History,* vol. 44, 2010, pp. 166–167.

20 T. Estes, 'Shaping the Politics of Public Opinion: Federalists and the Jay Treaty Debate', *Journal of the Early Republic*, vol.20, no. 3, Fall 2000, p. 399.

controversial debate followed, which provides insight into how Federalists and Republicans tried to shape public opinion and reveals the mechanism of discourse in the early republic's public sphere. A large part of the debate was carried out in newspapers revealing the deep fission between supporters (Federalists) and opponents (Republicans).[21]

The debates on the Jay Treaty illustrate that foreign affairs played a leading role in domestic and party politics. Studying the arguments used on both sides, one finds some interesting details on the shape of Asian commerce at the time. As most journeys to China stopped in India and other Indian Ocean destinations to participate in the Indian country trade, the East Indies trade was a very complex trade system. Restricting America's commercial relations to direct trade, meaning that ships could only pursue business in India when they returned directly to an American port, shows that Britain dreaded the competition of private American merchants in their lucrative trade. A comment against the Jay Treaty published in the *American Minerva*, underlines this. The author writes that '[t]he merchants who are certainly the most competent judges on these matters, contend that the trade of the United States to the East Indies is placed on a much worse footing than before'.[22]

The country trade, also known as the local trade, was a gainful business opportunity conducted by many English East India Company servants who privately traded between India and Canton. American merchants frequently participated in the country trade as well. Hezekiah Pierrepont approximated that the combined value of the country trade to China reached $1 million annually.[23] In his notes from 1798, he estimated that eight to nine local ships moved every year between Bombay and Canton and another one or two local ships regularly went from Calcutta to China with cargoes of opium, pepper, and tin. At least one ship was also employed between Pulo Penang and Canton, also bringing tin and pepper. According to Pierrepont, ships from Bombay often stopped at Calcutta on the return voyages taking in sugar, rice, coarse jute fabrics, and piece goods meant for the Malabar Coast and Bombay. The ones returning directly to Bombay brought cargos of sugar, sugar candy, raw and wrought silk, nankeens, chinaware, fireworks, quicksilver, camphor, and

21 J. Charles, 'The Origins of the American Party System', *The William & Mary Quarterly*, Third Series, vol. 12, no. 4, October 1955, p. 583.

22 American Minerva, Friday, 31 July 1795, New York Historical Society.

23 H. Pierrepont, Notes on the trade of China made at Canton 1796, Hezekiah Beers Pierrepont Miscellany, Volumes, Constable-Pierrepont papers. Manuscripts and Archives. The New York Public Library. Astor, Lenox, and Tilden Foundations.

gold from China. The country trade was mainly run by Persian merchants in Bombay[24] and British merchants and supercargoes like the houses of Robert Hamilton, Beale & Reid, and Dummond Sparks.[25]

Common ports of interaction in the Indian Ocean system were the Isle of France, Pulo Penang, and Batavia. Pierrepont called the Isle of France 'The Gibraltar or Key of India' as it was a great commercial hub for Asian goods trading to the Coast of Malabar, the Coromandel Coast, Bengal, Sumatra, Batavia, China and the coast of Africa. Excited by the profits made in the country trade, Constable and his partners considered sending their own agents to the Isle of France. There the agent was to obtain goods from India via the country trade, which would then be brought to China or straight back to New York.[26]

The Isle of France was also a commercial hub for slaves. A merchant from the island suggested engaging in slavery to Constable in 1784. He argued that 'negroes' could be procured from Mozambique and that some had been sent to Saint-Dominique. 'They cost 25 to 30 Indian Dollars which with cost for freight and charges ends up being 50 Dollars. Two-thirds of their price are usually paid for in Dollars, one third is paid in goods such as canon powder.'[27] The remaining documents do not tell how Constable responded to this letter but there is no indication that he became involved in the slave trade.

Many times, it was possible for the captains and supercargoes to dispose of their outbound cargo at the Isle of France and purchase return cargos for cheap prices, saving them the lengthy trip to India and Canton. Shipping equipment like spars, boards, planks, iron, and nails but also provisions like ham, butter, cheese, and salted beef and pork were welcomed goods on the island. Further demand existed for olive oil, painter's oil and colors, turpentine, cordage, canvas sheets, copper, Madeira wines, white wines and porter, and English manufactures such as clothes, shoes, gloves, umbrellas, paper, musical

---

24 'Persees' was the contemporary term for the community of ancient Persians at Bombay and Surat. J. Pinkerton, *A General Collection of the Best and Most Interesting Voyages and Travels in All Parts of The World*, London 1811, p. 220.

25 H. Pierrepont, Notes on the trade of China made at Canton 1796, Hezekiah Beers Pierrepont Miscellany, Volumes, Constable-Pierrepont papers. Manuscripts and Archives. The New York Public Library. Astor, Lenox, and Tilden Foundations.

26 'Extract from a letter to John Bondfield,' 12 February 1784, William Constable Correspondence, Constable Papers, Pierrepont papers. Manuscripts and Archives. The New York Public Library. Astor, Lenox, and Tilden Foundations.

27 'Extract from a letter to John Bondfield', 12 February 1784, William Constable Correspondence, Constable Papers, Constable-Pierrepont families papers. Manuscripts and Archives. The New York Public Library. Astor, Lenox, and Tilden Foundations.

instruments, and glass wares.[28] Hezekiah Pierrepont's strategy to dispose of his goods included renting a warehouse adjacent to the public place where he displayed samples of his available articles. He was surprised that 'as soon as the door opened the people of all sorts flocked in.'[29] He managed to sell the bulk of his cargo in only four days. Another way was to dispense the cargo to a local agent who would then provide the return cargo. During the French Wars, Americans profited enormously as neutral carriers. Between 1793 and 1810, 521 of 789 foreign ships that arrived at the Isle of France were American.[30] After the British captured the island, American commerce with Mauritius slowed down and of the 100 vessels arriving between 1810 and 1815 only seven were American.[31]

Pulo Penang (Prince of Wales Island) in the Straights of Malacca was another port that most vessels to China laid land at, as it was a commercial nexus linking the Straights of Malacca, the Malayan peninsula and the coast of Sumatra. It was a welcome port of shelter from the Monsoon winds and a place to take in provisions. The island produced an abundance of timber and pepper, which was usually taken on as cargo for China. The Straits of Malacca was, however, frequently visited by pirates, and Pierrepont especially warned against the 'proas' (Sulu pirates) who he believed sometimes had more than 50 pirate boats in the strait.[32]

Another port in the Indian Ocean trade was Batavia, and especially after 1795, Americans benefited from the commerce. The blocking of British ships to put in at Batavia by the Dutch forced Batavia's colonists to ship their goods in neutral American ships to Europe. Consequently, American trade with Batavia and Sumatra surged and between 1796 and 1807, 378 of the 586 long-distance arrivals at Batavia were American.[33]

---

28 H. Pierrepont, Notes on the trade of China made at Canton 1796, Hezekiah Beers Pierrepont Miscellany, Volumes, Constable-Pierrepont papers. Manuscripts and Archives. The New York Public Library. Astor, Lenox, and Tilden Foundations.

29 'Notes on the commerce of the Isles de France and Bourbon, Bombay, Pulco Pinang and the Malay Settlements 1796', in H. Pierrepont, Notes on the trade of China made at Canton 1796 Hezekiah Beers Pierrepont Miscellany, Volumes, Constable-Pierrepont papers. Manuscripts and Archives. The New York Public Library. Astor, Lenox, and Tilden Foundations.

30 Fichter, *So Great a Proffit*, p. 156.

31 Fichter, *So Great a Proffit*, p. 156.

32 H. Pierrepont, Notes on the trade of China made at Canton 1796, Hezekiah Beers Pierrepont Miscellany, Volumes, Constable-Pierrepont papers. Manuscripts and Archives. The New York Public Library. Astor, Lenox, and Tilden Foundations.

33 Fichter, *So Great a Proffit*, p. 150. Fichter used data from Batavian shipping records.

An example of how American captains and supercargoes made use of the ample Indian Ocean trade possibilities is found in a letter from Peter Hodgkinson to Robert Morris in 1789. Hodgkinson had left New York in December 1788, sailing as supercargo of the ship *Jay* to the East Indies. The ship first sailed to Madeira to take in wine for the Coromandel Coast. From the coast it proceeded to Tranquebar, Pondicherry, and Madras where it cleared some of the cargo. From Madras the ship then sailed to Batavia in hopes of selling the remaining wine before continuing to the Eastern Route to Canton. On their way to Batavia, it also stopped at Sumatra but the supercargo could not find any opportunity to sell the wines either. Since the market for wine in Batavia was also not very fruitful and the ship could not dispose of its cargo, Hodgkinson decided not to continue to Canton but to load a cargo of sugar for Bombay, Surat, and the Coast of Malabar. There it would wait until the next year and sell the wine for a cargo of cotton which was then to be shipped to China.[34]

The Indian Ocean was new and exotic not only for those consuming the products at home but also for the Americans sailing there for the first time. Samuel Ferguson's journal from his voyage to Bombay and Canton in 1795 offers great examples of what an astonishing experience it was for him. Yet at the same time, it is an intriguing depiction of the lifestyles of the merchants living there. In his journal he describes his arrival in Cape Town with great detail, covering the townscape and inhabitants:

> The houses many only one story high and few above two with flat roofs principally and neatly whitewashed or painted with Green window shutters have a very cool and neat appearance [...] about the middle of the town is a square which is uses as a market for Vegetables & fruits—at the upper part of the town next to the Sugar load are extensive gardens belonging to the Company together with a spacious house which the Governor occupies [...] the people seem to retain their European manners in great measure and from what I had an opportunity of seeing consider them friendly kind & hospitable—their politeness we considered rather troublesome whether it was from being immediately from Philadelphia where taking of the hat is not used or not I can't say but it struck us as a bad custom to have our hats to take of [sic] to every one we met as they did to us being strangers[35]

34 'Peter Hodginson to Robert Morris, 5 December 1789', William Constable Correspondence, Constable Papers, Constable-Pierrepont family papers. Manuscripts and Archives. The New York Public Library. Astor, Lenox, and Tilden Foundations.

35 'Samuel Ferguson Trip to Bombay 1793–1795', Series IV Diaries, Ferguson family papers. Manuscripts and Archives. The New York Public Library. Astor, Lenox, and Tilden Foundations.

Upon his arrival, Ferguson was invited to the Governor's habitation, which was in a fortress at the head of the bay. The governor struck him as a very likeable man and they had a pleasant conversation on business whereby the governor provided him with some business tips, suggesting going to Surat for cotton. He also visited a farm about 12 miles outside the town to taste and buy wine and have dinner. All in all, Ferguson's visit to the Cape of Good Hope had been a very rewarding experience for him although he maintained, '[t]his not the country I would of all others fit my residence in and by no means in the town.' From South Africa the vessel continued to Bombay where it was greeted with much joy as it was the first vessel to arrive that season and it had been unclear if, because of the war, Americans would be able to come at all. In Bombay Ferguson was shocked about the amount of servants that were put in service to him.

> [We were] immediately provided with such a train of servants as really threw me into a kind of fever every time I saw the lounging rabscallions—I was provided with a Persee to wait on my person a Misol or Umbrella bearer, A Palankeen and four men to carry me when ever I went out. I would gladly have dispensed with this last luxury but all our party were accommodated in this manner and 'twould not have done for me to be singular. I therefore only discharged my Misol and have since found I could not have done without a Panlankeen [sic].[36]

Ferguson's report of his travels ended in Bombay even though the ship proceeded to Canton where it arrived on 31 August 1794, and obtained a cargo of silks and nankeens, teas, and chinaware. The journal is an interesting read on the cultural encounters during such a journey and reveals Ferguson's cosmopolitan attitude, interest and curiosity.

Commodities

The commodities Americans exported from the East Indies were mainly teas and manufactured goods like textiles and chinaware. To a lesser extent they also exported sugar, pepper, rhubarb, spices, and quicksilver. The teas imported were Souchong and Bohea black teas and Hyson, Hyson Skin, and Gunpowder green teas. While before the 1790s cheaper Bohea tea was the main import, in the two decades after 1795 there was a noticeable shift towards the better

---

36 'Samuel Ferguson Trip to Bombay 1793–1795', Series IV Diaries, Ferguson family papers. Manuscripts and Archives. The New York Public Library. Astor, Lenox, and Tilden Foundations.

quality Souchong and Hyson teas and a general trend towards more green teas.[37] In his 1798 *Notes on the China Trade*, Pierrepont describes his observations for American consumption of Chinese teas. He calculated that Americans had an annual consumption of three million pounds of tea and Great Britain and its dependencies 18 to 20 million pounds. He also elaborated on detailed descriptions of the teas on the American markets. The teas listed were: Hyson Tea, Hyson Skin, Gunpowder (superior Hyson Tea), Young Hyson, Singlo & Twankay ('Common Green Teas in general under consumption in England'), Souchong ('first quality black tea') Anchoy Souchong ('This is a Tea passing on the Americans & others who are not skilled in Teas for real Souchong as in fact it has the appearance & flavor of a Tea of high quality'), Congon & Campoi ('black tea in general use in Europe') and Bohea Tea.[38]

According to Fichter, Americans bought more than $40 million worth of goods from India between October 1794 and 1815, and spent $31 million on Chinese 'piece goods.'[39] Most of these commodities were cloths (nankeens), porcelains, and silk. Pierrepont's notes confirm the great demand for textiles. 'The Americans are the greatest purchasers of Nankeens—They take rising one Million pounds annually.' Silks also answered well on the American market, especially 'Black Taffety' (taffetas), 'Sattni' (satins), lustrings, ribbons, handkerchiefs, and sewing silks 'with every variety of fancy.' Other goods from China that were in demand were sugar, cassia buds, oil of cinnamon, musk, rhubarb, quick silver, vermillion, mother pearl shells, matts, window blinds, umbrellas, and fans.[40]

As there were only few American goods that responded well in the East Indian markets, merchants had to be creative in obtaining articles to trade. Most merchants decided to bring European commodities, particularly alcoholic drinks like wine, beer and porter. The European community in India also desired salted provisions. It was important to arrive before the ships of the East India Company, which were usually stocked with them. Ships and 'marine stores,' like iron, lead, and copper were also in demand in India. Ships of high capacity, which were used in the trade between India and China, were especially preferred.[41]

---

37 Fichter, *So great a Proffit*, p. 92f.

38 H. Pierrepont, Notes on the trade of China made at Canton 1796, Hezekiah Beers Pierrepont Miscellany, Volumes, Constable-Pierrepont papers. Manuscripts and Archives. The New York Public Library. Astor, Lenox, and Tilden Foundations.

39 Fichter, *So great a Proffit*, p. 94.

40 H. Pierrepont, Notes on the trade of China made at Canton 1796, Hezekiah Beers Pierrepont Miscellany, Volumes, Constable-Pierrepont papers. Manuscripts and Archives. The New York Public Library. Astor, Lenox, and Tilden Foundations.

41 Henry Trail informs William Constable in a letter from Calcutta on 12 August 1789, on the market. He writes, 'Of Consumable Articles a Considerable part should consist of light

Being attentive to the freights of other ships was important for a supercargo in order to prevent gluts at the home market and achieve better prices. In 1794 Samuel Ferguson, supercargo on the *Atlantic,* sent a letter to his company in Philadelphia speculating about the shipments of the other American vessels that had gone to Canton that season: 'From the Secret Manner in which Business is conducted here it's impossible for us to say correctly what funds they have or of what Articles their return Cargoes will Consist.' He also wrote that there were some ships 'short of funds and their Cargoes will consist of Bohea and other trash of common teas they being the only articles that can be obtained on Credit here by those who come short of funds and are without friends here which appears to be the case with most of the New England ships.'[42]

Silver was the main good American merchants brought to trade with the East Indies. For centuries, Asia had been demanding silver from Europeans in exchange for luxury goods. According to historian Alejandra Irigoin, 98.2 million pesos worth, or 2,432 tons of silver were brought to China between 1719 and 1785: 37 percent was organized by English intermediates and 35 percent by the Dutch and French. After 1785 the United States became the prime importer of silver to China.[43]

Most of the silver that was shipped to China came from Spanish America. Examining custom records of Long Island, Irigoin noticed that the re-export trade to the Caribbean and South America was a welcome means to increase specie importation.

> Half of the cargoes to South America were re-exports of Spanish or French wines; textiles from France and German territories, Scandinavian cordage and sailcloth; Russian duck and tar; cotton goods from India; and

---

French Wines made up in Cases of 4 or 6 Dozen each. 5 or 600 of there would find a ready Sale. 100 of the best small Beer and the same quantity of Porter. Cheese, Hams, and Pickles if they arrive in high Preservation are also articles that would immediately be taken off, altho' the quantities of either should not be Considerable, unless you could depend upon their early arrival, that is to say before any of the English ships, which are always abundantly provided with every thing of the kind.' 'Henry Trail to William Constable', 12 August 1789, William Constable Correspondence, Constable Papers, Constable-Pierrepont family papers. Manuscripts and Archives. The New York Public Library. Astor, Lenox, and Tilden Foundations.

42 Samuel Ferguson to Philip Nichlin & Co., Canton, 2 November 1794, Series III Diaries, Ferguson family papers. Manuscripts and Archives. The New York Public Library. Astor, Lenox, and Tilden Foundations.

43 A. Irigoin, 'The End of a Silver Era: The Consequences of the Breakdown of the Spanish Peso Standard in China and the United States, 1780–1850', in *Journal of World History,* vol.20, no. 2 June 2009, p. 210.

> silk, nankeens (cotton), silk piece goods, and porcelain from China. Specie and a variety of products from the West Indies and Spanish America returned to Rhode Island.[44]

France's invasion of Spain and the Spanish American revolutions strengthened America's position in the trade by opening up new avenues of silver supply for Americans in ports like Havanna, Buenos Aires, Veracruz, Valparaiso, Callao, and San Blas. Between 1803 and 1805 American vessels trading with South American and Caribbean ports far surpassed the number of British ships.[45] In *the merchants*' records no entries for silver from Latin America were found; however, this does not mean that there was not any silver shipped. It is very likely that silver, if shipped from Latin America would not have been registered in the official records, in fear of the ship being captured by French and British ships in the West Indies.

The need for a steady supply of silver was so important for the trade with China that American merchants participated in a variety of undertakings to obtain the metal. The Pierrepont family, for instance tried to enter the Manila-Acapulco trade by sailing Hezekiah B. Pierrepont's ship, *Seramis*, between the Philippines and Mexico. John Pierpont, Hezekiah's brother, had thought up the idea during a journey to China when he heard of slim trade prospects in Canton caused by a glutted market and too many American ships. Searching for new business opportunities he learned about a possibility of participating in the silver routes between Manila and Acapulco. In Manila, he received the Governor's permission with the understanding that the ship was to bring the goods and cargo of several ships in Manila to Acapulco in exchange for silver and that he used local crews only. But John Pierepont experienced a variety of obstacles by Manila merchants who tried to stop the voyage claiming that a foreign ship should not be allowed to sail the silver galleon routes. He placed the ship under a Spanish captain and after numerous quarrels with the Spanish crew the ship ultimately managed to sail from Manila in March 1802 with a cargo worth $1.5 million.[46] However, John was disappointed by the outcome of the voyage. Having stayed in Manila, he relied entirely on the management of the Spanish crew who encountered a bad market in Acapulco, which forced

44 Irigoin, *The End of a Silver Era*, p. 216.

45 Irigoin, *The End of a Silver Era*, p. 217.

46 'John Pierpont to Hezekiah B. Pierpont', 14 March 1802. The letter is a copy made in 1941. Hezekiah Beers Pierrepont Correspondence, Pierrepont Papers, Constable-Pierrepont family papers. Manuscripts and Archives. The New York Public Library. Astor, Lenox, and Tilden Foundations. See also Block, *New England Merchants*, p. 335.

them to stay longer than expected in order to sell their goods. Leaving most of the cargo unsold, the ship could only bring $500,000 in specie instead of the expected four or five million silver dollars.[47]

An audacious scheme that involved the channeling of Mexican silver to the United States was developed by the New York merchants Archibald Gracie, Oliver Wolcott, and David Parish. The silver was needed to pay the terms of a Spanish treaty made between Spain's Charles IV and Napoleon. A French banking house was entitled and permitted with the exclusive rights to pay the debt through Mexico and the merchant companies Hope & Co. and Reid, Irving & Co. were engaged to help in the exchange. David Parish was sent to New York as the agent of Hope & Co. and obtained office space in Archibald Gracie's counting house. Gracie's friendship with Rufus King and Gouverneur Morris, both former American ambassadors to France and Great Britain, might have helped him get involved in the promising commercial arrangement.[48] (He, as well as John Craig of Philadelphia and the Olivers of Baltimore were among the American merchants whose ships went to Mexico.[49]) They organized a method to transfer gold and silver from Vera Cruz to New Orleans through the Gulf of Mexico. As British ships were patrolling Atlantic and Caribbean waters, neutral American ships, although still frequently seized, were less at stake than French and Spanish ships. Gracie employed several small but quick 100-ton boats in regular service between Vera Cruz and New Orleans. The schooner *Aspasia* was the first ship to undertake the risky journey to Vera Cruz loaded with British and German dry goods, returning with a cargo of more than $50,000 in silver dollars. Between March 1806 and August 1807, at least six ships were regularly sailing between the two ports carrying up to $150,000 in silver and gold. Historian Peggy Liss estimates that about $28 million worth of specie was brought from Mexico. Most of the silver was processed through American trading channels and banks or was converted into American commodity and shipped to Europe as neutral freight.[50]

The large amounts of specie needed to enter the East Indies trade constituted a relative high burden of entry and made it more difficult for less affluent

47 'John Pierpont to Hezekiah B. Pierrepont', 26 March 1803. Hezekiah Beers Pierrepont Correspondence, Pierrepont Papers, Constable-Pierrepont family papers. Manuscripts and Archives. The New York Public Library. Astor, Lenox, and Tilden Foundations.

48 S.E. Lyman, *Archibald Gracie and his Mansion*, unpublished manuscript, New York Historical Society cited in M. Black and J.R. Olshansky, *New York City's Gracie Mansion: A History of the Mayor's House*, New York, J.M. Kaplan Fund, 1984, pp. 36–38.

49 P.K. Liss, *Atlantic Empires: The Network of Trade and Revolution, 1713–1826*, Baltimore, Johns Hopkins University Press, 1983, p. 117.

50 Liss, Atlantic Empires, p. 117.

merchants to join the trade. In *his Notes on the China Trade*, Pierrepont registered several possible ways for merchants to acquire silver without having to draw dollars from U.S. circulation. His first suggestion was to create funds in London through shipments of produce from America and the West Indies to Europe. From these funds merchants could take out silver dollars either in London or at other European ports. Second, they could lodge a fund in London and order a credit at Lisbon or Cadiz for the amount. Additional shipments of provisions to these ports could have been made to add to the credit. The proceeds of these shipments and the fund in London would then be converted to silver in Lisbon or Cadiz, granted that there were not any restrictions on the exportation of silver from those ports, which was possible during war. A fourth possibility was to negotiate with the bank of St. Charles to obtain an order and permit to receive silver at Havana, Vera Cruz, Lima, Acapulco, or Manila payable with bills drawn at 6 to 12 months of sight. If such a negotiation was entered, it was most likely that silver dollars could be obtained at 45 or 50 Pound Sterling per dollar. According to Pierrepont, this was the common financing habit of Swedish and Danish merchants and a suitable method for Americans.[51] A further option for funds in China was to negotiate bills at Canton on London. If goods were purchased by this means of payment they were usually 10 to 15 percent higher than when they were paid for in silver dollars.[52] It was also possible to take tea on respondentia[53] and bottomry bonds, which Pierrepont saw as a ruinous enterprise. He recommended, however, to always carry bills of exchange or have established credit, so in the unlikely event of the exchange rate falling, one could get a profitable course.[54]

---

51 H. Pierrepont, Notes on the trade of China made at Canton 1796, Hezekiah Beers Pierrepont Miscellany, Volumes, Constable-Pierrepont papers. Manuscripts and Archives. The New York Public Library. Astor, Lenox, and Tilden Foundations.

52 H. Pierrepont, Notes on the trade of China made at Canton 1796, Volumes. Hezekiah Beers Pierrepont Miscellany, Volumes, Constable-Pierrepont papers. Manuscripts and Archives. The New York Public Library. Astor, Lenox, and Tilden Foundations.

53 A respondentia bond was a loan on the security of a cargo compared to a bottomry bond, a loan on the security of a vessel. A loan was taken out, usually at a high interest rate, but only to be repaid when the secured property arrived safely. The respondentia bond was more than a sole insurance contract as it also incorporated a financing component. See H. Benett, *The Law of Marine Insurance*, Oxford, Oxford University Press, 2006, p. 1; S. Go, *Marine Insurance in the Netherlands, 1600–1870: A Comparative Institutional Approach*, Amsterdam, Aksant, 2009, p. 24.

54 H. Pierrepont, Notes on the trade of China made at Canton 1796, Volumes. Hezekiah Beers Pierrepont Miscellany, Volumes, Constable-Pierrepont papers. Manuscripts and Archives. The New York Public Library. Astor, Lenox, and Tilden Foundations.

For merchants who could not come up with large sums by themselves, joining with others or renting freight on vessels bound for Asia was the best strategy for avoiding risk. Different partners, each bringing shares to the business, assembled most of the merchant companies. For East Indies tours, it was sometimes necessary to bring in further partners, allowing several merchant firms to join for a tour. Although this was not a new business model—collaborative enterprises in long distance shipping and joint ownerships had been a long tradition in oversea commerce—shipping other peoples' silver was a new form of business. Merchants often collected amounts of silver from others to make a shipment to China. The organizing merchant was entailed to commission and a percentage on the net profits. This enabled smaller merchants to join the trade. It also allowed merchants to reduce risks, as they could spread their investments on several ships.[55] According to Fichter, the fee structure of these undertakings 'resembled the two-and-twenty of modern-day hedge funds.'[56] The method delegated great responsibility into the hands of the supercargo, who had to manage the cargoes of several shareholders. In return, the supercargoes usually obtained a commission of three percent of the return cargo and sometimes were allowed some freight space for their own businesses.

In the 1800–01 season, Isaac Bell undertook a voyage as supercargo of the ship *Industry* where he managed the cargo of New York firms Archibald Gracie; Nehemiah Rogers & Isaac Bell; John Murray & Son; and Welling & Francis. Each of their outbound cargoes consisted of silver but also furs and ginseng.[57] In 1805 the vessel *Virginia* dispatched from New York to the East Indies, carrying a cargo of Spanish silver dollars, of which 5000 were to be invested for Archibald Gracie, 15,000 for Moses Rogers and 50,000 for Oliver Wolcott & Co.[58] Similarly, Gouverneur & Kemble loaned $30,000 and the ship *Hancock* to William McCarty, a Philadelphia merchant who had settled in L'Orient, for a trading voyage to the Isle of France and the Malabar Coast. The firm asked for an interest rate of 22 percent on ship and cargo and 12 percent should the ship not get further than the Isle of France.[59]

---

55 Fichter, *So great a Proffit*, p. 119f.

56 Fichter, *So great a Proffit*, p. 119.

57 'Isaac Bell from Canton', 2 December 1801, Isaac Bell Letterbook 1790–1856, Isaac Bell Papers, Butler Library, Columbia University in the City of New York.

58 'Oliver Wolcott to Solomon Ingraham, Master and William Taylor Supercargo of the ship Virginia', 12 January 1805, Oliver Wolcott letterbook 1803–1808. Manuscripts and Archives. The New York Public Library. Astor, Lenox, and Tilden Foundations.

59 'Gouverneur & Kemble to Henry Beare, Esq. in Hamburg', 16 July 1796, Gouverneur & Kemble Letterbook 1796–98 Manuscripts and Archives. The New York Public Library.

In order to lessen their silver exports, American merchants tried to find other goods suitable for the East Indian markets. With the opening of the China trade, merchants learned quickly that they could sell furs for higher prices in China than in Europe. As New York had always been an important hub for the fur trade, they benefited from its existing infrastructure. Sea otter had been recently discovered on America's northwest coast and many merchants started to send their own vessels to hunt for otter skins. The costs of these voyages, also known as the maritime fur trade, were relatively small compared to the high prices that could be obtained for furs in China. Pierrepont recommended undertaking a voyage to the northwest prior to a China trip. He suggested sailing along the northwest coast for sea otter furs or the Falkland Islands or the islands of Saint-Paul and Amsterdam for seal skins:

> A China Voyage might be assisted by an adventure to the North West Coast of America from Latt 32 to 56 for Sea Otter Skins & other Furs which are always in demand and a ready money article [...] A Sealing Voyage to the Falkland Island and Islands of St. Paul [sic] and Amsterdam for Seal Skins might be made to cooperate with a China voyage as the Market at Canton will in general be the best for that article if furnished in moderate quantities, for large quantities will destroy the Market. 15 to 20,000 Skins would at any time bring as much money as double the quantity.[60]

William Constable, too, decided in 1789, after he had previously achieved great profits with furs bought in London, to send two brigs to the Falkland Islands to catch animal skins, preferably seal skins.[61] The ships returned in 1790, bringing a cargo of fourteen thousand skins, which were prepared and 'half dressed as

---

Astor, Lenox, and Tilden Foundations In the same letter, the company orders a fashionable silver tea set from London for personal use.

60 H. Pierrepont, Notes on the trade of China made at Canton 1796, Hezekiah Beers Pierrepont Miscellany, Volumes, Constable-Pierrepont papers. Manuscripts and Archives. The New York Public Library. Astor, Lenox, and Tilden Foundations.

61 William Constable wrote to Morris in December 1789: 'My reason is that I have now before me the Sales of 12,000 sold at Canton in November 1788 (which were caught at Falkland Islands) ... Some of the Captains would carry them upon very reasonable terms & no doubt a very handsome profit could be made on them,' William Constable to Morris, 1 December 1789, William Constable Letterbooks 1790–1791, Volumes, Constable-Pierrepont families papers. Manuscripts and Archives. The New York Public Library. Astor, Lenox, and Tilden Foundations.

a means of preserving them against the worms'[62] and sent to Canton in the *America*. The trip proved to be very successful and Constable sent out his ship *Patty* for several years to catch sealskins and whale oil. For other furs, like beaver and rabbit, Constable relied on the house of Phyn, Ellice & Inglis in Montreal. In 1790, he closed a deal with Alexander Ellice who had recently left London to run the firm's branch in Montreal. The company had managed to achieve a near monopoly on all furs exported from the Northwest and Constable signed an agreement by which he would provide flour, rum and sugar in exchange for ashes, furs and ginseng.[63] Constable even debated undertaking a China voyage by way of the Northwest coast of America. In 1786, he had received a letter from Morris that included charts and drawings of America's coastline with samples of the furs that could be obtained along the coast, which were mostly sea otter skins. Constable however decided against the voyage and preferred to sail to the East Indies on the common routes.[64]

In July 1797, Gouverneur & Kemble prepared their ship *Maryland* for a seal catching mission. 'We are fitting out a very fine Ship about 300 tons on a Whaling and Sealing Voyage into the South Seas, calculated to go around Cape Horn.' They hired a crew of 40 to 50 men for the 18-month voyage. The ship was supposed to make a stop at Bedford, where they planned to buy '100 tons prime iron hooped casks, 100 tons of wooden iron hooped casks, 3 boats and oars, 50 harpoons, 20 lancets and 10 spades'[65] from their contact.

A China voyage along the Northwest Coast was a popular journey completed by many American merchants to China, especially New England traders. According to James Gibson, between 1788 and 1826, American ships undertook at least 127 voyages between the United States and China via the Pacific.[66] A typical journey to the Northwest Coast took about six months and the vessels usually left in autumn, sailed around Cape Horn with a few stops at the Falkland Islands, Galapagos Islands, or Valparaiso and arrived at the Northwest Coast in early spring, just in time when the Native Americans returned to

---

62 William Constable to Morris, 1 December 1789, William Constable Letterbooks 1790–1791, Volumes, Constable-Pierrepont families papers. Manuscripts and Archives. The New York Public Library. Astor, Lenox, and Tilden Foundations.

63 Davis, *William Constable*, p. 104.

64 Davis, *William Constable*, p. 135.

65 'Gouverneur & Kemble to William Roach and Sons, Nantucket', 1, July 1797, Gouverneur & Kemble letter book 1796–1798, Manuscripts and Archives. The New York Public Library. Astor, Lenox, and Tilden Foundations.

66 James Gibson, *Otter Skins, Boston Ships, and China Goods: The Maritime Fur Trade of the Northwest Coast, 1785–1841*, Seattle, University of Washington Press, 1992, p. 56.

the coast from their inland winter camps. The ships then spent all spring and summer sailing along the coast, from the Columbia River to Sitka, trading for skins.[67]

Gibson describes the trade in the following manner: navigating along the coast and Inside Passage, the crew looked for an inlet to anchor. Once they found one, they fired a cannon to signal their arrival, which would cause the Native Americans to come on canoes to the ships bringing furs to barter. The American sailors had American and British products on board such as cloth, iron, and glass that they exchanged for the furs. Once a trade was completed, the captain would lift anchor and sail to the next inlet, where the procedure was repeated. When they had collected enough furs, usually in late summer when the Native Americans retreated back inland, the sailors took off to China. On their way they stopped at Hawaii, where they recharged with water, wood, salt, and provisions. From Hawaii the captains sailed across the Midwestern Pacific to the Strait of Luzon between Taiwan and the Philippines where they entered the South Chinese Sea and sailed up to Macao and Canton for the winter trading season. The return voyage was then followed along the common Indian and Atlantic Ocean routes.[68] Gibson estimates that an average of $62,673 worth of American goods was traded for furs, whereas the value of sea otter skins brought to Canton were worth five to six times as much, reaching an average of $350,000, bringing the Americans lucrative profits.[69]

As furs reduced the need for silver, they were a popular good that almost every American vessel had on board when it entered Canton. Market gluts resulted that made furs a less reliable commodity. In October 1801, Isaac Bell informed the company of John Murray & Sons for whom he tried to sell a cargo of furs shipped aboard the *Industry* to Canton that, '[t]he present state of the Market at Canton does not hold out any of the prospects for the sale of the Furrs [sic] as was contemplated when I left America.' This overabundance was caused by 'the great number of arrivals of the South Sea with Seal Skins and of North W. America with Sea Otters and a number more expected. Some of them have brought Beavers—which they have sold in way of trade for five dollars the piece.' He complained that although those furs did not exhibit good quality they had nonetheless weakened demand making it more difficult for him to achieve prices higher than four dollars. The market was so frustrating that Bell concluded not to send beaver again to China.[70]

---

67 Gibson, *Otter Skins*, p. 40ff.

68 Gibson, *Otter Skins*, pp. 44–58. See also Block, *New England Merchants*, p. 314f.

69 Gibson, *Otter Skins*, p. 58.

70 'Isaac Bell to John Murray & Son', 16 October 1801, Isaac Bell Letterbook 1790–1856, Isaac Bell Papers, Butler Library, Columbia University in the City of New York.

Compared to New England merchants, relatively few New York and Philadelphia houses pursued trade to China via the Northwest Coast with John Jacob Astor being the great exception.[71] New Yorkers seemed to have much better access to silver dollars, most likely from trade with Spain and Spanish America. Furthermore, sailing to the East Indies through the Indian Ocean allowed the employment of larger vessels, as they did not have to maneuver through the Inside Passage, and the participating in the Indian Ocean trade system. Gibson points out that in the 1800/01 season, two-sixths of the American vessels but only one-sixth of the American tonnage at Canton were from Boston and usually almost two-thirds of Boston's ships brought solely furs.[72]

Easier access to silver was probably also the reason why there were fewer New York merchants participating in the Levant opium trade compared to sailors from other American ports.[73] Opium was usually obtained from Smyrna and then smuggled into China. As Charles Stelle points out, the voyage to Smyrna was lengthy, and American merchants developed a business network, which allowed them to obtain opium in London and Mediterranean ports such as Leghorn and Gibraltar.[74] The British East India Company prohibited British privateers from bringing opium from Smyrna and thus eased the way for Americans to enter the market since there was less British competition.[75] Although Americans had participated in the opium trade as early as 1790, it became a more popular business after 1804. In the seasons of 1805 and 1807

71 Encouraged by his successful fur business, in 1811 Astor erected a permanent outlet in the Pacific Northwest, at Fort Astoria, located at the mouth of the Columbia River. His plan was that supporting stations in the interior would gather furs and bring them to Astoria, from where they would be shipped to Canton. A ship would sail annually from New York to supply the establishment with trading goods for the Native Americans and white trappers. Astor's plan however failed. The vessel which brought the pioneers was lost with its entire crew and the war between America and England put the establishment in danger of capture by the British. On 23 October 1813, the post and property were sold. *Dictionary of American Biography*, A Johnson (ed.) vol. 1, New York, Charles Scribner's Sons, 1928, p. 397ff.

72 Gibson, *Otter Skins*, p. 103. Gibson states that in 1799/1800, six of eight and in 1801/02 ten of the thirteen Boston vessels only brought furs, an observation that corresponds with Isaac Bell's remark on glutted fur markets.

73 On the early American opium trade see C.C. Stelle, 'American Trade in Opium to China prior to 1820.' *Pacific Historical Review* vol. 9, no. 4, December 1940, pp. 425–444; J.M. Downs, 'American Merchants and the China Opium Trade', *The Business History Review* vol. 44, no. 4, Winter 1968, pp. 418–442.

74 Stelle, *American Trade in Opium*, p. 439.

75 Stelle, *American Trade in Opium*, p. 429.

merchants imported 102, 108, and 150 piculs[76] of Turkish opium, which constituted a value between $50,000 and $100,000.[77] After the war of 1812, American opium imports increased even more. In the years between 1816 and 1818, Turkish and Persian opium accounted for almost half of the American imports to China and Americans delivered more than a third of the opium consumed in China.[78] The firms of Stephen Girard of Philadelphia, John Jacob Astor, Joseph Peabody of Salem, John Donnell of Baltimore and the Perkins of Boston were among the larger shippers. Perkins & Co. especially had their hands in the trade.[79] There is little evidence that the merchants of this study were engaged in the Turkish opium trade. Le Roy, Bayard & Co. traded frequently with Smyrna and Leghorn in the early decades of the nineteenth century. The price currents that they received from Smyrna list the prices for opium and a handwritten memorandum on different European and Asian commodities in their records also lists opium as a possible export commodity.[80] Whether the house actually engaged in the trade cannot be deduced from the remaining sources; however, there is evidence that some of *the merchants* participated in smuggling opium, which was obtained along Indian Ocean ports. In his *Notes on the China Trade*, Pierrepont describes that dollars and opium are the best exchange medium for trade at the Malaysian island Pulo Penang. Gouverneur & Kemble also advised Captain Swords of their ship *Sampson* to stop at Pulo Penang on the way to China to trade his wine for opium writing:

> There is at this place a great many of China Men and you will find a market for a considerable part if not the whole of the Wine—get rid of it if it is even in exchange for Opium from 300 to 350 Dollars per chest but prefer the Borniries Opium to that of the Patna. The Superintendant

76 A unit of weight used in some parts of Asia. One picul was equal to approximately 132 pounds or 60 kilograms.

77 In comparison, the English East India Company brought an annual average of 4000 chests of India opium to China. Downs, *American Merchants*, p. 421; Stelle, *American Trade in Opium*, p. 432.

78 Stelles, *American Trade in Opium*, p. 432.

79 For a detailed description of Perkinson's engagement in the trade see R.T. Van, 'Free Trade & Family Values: Kinship Networks and the Culture of Early American Capitalism', PhD Thesis, Columbia University, 2010.

80 See, for instance, the price currents from 22 September 1806 and 22 October 1806. A handwritten memorandum on different European and Asian ports lists opium as a possible export commodity from Smyrna. Bayard Correspondence 1751–1832, Bayard-Campbell-Pearsall families papers. Manuscripts and Archives. The New York Public Library. Astor, Lenox, and Tilden Foundations.

> Mr. Laight may accommodate [sic] you in this—he has always opium by him and either he or his house Scott&Co. purchase almost everything that comes to the Island and from whom you may generally count upon some freight.[81]

The opium acquired in Pulo Penang was then either disposed at a small smugglers' station outside of Macao at Lark's Bay or carried up the river to Whampoa, where it usually sold without difficulties to Chinese dealers.[82]

Ginseng was another commodity Americans brought to China as it is native to forests in East Asia and Eastern North America from Florida to Canada and from the Mississippi to the Atlantic.[83] Ginseng was used as a popular medical remedy in China. The *Empress of China* had made a considerable profit importing ginseng to China and many American merchants followed this example. According to Michael Block, the supply of ginseng became a source of income for many smaller towns and communities in upstate New York, Virginia, the mountain regions of western Massachusetts and the Connecticut River Valley from where ginseng was brought downriver to New York. The ginseng market was also reason for the foundation of a number of small towns in upstate New York in the 1780s and 90s like Rochester, Paris, Utica, and Clinton.[84] With the expansion of the ginseng trade, towns prospered and small manufacture industries developed. Block points out that in the town of Greenfield in Massachusetts, a 'ginseng preparation shop' was opened in 1791 after the town had been connected to the Connecticut River Valley trade.[85] New York's easy access to ginseng was a further reason why fewer merchants pursued the Atlantic and Indian Ocean routes instead of the Pacific trade. A large number of the ginseng supplies from western Massachusetts were shipped via the Connecticut River to New York instead of being brought overland to the seaports of New England.[86]

Although ginseng did not always sell well and markets in China were frequently exhausted, the right preparation could make an impact on the prices. As Hezekiah B. Pierrepont wrote in his notes:

---

81 'Letter to Capt. Swords, 25 January 1795', Gouverneur and Kemble, Letter book, 1794 May–1796 June, New York Historical Society Mss Collection.

82 Stelles, *American Trade in Opium*, p. 426.

83 Block, *New England Merchants*, p. 63.

84 Block, *New England Merchants*, p. 63.

85 Block, *New England Merchants*, p. 292.

86 Block, *New England Merchants*, p. 292.

> Gensang will always be demanded at Canton. But new modes of Curing & preparing it must be found out for in the state in which it is commonly sent from America it is of but little value compared with what it could be if prepared to resemble Tartar Gensang which is bright & of the color & clearness of Gum Senegal & hard solid & heavy & when broken is brittle & shows like a fine transparent gum. Of this kind I saw a small parcel which was gathered in the woods of America & cured by Dr. Hurst of New York which he sold for 100 Dollars per Catty in 1796 when the common sort would not bring more than 75 Dollar per picle [probably picul, L.S.][87]

The importation of ginseng to China was so immense that it changed prices and consumption patterns there, mitigating its status from a luxury good to a more accessible good that less affluent people could afford. Constable was informed of this trend by a business correspondent who wrote: 'We are told that in consequence of the Article becoming cheap in China the Common People are getting into the habit of using it in which Case we cannot form an idea to what Extent the Consumption will be.'[88] Gibson's statistics on the ginseng consumption in Canton, states that while Canton absorbed around 500 to 600 piculs before 1800, imports amounted to 800 piculs in the 1799–1800 season, 1,600 piculs in 1800–01 and 1,700 in 1801–02, with prices falling respectively from $400 to $190 in 1799 to $80 in 1801.[89]

How American merchants traded these common commodities for their outbound cargoes during an East Indies voyage will be detailed next.

Spanning a Net of Trade around the World—The Routes of the Ships *Washington, America,* and *Sampson*

The routes of William Constable's ship *Washington,* and Gouverneur & Kemble's ships *America* and *Sampson,* which sailed from New York to the Indian Ocean in 1791 and 1795, reveal the global network these East India bound vessels extended around the world, covering distances from New York to the Falkland

87 H. Pierrepont, Notes on the trade of China made at Canton 1796, Hezekiah Beers Pierrepont Miscellany, Volumes, Constable-Pierrepont papers. Manuscripts and Archives. The New York Public Library. Astor, Lenox, and Tilden Foundations.

88 'Undated Letter', Constable Papers, Wm. Constable Shipping Papers, Constable-Pierrepont papers. Manuscripts and Archives. The New York Public Library. Astor, Lenox, and Tilden Foundations.

89 Gibson, Otter Skins, p. 100.

Islands, South Africa, India, Malaysia, China, and Indonesia as well as several ports in Europe and the Caribbean. It uncovers how the New York merchants cleverly used a variety of different destinations to fit their ships for the trade, to acquire the best goods in the Indian Ocean, and to gain large profits in the re-export business. It also illustrates that they did not pass on any opportunity to make money and participated in a variety of businesses from the fur to the country trade, all of which were only possible by the information their vast networks of business partners supplied.

The *Washington* left New York early in 1791. Before the departure of a ship it was common for a merchant to hand captains and supercargoes instructions regarding the trade routes, commodity exchange, and customs of an Indian Ocean voyage. These letters detail the complex management and organization of the trading business. William Bell received, along with the letter, a bill of lading and an estimate of the sales of the cargo on 10 December 1790.[90] Equipped with 56 pipes of Madeira Wine, 400 cases of gin, pig iron, seals, and cordage, the *Washington* was set to sail for Bombay.[91] Constable's plan was to get to Bombay fast, 'being firmly Convinced that the Success of the adventure will, in a great measure, depend upon the ship's early arrival at Bombay; as by this means you will be certain of an advantageous Sale for your outward Investment before the Ships from Europe shall get in.'[92] The captain of the ship was Captain Hodgkinson who was also advised of the importance of a 'speedy passage.' Constable wanted the *Washington* to beat the European ships and to obtain a freight of cotton in Bombay for China.

For a smooth run of business in Bombay, Constable had written to his business partners Phyn, Ellice & Co. in London asking them to send a letter to John Forbes of Bombay recommending Bell. To save commission, Constable advised

90 'William Constable to William Bell, 10 December 1790', William Constable Letterbooks 1790–1791, Volumes, Constable-Pierrepont families papers. Manuscripts and Archives. The New York Public Library. Astor, Lenox, and Tilden Foundations.

91 The ship also carried a barrel of apples and nuts, which Constable sent to his correspondence partner Henry Forester Constable in Bombay. 'I send you a Barrell of apples which my mother has taken the pains to Paper and seal with Wax in hopes some of them will get to your hands—Mr. Bell will deliver you also a Barrel of Nutts which I fear will be rancid before you get them they will be a curiosity and I give them a chance,' 'William Constable to Henry Forester Constable, 10 December 1790', William Constable Letterbooks 1790–1791, Volumes, Constable-Pierrepont families papers. Manuscripts and Archives. The New York Public Library. Astor, Lenox, and Tilden Foundations.

92 'William Constable to William Bell, 10 December 1790', William Constable Letterbooks 1790–1791, Volumes, Constable-Pierrepont families papers. Manuscripts and Archives. The New York Public Library. Astor, Lenox, and Tilden Foundations.

Bell to hire a local broker and refrain from consigning the entire cargo to Forbes. Only in the case of unforeseen circumstances was Bell advised to rely on Forbes entirely. Instead Bell was supposed to sell his cargo on respondentia for payment in China to the merchants Pertonjee Bomanjee and Daddee Nerawanjee and obtain a freight of cotton from them. Otherwise the cotton cargo was preferably paid with bills of exchange drawn from London, which would preclude Bell from having to draw bills in China. According to Constable, the great advantage of being able to make purchases in China with silver outweighed the fees that had to be paid on such money advancement, even for a bad interest rate of nine percent. In Bombay, Bell had to collect information about the availability of large quantities of tin and pepper in Pulo Penang and, in case business prospects looked good, Constable recommended using his funds for pursuing business there instead of buying cotton in Bombay. Upon his arrival in Bombay, Bell was to send a letter to Mr. Laight at Pulo Penang to inform the latter about his intention and request a cargo of tin and pepper, desirably in the amount of 40 to 50 tons. Other possibilities for Bell were to sell the ship in Bombay, in the case that a war between Great Britain and Spain broke out which would likely bring a very advantageous profit on the vessel, or to charter it to an East India servant wanting to bring his family and effects to Europe in which case he was supposed to sail the ship to Ostend. The likelihood of such alterations was fairly slim and Bell's best chance was to proceed to Pulo Penang for the cargo of tin and pepper. From there he was also to write to Mynheer Inglehead Shabendar of Batavia asking for sugar and pepper which he could obtain on his journey back from China. Constable was optimistic that Mynheer Inglehead was able to help since he was the 'Governor's son in law and the head of the department of trade.'[93]

As William Bell had already made two journeys to China prior to the *Washington* trip, he was well aware of business practices in Canton so Constable had no need to instruct him in those issues. Constable relied on Bell's perfect understanding of the American markets and advised him to base his judgments on what others were shipping. Constable recommended that Bell not bring Bohea tea, even though it was an 'unfailing article,' because a large cargo of the tea was expected to arrive on the ship *President*. Constable expected, that two or three Swedish ships would sail to Canton that year as well and interfere with business, as the duty from Europe on Bohea tea was relatively low. Bell was advised to pay close attention to European politics since prices could increase

93 'William Constable to William Bell, 10 December 1790', William Constable Letterbooks 1790–1791, Volumes, Constable-Pierrepont families papers. Manuscripts and Archives. The New York Public Library. Astor, Lenox, and Tilden Foundations.

because of Russian participation in the French Revolutionary War. In case of an outbreak of war between Spain and Great Britain, Bell was encouraged to bring as much Hyson tea as possible. Since Souchong and common green tea were of little demand in the United States but sold better in Europe, Bell was told to judge how much to take according to the shipments of the British East India Company. Constable expected to sell a large quantity of the teas to Ostend and Amsterdam, advising Bell to bring teas suitable for those markets. In the case that large quantities of Bohea Tea was shipped to the United States by other vessels, the purchase of sugar and pepper was more advisable. Constable wrote, 'The Consumption of Sugar in our Country is immense and from the distracted State of the French Colonies and the chance of a British War you may calculate upon 8 Dollars as an average price.'[94] Nankeens were also considered good articles and, if they were of good quality, they were expected to sell for five pounds sterling in Europe and the West Indies.

Attached to the letter was an estimated cost calculation of the *Washington* and her cargo: the London investment to draw in Bombay would bring Bell £9000 or $40,000. Together with the sales of the 56 pipes of Madeira wine, worth $5600; the 400 cases gin ($1600); the pig iron ($4400); and cadage ($2400) Bell had an estimated amount of $54,000 of which $2000 were deducted for petty charges and expenses. For the 750 candy units of cotton, Constable approximated getting $30 a unit minus $1125 for commission which totaled $21,735. For the respondentia bond taken in Bombay ($30,000 at a rate of 9 percent), $2700 needed to be paid in commission. In Pulo Penang, he estimated paying $15 per parcel for 500 parcels of tin totaling $7500 and for the 400 parcels of pepper a total of $6000. Additionally he estimated he needed $1600 for a respondentia bond taken in the Straits of Malacca on $20,000 with an eight percent interest rate. This would leave Bell in Canton with a capital of roughly $116,416 consisting of the $54,000 from Bombay (sales and investment from London), the $21,375 for the cotton, $3375 for the sale of the tin and pepper, $6666 for the sale of the seal skins at $1 per skin and the 31,000 Spanish silver dollars that were brought from New York. From this money $8416 was deducted for duty and expenses, which would give Bell a fund of $108,000 to be invested for Chinese goods: an estimated $46,000 for 1000 chests Bohea Tea, $20,000 for 500 chests Hyson, $18,000 for 500 chests Single Souchong, $12,000 for nankeens, $7000 for silk and chinaware and $5000 for commission. For the sales of the goods in New York, Constable calculated a return of $177,500 which included

94 'William Constable to William Bell, 10 December 1790', William Constable Letterbooks 1790–1791, Volumes, Constable-Pierrepont families papers. Manuscripts and Archives. The New York Public Library. Astor, Lenox, and Tilden Foundations.

$85,000 for the Bohea Tea, $29,000 for the Hyson, $27,000 for the Souchong, $22,500 for the Nankeens and $14,000 for the silk and chinaware. After the subtraction of about $7500 he would be left with net proceeds of $170,000. For the cost of the cargo he estimated $130,000, which would leave him $40,000 net gains. After subtracting another $7000 for interest on his advance in London he would have $33,000 profit or about 30 percent on the capital.[95]

In reality, Bell and Hodgkins arrived in Bombay later than expected as they were caught in a heavy storm and had to stop at Isle of France for repairs. They were nonetheless able to sell their cargo for a very good price to John Forbes. Opting against the purchase of cotton, they stopped at Pulo Penang where they picked up the tins and pepper, which along with the sealskin were readily sold in Canton in November 1791. On their return voyage they went to Batavia for sugar and pepper. The *Washington* arrived in New York in May 1792. Her cargo of Chinese goods, sugar and pepper sold readily, yielding the largest return any East Indies voyage had ever made until that point.[96]

Gouverneur & Kemble undertook a similar voyage in 1795. Encouraged by the success of their previous East Indies journeys, they decided to send out two vessels in the 1795–96 season to India and China.[97] Although the firm complained about the high exchange rate of 9.5 percent for bills and heavy insurance premiums due to the European wars, the business still seemed to be lucrative enough to invest into a second vessel.[98] Both the *America* and *Sampson* were dispatched in February 1795. Captain Howe, Joseph Gouverneur and Peter Cruger as supercargoes sailed with the *America*. Captain Swords was supercargo and captain on the *Sampson*. For Gouverneur and Cruger it was their first trip as supercargoes, so the instructions from the firm were very precise.

---

95 'William Constable to William Bell, 10 December 1790', William Constable Letterbooks 1790–1791, Volumes, Constable-Pierrepont families papers. Manuscripts and Archives. The New York Public Library. Astor, Lenox, and Tilden Foundations.

96 'Constable to James Constable, 18 June 1793', William Constable Letterbooks 1793–1794, Volumes, Constable-Pierrepont families papers. Manuscripts and Archives. The New York Public Library. Astor, Lenox, and Tilden Foundations and Davis, William Constable, pp. 167–168.

97 'Gouverneur & Kemble to Daniel Beale, 1 November 1794', Gouverneurand Kemble, Letter book, 1794 May–1796 June, New York Historical Society Mss Collection. The letter also mentions some of the returns of the cargos of the ships *America* and *Washington* which were sent to Canton in 1795. Daniel Beale received half of the net prices of the sales of silks and nankeens which came to a value of $97,617.

98 'Gouverneur & Kemble to Daniel Beale, 1 November 1794', Gouverneur and Kemble, Letter book, 1794 May–1796 June, New York Historical Society Mss Collection.

Both ships were sent to Bombay first, where they were advised to stay at a hotel, which was cheaper than hiring a Dubash[99] and other servants. Their first task in Bombay was to purchase a freight of cotton. The local contacts in Bombay were Pertonjee Bomanjee and Daddee Nerawanjee, the same men used by William Constable. The supercargoes carried letters for Bomanjee and Nerawanjee from the company in New York. The outward investment comprised of Swedish confined bar iron along with specie; the former was supposed to be sold in Bombay provided it would sell for at least $6.5 per parcel and could be retained in the ship until it reached Whampoa. Otherwise they were instructed to try to sell the iron to a country ship since, according to Gouverneur & Kemble, there was always demand for iron in Macao or Manila. In Bombay the supercargoes had to show their managing qualities for the first time since finding the right moment to sell specific goods was a tricky affair. Negotiations with the local merchants for the cotton could constitute another challenge and they were advised to exercise their best judgment at all times. For the cotton they were to receive a respondentia bond at $50 per candy with a premium of ten percent. Gouverneur and Cruger carried $64,595 for the Chinese merchant Shyshingua, which the latter had loaned to the firm during the *America*'s previous voyage. If they wanted to, they could loan that money as respondentia to other merchants provided they could obtain at least a ten percent return. They needed, however, to consult with Bomanjee and Nerawanjee first, to ensure that the signers of the bonds were trustworthy. According to Gouverneur & Kemble money was in high demand in Bombay and they could loan it to very favorable conditions with high premiums and a return period of only 31 days instead of the usual 61.

On their way to China they were advised to stop at Pulo Penang where they were instructed to try to purchase tin or opium to bring to China. If both were not available they should try to obtain betel nuts and rattans, two commodities in high demand on the Chinese markets.[100] The importance of time management was explicitly highlighted and they were instructed to 'by no means create delays' or to be in such a hurry as to miss a great business opportunity. Upon their arrival in Canton, they had to search for a factory able to accommodate both ships. They carried a letter for the security merchant, Shypingea,

99 A Dubash was a local broker who usually supplied all the provisions and personnel for the foreign trading houses.

100 'Gouverneur & Kemble to Joseph Gouverneur and Peter Cruger, 20 January 1795', Gouverneur and Kemble, Letter book, 1794 May–1796 June, New York Historical Society Mss Collection.

who was their first merchant of choice. In case they were not happy with his suggested terms and prices, they could then begin negotiations with another merchant, Ponguea. The supercargoes were instructed to immediately contact a merchant named Sychon and order chinaware, as the china required time to be painted.

The negotiation of the contract with their security merchant was a very important task that would test the supercargoes' skills. They were advised to retain the iron to get a more advantageous price for it. They also had to ascertain their bills of exchange to draw from London, which they would use as a means for paying. The bills were drawn in Joseph Gouverneur's and Peter Cruger's name from Smith & Atkinson in London with a length of twelve months, in the amount of £10,239.14.[101] The following goods were requested from China (as listed in the original document).

For the *America*
1000 Chests Bohea Tea
600 Half Bohea Tea
1000 Bags Sugar 500 picul
200 chests Hyson
100 chests Gunpowder
200 chests Young Hyson
500 chests Hyson Skin
100 chests of best Ankoy Souchon
20 Boxes Rhubarb
50 Boxes Good Cashia
100, 000 Pieces of Good Yellow Nankeens of second chop

For the *Sampson*
600 chests Bohea Tea
400 Half chests Bohea Tea
600 Bags Sugar 300 picul
50 Chests Gun Powder Tea
100 Chests Hyson Gornu
200 Chests young Hyson
500 Chests Hyson Skin
50 Chests of Ankoy Souchon
50 picul Quicksilver

101 'Gouverneur & Kemble to Smith & Atkinson, 8 December 1796', Gouverneur and Kemble Letter book, 1794 May–1796 June, New York Historical Society Mss Collection.

20 picul Rhubarb
100 picul Caskia
20 boxes Vermilion
40 picul Camphine
50,000 pieces Yellow Nankeens[102]

Cruger and Gouverneur were to pay $64,595 Dollars to Shyshingua for the cargo and obtain a new credit ($60,000 on the *America* and $40,000 on the *Sampson*) to pay back within two years.[103] Additionally, the supercargoes were advised to buy first quality Hyson tea, which was hard to find and produced only in small quantities because of the British monopoly. Hong merchants of Canton usually did not have access to the fine Hyson tea so the supercargoes had to turn to silk merchants. In case they were able to get some tea of excellent quality, they would have to deposit it somewhere until their other business was finished as not to offend the Hong merchants, who were usually responsible for all of a ship's tea provisions. Being present for the weighing of the tea in Canton was of the utmost importance, and they were to constantly oversee the smooth procedure of business. Their finances required some special tactics. The $64,595 obligation for Shyshingua was made payable for January 1796. If they loaned out the money in Bombay they had to make sure that they calculated the necessary time needed to retrieve it back, in order to make the payment to Shyshingua on time. As soon as the first set of chinaware was ready, they were instructed to equip the *Sampson* with it, so that the vessel could make an early dispatch back to New York.[104]

The *Sampson* and *America* returned to New York in May 1796. Their cargos were readily expected and many applications to purchase the goods had been made to Gouverneur & Kemble by local merchants before their arrival.[105] The supercargoes had been able to obtain the goods that the company ordered,

102 'Gouverneur & Kemble to Joseph Gouverneur and Peter Cruger, 20 January 1795', Gouverneur and Kemble, Letter book, 1794 May–1796 June, New York Historical Society Mss Collection.

103 'Gouverneur & Kemble to Shyhingua, February 1795', Gouverneur and Kemble, Letter book, 1794 May–1796 June, New York Historical Society Mss Collection. In the letter Gouverneur & Kemble expressed their discontent of the quality of the Congs and Souchon teas and some nankeens from the former voyage of the *America*.

104 'Gouverneur & Kemble to Joseph Gouverneur and Peter Cruger, 20 January 1795', Gouverneur and Kemble, Letter book, 1794 May–1796 June, New York Historical Society Mss Collection.

105 'Gouverneur & Kemble to William Buckley, 9 April 1796', Gouverneur and Kemble, Letter book, 1794 May–1796 June, New York Historical Society Mss Collection.

leaving Gouverneur & Kemble with a large variety of china, nankeens, rhubarb, sugar, and teas. New York merchant James Morewood anticipated that the *Sampson* would overflow New York's market with India goods. He wrote to Samuel Ferguson, who was at that point still a merchant in Philadelphia, to cancel his planned assignment of silks and nankeens as a 'ship has a pretty considerable quantity of both these articles which it is presumed, will soon sink this market for them to a level of yours.'[106]

Gouverneur & Kemble's plan was to then send the *Sampson* with freight straight to Amsterdam and afterwards to London, where the ship would get coppered.[107] Haro Coster was their contact person in Amsterdam. Gouverneur & Kemble advised captain Rooke to rely entirely on Coster's judgment. In case he encountered trouble with one of the parties at war, he had to show a manifest accompanying the bill of lading, which stated that all articles on board were American property.[108] The *Sampson* set sail to Amsterdam in July 1796 and the journey went as planned.[109] The vessel returned to New York in early March 1797 and was immediately sent on another East Indies voyage to India and China, with Captain Rooke and Joseph Gouverneur as supercargo carrying cargo amounting to $82,530, consisting mainly of silver and Madeira wine from the house of Newton, Gordon & Murdoch.[110] Although both the *America* and *Sampson* had brought satisfying cargoes from the East Indies, sales were slow. After calculating the enormous capital needed for two voyages and selling the *America*, Gouverneur & Kemble decided to employ only one of their vessels in the Asia trade.[111]

The voyages of the *Washington, America,* and *Sampson* are great examples of East Indies voyages. They illustrate the cost calculations companies made

106 'J. Morewood to Samuel Ferguson, New York, 6 June 1796', Series II: Business Records, Ferguson family papers. Manuscripts and Archives. The New York Public Library. Astor, Lenox, and Tilden Foundations.

107 'Gouverneur & Kemble to Smith & Atkinson, 18 April 1796', Gouverneur and Kemble, Letter book, 1794 May–1796 June, New York Historical Society Mss Collection.

108 'Gouverneur & Kemble to John Rooke, 16 July 1796', Gouverneur and Kemble, Letter book, 1794 May–1796 June, New York Historical Society Mss Collection.

109 'Gouverneur & Kemble to Smith & Atkinson, 6 July 1796', Gouverneur & Kemble letter book. Manuscripts and Archives. The New York Public Library. Astor, Lenox, and Tilden Foundations.

110 'Gouverneur & Kemble to Smith& Atkinson, 2 March 1796', Gouverneur and Kemble, Letter book, 1794 May–1796 June, New York Historical Society Mss Collection.

111 'Gouverneur & Kemble to Richard Jennings, 29 August 1796', Gouverneur & Kemble letter book 1796–1798. Manuscripts and Archives. The New York Public Library. Astor, Lenox, and Tilden Foundations.

in advance of and during voyages. Market demands dictated the goods desired from the East. Their estimation was based on information about annual consumption in the United States, the numbers of vessels sailing to the East, and the sales of previous seasons. Price information and commodity memorandums from other ports also played an important role. Credit arrangements and participation in local trade helped to reduce the necessity of silver.

The opening of the East Indies trade brought a plethora of new global business opportunities to *the merchants*, virtually spreading their enterprises around the world. Within a short period they managed to establish new global relationships and integrate different markets and commodity chains into their home market. They were successful managers of a complex trade system. They were also people of the moment, using every opportunity to make money. They proved themselves to be flexible and elegant actors who could easily adjust to changing global conditions. Just how much these conditions continued to work in their favor will be examined next.

Trade with Europe

America's entrance into Asian trade networks shortly after the American Revolution and the establishment of an important branch of commerce with the East Indies is an example of how changing global patterns benefitted American merchants. But American merchants also profited from another late eighteenth century crisis: the European wars.

When France declared war on Austria in 1792, Americans were quick to announce their neutrality. Although the United States was legally bound to France through the Treaty of Alliance, issued in 1778 during the American Revolution, the war-weary nation had no intentions to militarily support the French cause. President Washington recognized the slim chances of winning and feared the consequences of another strenuous war for the young republic. He declared a 'policy of non-intervention' arguing that since France was the aggressive power, the U.S. was not bound to the treaty, which was 'defensive in nature.'[112] The decision to stay neutral brought along new economic opportunities resulting in a boom in America's export business in the years following. The value of exports increased almost five-fold from \$20.2 million in 1793 to \$94 million in 1801, reaching a peak of \$108.3 million in 1807.[113]

112 G.H. Williams, *The French Assault on American Shipping, 1793–1813: A History and Comprehensive Record of Merchant Marine Losses*, Jefferson, McFarland & Co., 2009, p. 2.

113 Williams, *French Assault on American Shipping*, p. 2.

The United States profited from its neutrality in two ways. Firstly, the export shipping of domestic products, particularly wheat, flour, and other foodstuffs boomed as Europe faced several bad harvests and needed large supplies of wheat for its armies. Spain, Portugal, and Great Britain were major buyers of crops as were the West Indies. The demand for marine and forest products like lumber, naval stores, and ashes rose as well.[114] By 1790, flour was the United States' top export article listing before tobacco and rice, the pillars of the old export trade. Even though it would soon be replaced by tobacco, for about ten years flour and wheat constituted the foundation of its export commerce.

A second opportunity lay in the fact that American merchants were now able to take over the carrying trade from the belligerent European powers. Within only three years, from 1790 to 1793, the value of re-exports quadrupled from $539,000 to $2,110,000. In 1794 it tripled again, reaching a value of $6,526,000, which expanded to $26,300,000 in 1796, and peaked at $60,283,000 in in 1806.[115] During those fifteen years, the re-export business reached a combined value of $439 million. The re-export business was comprised of several trade channels. For one, it included the shipping of European goods to the West Indies. Another sector consisted of the re-exporting of East Indies goods to Europe and the West Indies, and a third accounted for West Indies goods that were brought to Europe. The war forced the European motherlands to lift their restrictions requiring colonial goods to go through the mother country before being shipped to other destinations. Before the war, Havana sugar, for example, could not have been shipped to Bordeaux or Hamburg unless it went through Spain. Because of that change, it became possible for American shippers to bring sugar directly to non-Spanish ports.[116] The contribution of the re-export business to America's economic landscape was enormous. From 1800 to 1805, American merchants re-exported a yearly average of more than 37.6 million pounds of coffee, 4.2 million pounds of pepper, and 72.7 million pounds of sugar. The numbers even increased in the years 1806 and 1807, reaching an average of 45 million pounds of coffee and 144.5 million pounds of sugar.[117]

New York's merchants were active in numerous branches of the European trade, speculating heavily on Europe's wars and crises. William Constable employed several of his ships, the *Carleton, Ellice, Fame, Grange, Nancy, Perservance,* and *Peter* between New York and Europe. The *Carleton, Ellice,* and *Peter* regularly voyaged to England; the others went to ports on the continent. He maintained close ties to the firms David Gregoris and Son in Dunkirk, France;

114 North, *Economic Growth*, p. 40.

115 Nettels, *Emergence of a National Economy*, p. 235.

116 Marzagalli, *Transatlantic Trade Networks*, p. 823.

117 North, *Economic Growth*, p. 230.

the Wilikings, Jacob van Staphorst, and Hubbard & Co. of Amsterdam; George Keith & Co. of Ostend; John Parish & Co. of Hamburg; Chalmers and Cowie of London; and Le Couteulx & Co. of Paris. Constable started exporting wheat and flour to Europe in 1789, after hearing of the bad harvests on the continent. He sent several brigs and sloops to Pennsylvania, Maryland, and Virginia to purchase flour and wheat which was shipped to Europe, in particular, France.[118] The years between 1789 and 1793 proved to be so lucrative for American provisions trade that Constable saw himself in ever-greater need to obtain those large cargoes. He wrote numerous letters to merchants asking to buy wheat, flour, rice, and tobacco and, as it was becoming more difficult to obtain the amounts of wheat needed, he decided to grow his own wheat and build a flourmill. He even wrote to London to send him a miller, as it was impossible for him to find one in the United States.[119] Constable did not only ship flour: re-exports also accounted for large parts of his shipments. In the early 1790s he made large profits while shipping teas and nankeens to Amsterdam. The sloops *Grange* and *Nancy*, which were dispatched to Amsterdam in September and December 1790, carried a combined cargo of almost two thousand chests of Hyson and Souchong tea. The *Grange* went to Amsterdam where her cargo was disposed to Jacob van Staphorst and in Dunkirk the *Nancy* went to David Gregorie and Sons of Dunkirk. Constable had already dispatched the *Grange* to Ostend with a cargo of 600 chests of Hyson tea and 400 chests of Souchong earlier that year.[120] He counted a profit of £10,000 from his tea exports to Amsterdam and hoped a war between Britain and Spain would raise the prices for goods from China.[121]

118 In 1789, the *Bell, Commerce, Industry, Maria, Peggy Wallace,* and *Russell* all brought freights of wheat and flour to France. In 1791, Constable included other vessels: the *Adventure, Carleton, Eagle, George, Grange, Gratton, Margaret, Nancy,* and *Perservance*. Davis, *William Constable,* p. 194.

119 'Constable to John Portius, 12 January 1790', William Constable Letterbooks 1790–1791, Volumes. Constable-Pierrepont families papers. Manuscripts and Archives. The New York Public Library. Astor, Lenox, and Tilden Foundations. Most of those mills were large-scale enterprises purchasing wheat from farmers outside of the community and selling the flour to distant markets. Three elements were necessary for their successful operating: a steady wheat supply, abundant water, and access to distant markets. See B. Hunter, 'Wheat, War, and the American Economy During the Age of Revolution', pp. 508–509.

120 'William Constable to Morris, 30 July 1790', William Constable Letterbooks 1790–1791, Volumes, Constable-Pierrepont families papers. Manuscripts and Archives. The New York Public Library. Astor, Lenox, and Tilden Foundations.

121 'William Constable to Gouverneur Morris, 6 Oct 1790', William Constable Letterbooks 1790–1791, Volumes, Constable-Pierrepont families papers. Manuscripts and Archives. The New York Public Library. Astor, Lenox, and Tilden Foundations.

Gouverneur & Kemble were also heavily involved with the Europe trade in the 1790s. During 1794 and 1798, they had several ships—the *Briseis, Diana, Franklin, Nancy, Ellice, Oliver,* and *Friendship*—regularly sailing from New York to London, Bordeaux, Amsterdam, and Hamburg, but also to Havre, Leghorn, Ostend, and Lisbon.[122] Their main business partners were Smith & Atkinson in London; Jonathan Jones in Bordeaux; DeChapearouge in Paris; Mallhuessen & Sillem in Hamburg; and P. & C. Van Eeghen, Haro Coster, and Hope & Co. in Amsterdam. From the existing records there is evidence that Gouverneur & Kemble were involved in the wheat trade to Europe; however, they abandoned the trade in the mid-1790s when prices of wheat and flour spiked. In a letter to Smith & Atkinson, they wrote that they had been in the 'habit of shipping wheat from this country, in particular to the Portugal market' but stopped due to the speculative character of the trade. They did, however, point out that they were not opposed to sending out a vessel 'when favorable opportunities' presented themselves.[123]

During 1794 and 1798, the trade with three continental European ports, Bordeaux, Hamburg and Amsterdam, seemed to be of special importance to the firm. The general character of the Hamburg and Amsterdam trade can be demonstrated by the example of the ship *Briseis*, which was dispatched to Northern Europe in February 1796. Gouverneur & Kemble and the firm Rutgers, Seaman & Odgen, organized the ship in a joint venture; Benjamin Seaman sailed with it as supercargo. The cargo consisted mostly of sugar and indigo from the West Indies. In a letter to Seaman on 1 February 1796, the firm gave precise instructions on how to organize the trade. Seaman was advised to either go to Amsterdam or Hamburg depending on the better market. He could obtain market information while stopping in Cowes at the Isle of Wight in the English Channel. Seaman carried letters to Van Eeghen of Amsterdam and De Chapeaurouge and John Parish in Hamburg. It was of great importance to bring the necessary paperwork and acquire depositions and certificates for the cargoes, as the company needed the papers to obtain rebates on the duties. For the outbound cargo he was counseled to bring Geneva wine, gunpowder, Osnaburgs (coarse flax, tow, or jute fabrics), coffee bags made from coarse textiles and harlem stripes (linen). In case he could not obtain a proper cargo or needed more ballast he was encouraged to load 'good hard Bricks.'[124]

122 The ships *Briseis, Diana, Franklin, Nancy, Ellice, Oliver, Friendship, Diana,* and *Franklin* regularly went to Bordeaux.

123 'Gouverneur & Kemble to Smiths & Atkinson, 2 January 1796', Gouverneur & Kemble letter book. Manuscripts and Archives. The New York Public Library. Astor, Lenox, and Tilden Foundations.

124 'Gouverneur & Kemble to Benjamin Seaman, 1 February 1796', Gouverneur and Kemble, Letter book, 1794 May–1796 June, New York Historical Society Mss Collection.

The credit for the goods was supposed to be sent via Parish to Smith & Atkinson. Linen and coarse textiles were the most desired goods from Hamburg. In a letter from Gouverneur & Kemble to Henry Beare in Hamburg, they asked for hemp, iron, cordage, tallow, window glass, linen nankeens, stripes, and coarse textiles suitable for coffee bags, as well as Dutch creme cheese.[125]

American exports to Hamburg boomed in the 1790s and the number of ships entering the city increased more than six-fold from 1791 to 1798. In 1799 almost 200 American ships arrived in Hamburg.[126] Additionally, the number of ships sailing under American flags also rose drastically. Many captains from other countries used the American flag to protect their vessels from belligerents. American administrators, however, did not inactively watch the misuse of their flag and prompted more drastic measures for its protection. In 1793, John Parish, American consul to Hamburg, declared that all American ships had to deliver their papers and certificates immediately to the consul upon their arrival in Hamburg's port, and urged the Hamburg senate to forbid allowing vessels in the custom house if they were unable to show a certificate signed by the American consul.[127]

The French Revolutionary Wars gave Hamburg an unexpected trade boom when French and Dutch merchants started to ship their colonial goods to Hamburg. The city rose to become one of the most important transshipment points for colonial goods on the European continent. The harbor was also an important German wheat channel to middle and southern Europe. French supplies, however, ceased during the 1790s when France became more entangled in the war and lost its West Indian territories. France still exported about 23,000 barrels of sugar to Hamburg in 1790 (England brought only 4828), but it reduced those numbers to 291 in 1795 whereas England brought 25,390 barrels in the same year. The United States and England then took the lead as Hamburg's main suppliers of West Indian commodities.[128]

When the Netherlands were brought into the war, Hamburg's economy boomed even more and almost all of continental Europe's West and East Indies

125 'Gouverneur & Kemble to Benjamin Seaman, 1 February 1796', Gouverneur and Kemble, Letter book, 1794 May–1796 June, New York Historical Society Mss Collection. Russian goods were mainly hemp, flax, tar, iron, and duck linen. In the same letter, the firm orders a fashionable silver tea set from London for personal use.

126 Baasch, E., *Beiträge zur Geschichte der Handelsbeziehungen zwischen Hamburg und Amerika; Festschrift der Hamburgischen Amerika Feier*, Hamburg, L. Friederischen & Co., 1892, pp. 67–68.

127 Baasch, *Beiträge zur Geschichte der Handelsbeziehungen zwischen Hamburg und Amerika* p. 68.

128 Baasch, *Beiträge zur Geschichte der Handelsbeziehungen zwischen Hamburg und Amerika*, pp. 71–74.

products went through the city. In the late 1790s, however, France increasingly captured American vessels, which made it riskier for American merchants to send ships to Europe. Trade was also interrupted shortly in 1801 by the occupation of Hamburg by the Danish and the blockage of the Elbe by the British. In 1802 and 1803, only 56 and 32 American ships, respectively, docked in Hamburg as a majority of American merchants began to prefer Amsterdam over Hamburg. In 1804, 161 American ships arrived in Amsterdam compared to 87 in 1803.[129] When the French captured Hamburg in 1806, the situation became even more precarious, hindering commerce substantially.

Letters to Samuel Ferguson from Krüger & Orth, his business partners in Hamburg, bear example of this uncertainty. From 1805 to 1807 Ferguson & Day shipped West and East Indian goods worth more than $63,000 to Krüger & Orth in Hamburg, mainly sugar and coffee but also Indian textiles. On 28 November 1806, Ferguson received a letter from Krüger & Orth informing him of the occupation of Hamburg; it brought their business operations to a temporary standstill. The Hamburg company asked Ferguson not to make use of the credits they had recently drawn. Since no vessels were permitted at Hamburg's port, Krüger & Orth advised sending letters via Copenhagen and Gothenburg.[130] Other businessmen were quick to make use of the dire situation in Hamburg. On 16 December 1806, Westrik & Co. of Amsterdam sent a letter to Ferguson asking him to assign his cargo to Amsterdam rather than Hamburg:

> The great Events who [sic] have taken place on the Continent have changed the Situation of our market who [sic] is in this moment particularly favorable for Colonial products notwithstanding the little Demand for Germany in this Season. We take the liberty to give you at the Bottom our actual price, desiring much that you will be pleased to address us your Cargo destined for Hamburg where we fear that will Come great disastrous fruits of Circumstances. We are in the occasion, by our extended relation to procure you the highest prices and recommending us in your friendship ...[131]

---

129 Baasch, *Beiträge zur Geschichte der Handelsbeziehungen zwischen Hamburg und Amerika*, pp. 76–82.

130 'Krüger & Orth to Samuel Ferguson, Hamburg 28 November 1806', Ships: *Henrietta Charlotte, Margareth, Ocean, Argus*, Account with Krüger & Orth, Series II: Business Records, Miscellaneous 1794–1817, Ferguson family papers. Manuscripts and Archives. The New York Public Library. Astor, Lenox, and Tilden Foundations.

131 'Westrick & Co. to Samuel Ferguson, Amsterdam, 16 December 1806', Series II: Business Records, Miscellaneous 1794–1817, Ferguson family papers. Manuscripts and Archives. The New York Public Library. Astor, Lenox, and Tilden Foundations.

The letter highlights the fine line between one merchant's misfortune and another's fortune brought about by the European Wars. It also reveals merchants' opportunistic character and their immediate flexibility to shift business plans and adapt to new patterns of trade, even those arising during war.

Similar trends like those in Hamburg happened in Bordeaux, when American shipping increased substantially after 1793. Commerce between Bordeaux and the United States before 1793 was small as Bordeaux focused on other destinations in the Atlantic world and showed relatively little interest in trade with North America. Silvia Marzagalli underlines that throughout the 1790s only 30 to 40 U.S. ships entered Bordeaux's port each year and only a few of Bordeaux's vessels stopped at ports in the new republic. With the beginning of the French wars commerce changed significantly, making Bordeaux one of the major destinations for American sailors and the most important French harbor for American commerce. In 1795 more than 350 American ships had arrived there. Before 1793 most of the American ships entering Bordeaux came from southern ports bringing tobacco, rice, and staves. These journeys were usually done on New England vessels, which had gone to the South to load cargo before crossing the Atlantic. The range of items shipped to Bordeaux widened after 1793 and included goods from the East and West Indies, with sugar and coffee being the main commodity. Some ships proceeded from Bordeaux to other European destinations, most frequently Hamburg. The return cargo usually consisted of wine and brandy, which was hitherto often re-exported to destinations in the West and East Indies.[132]

Gouverneur & Kemble's brig *Diana* was an American ship sailing between New York and Bordeaux on a regular basis. In 1796, the *Diana* was sent to Bordeaux with a cargo valued at $46,670. Samuel Gouverneur sailed with her as supercargo. Originally the *Diana* was supposed to go to India but business with Bordeaux appeared so promising that the company changed course.[133] The ship was loaded with colonial goods for the French market and sought to bring back wine and brandy. For the outbound cargo Gouverneur was advised to draw credits through the houses of Haro Coster in Amsterdam and Parish in Hamburg. He also carried letters signed by the English and French councils in case the vessel entered into conflicts with those powers. The journey went smoothly at first, leaving the company at home with great expectations. In December 1796, however, they learned that Samuel Gouverneur had decided

132 Marzagalli, *Establishing Transatlantic Networks*, pp. 812–822. Until 1793 Le Havre used to be the first destination for American merchants.

133 'Gouverneur & Kemble to Smiths & Atkinson, 8 December 1796', Gouverneur & Kemble letter book 1796–1798. Manuscripts and Archives. The New York Public Library. Astor, Lenox, and Tilden Foundations.

to continue onto the West Indies instead of sailing straight home as he anticipated great profits for the French wines and brandy on the islands. It was a bold decision, which left the company in New York furious as the ship had no insurance for such an undertaking and the West Indian waters were unsafe due to the ongoing wars between the European powers. The company expected to lose the ship entirely. A letter to Jonathan Jones in December 1796 expressed the New York company's anger, accusing Jones of not properly advising Samuel Gouverneur.[134] Luckily the *Diana* made it safely to Guadeloupe in a 34 days which relieved the company at home; the ship's safe arrival meant they could expect profitable business, as prices for sugar and coffee had been high in Europe in 1796 and 1797.[135] Samuel Gouverneur expected to sell the wine and brandy and, if necessary, draw an additional credit to obtain a cargo of $60,000 worth of coffee and sugar, goods that the company planned to immediately dispatch to Bordeaux in another voyage of the *Diana*. In the meantime, they sent their ship *Franklin* off with a cargo of sugar, coffee, and cotton worth $50,000 to Bordeaux. But the situation in the West Indies left Gouverneur & Kemble worrisome. French and English ships were at the time capturing many ships coming from Caribbean ports, which made business for American merchants riskier.[136] The *Diana* indeed was captured and held in the Caribbean by a British privateer but luckily was released after one month and allowed to sail back to New York where she arrived in April 1797. The costs for her release amounted to $2,000, which was partly paid by the insurance obtained for her voyage from Guadeloupe to New York.[137] Despite the trouble in the Caribbean, she was immediately outfitted for another journey to Bordeaux with a cargo of coffee, cocoa, and cotton worth more than $23,800, and a cargo of nankeens worth $50,000 shipped on a joint account with Nicholas Cruger and William Edgar. The money received for it was to be channeled back to New York through the hands of Mallhuessen & Sillem of Hamburg and Dan Crommelin & Sons of

134 'Gouverneur & Kemble to Jonathan Jones, 26 December, 1796', Gouverneur & Kemble letter book 1796–1798. Manuscripts and Archives. The New York Public Library. Astor, Lenox, and Tilden Foundations.

135 'Gouverneur & Kemble to Smiths and Atkinson, 14 January 1797', Gouverneur & Kemble letter book 1796–1798. Manuscripts and Archives. The New York Public Library. Astor, Lenox, and Tilden Foundations.

136 'Gouverneur & Kemble to Jonathan Jones, 2 February 1797', Gouverneur & Kemble letter book 1796–1798. Manuscripts and Archives. The New York Public Library. Astor, Lenox, and Tilden Foundations.

137 'Gouverneur & Kemble to James Crawford, 24 June 1797', Gouverneur & Kemble letter book 1796–1798. Manuscripts and Archives. The New York Public Library. Astor, Lenox, and Tilden Foundations.

Amsterdam.[138] Unfortunately, the French government confiscated the cargo of nankeens and held them at the port of Bordeaux. Jones tried to manage their release. This, along with the higher prices for Brandy, had brought the company less money than calculated and neither the *Diana*, which returned to New York in September 1797, nor the *Franklin* had made the profits expected of them. Gouverneur & Kemble expressed their disappointment in a letter to their Hamburg correspondents Mallhuessen & Sillem.[139] However, the *Diana* was dispatched immediately for another voyage to Bordeaux and returned in early spring 1798 bringing a cargo of Brandy, which made a 'handsome voyage.'[140]

Le Roy, Bayard & Co.'s remaining business papers illustrate that their company, too, was substantially involved in trade with Northern European ports like Havre and Hamburg and with a variety of Mediterranean ports, most notably Naples, Leghorn, Marseilles, Barcelona, Malaga, Alexandria, and Smyrna. Their business records entail letters with correspondents as well as several memorandums and price currents from these ports through the year 1819. Many of these memorandums list great demands for provisions like rice, flour, wheat, and Indian corn, as well as coffee, sugar, dye goods, and cotton and even also East India goods like teas, textiles, and pepper. Goods exported from the Mediterranean usually included wines, fruits, olive oil, raisins, figs, and drugs.[141]

The company's commercial engagement in the Mediterranean sea, reaching as far as Alexandria and Smyrna, is an example of how quickly American merchants managed to expand their trade routes. During colonial times, the United States had already traded with the Mediterranean world through British merchants on a steady basis and many merchants were familiar with the

---

138 'Gouverneur & Kemble to Samuel Gouverneur, 7 May 1797', Gouverneur & Kemble letter book 1796–1798. Manuscripts and Archives. The New York Public Library. Astor, Lenox, and Tilden Foundations.

139 'Gouverneur & Kemble to Mallhuessen & Sillem, 18 September 1797', Gouverneur & Kemble letter book 1796–1798. Manuscripts and Archives. The New York Public Library. Astor, Lenox, and Tilden Foundations. Here the sources are conflicting as the company writes in a letter to Jonathan Jones that the sales of the *Diana* have brought them funds of at least $20,000 to $30,000. 'Gouverneur & Kemble to Jonathan Jones, 1 October 1797', Gouverneur & Kemble letter book 1796–1798. Manuscripts and Archives. The New York Public Library. Astor, Lenox, and Tilden Foundations.

140 'Gouverneur & Kemble to James Murphy, 12 March 1798', Gouverneur & Kemble letter book 1796–1798. Manuscripts and Archives. The New York Public Library. Astor, Lenox, and Tilden Foundations.

141 'Invoice of Merchandize, 10 November 1805', William Bayard Accounts & Papers, 1805 June-December, Bayard-Campbell-Pearsall families papers. Manuscripts and Archives. The New York Public Library. Astor, Lenox, and Tilden Foundations.

business structures.[142] When in the late eighteenth and early nineteenth century many of the Mediterranean regions underwent changes as a result of accelerating economic and demographic growth, Americans profited highly from these increasing business opportunities. Demand for wheat, sugar, and coffee increased in the European as well as in expanding Ottoman markets. The Tuscan port city Leghorn (formerly Livorno) emerged as a central commercial hub for Mediterranean shipping where merchants of different countries brought European, Caribbean, American, and Ottoman goods together.[143] In the 1810s, Le Roy, Bayard & Co. kept regular business with Leghorn to which they shipped mainly coffee, sugar, cotton and dyewoods, rice and flour, pepper, and East Indies textiles. Return commodities from Leghorn included olive oil, anchovies, capers, and olives.[144] One of the ships was their schooner *Fanny.* Credits were arranged through the Baring Brothers.

How significant the Mediterranean trade had become for the new republic is apparent in the fact that the United States decided to deploy its naval force to protect American merchants against the Barbary Pirates in the wars with Tripoli in 1801 and Algeria in 1815. The pirates from the North African shores had increasingly seized American vessels going through the Strait of Gibraltar. It is presumed that part of the reason the U.S. government sent its navy was the high profits that were achieved with trade in the region and the willingness by the government to protect and enhance commerce.[145]

Considering *the merchants*' engagement in the European trade, the following assertions explain their success: first, the wars in Europe did not constitute an obstacle but were rather a welcomed circumstance. Their performance as neutral suppliers of foodstuffs and luxury products to which the Western world had become accustomed in Europe and the West Indies, promoted them to

---

142 An excellent read about American trade with the Mediterranean is *Rough Waters: American Involvement with the Mediterranean in the Eighteenth and Nineteenth Centuries, Research in Maritime History, No. 44,* S. Marzagalli, J.R. Sofka and J.J. McCusker (eds.), St. Johns: International Maritime Economic History Association, 2010.

143 A.J. Antonucci, 'Consuls and Consiglieri: United States Relations with the Italian States, 1790–1815', in S. Marzagalli, J.R. Sofka and J.J. McCusker (eds.), *Rough Waters: American Involvement with the Mediterranean in the Eighteenth and Nineteenth Centuries, Research in Maritime History,* No. 44, St. Johns: International Maritime Economic History Association, 2010 p. 79.

144 'Letter from Mott to Bayard, 23 November 1816, Bayard Correspondence 1751–1832', 1816 June-December, Bayard-Campbell-Pearsall families papers. Manuscripts and Archives. The New York Public Library. Astor, Lenox, and Tilden Foundations.

145 See Sofka, *Jeffersonian Idea,* p. 163; G. Fremont-Barnes, *The Wars of the Barbary Pirates: To the Shores of Tripoli: The Rise of the US Navy and Marines*, Oxford, Osprey, 2006, p. 13.

powerful trading partners. Their flexibility in reacting to the shifting policies of belligerent European powers enabled them to circumnavigate restrictions and bring forward new trading patterns. A net of partners and information correspondents was a crucial prerequisite for success. Remarkably, *the merchants'* collaboration with business partners did not stop at national borders. Quite the contrary, despite the ongoing wars, the merchant class across Europe and the Americas found ways to work cooperatively, channeling money and information across national borders—even among warring countries. A most striking circumstance in *the merchants'* trade with France is that it was accomplished in almost all cases with the help of British, Dutch, and German banking houses. Their transnational teamwork is thus an example of the global coordination and interaction in overseas trade. America's commercial expansion to Europe was the result of favorable global circumstances that opened room for agency. Yet, there is one event that perhaps best shows how quickly American merchants used a global crisis to their advantage: the Haitian Revolution.

The West Indies Trade

Shortly after the American Revolution, American merchants were facing meager business opportunities as large parts of the West Indies trade were restricted by the European powers who banned Americans from trading with their colonies. Before the war, commerce with the British West Indies was the principal mode of economic engagement of most American port cities. Twenty to twenty-five percent of all vessels from Boston, New York, Philadelphia, and Charleston were trading with the British Antilles in the years from 1768 to 1772.[146]

After independence, business did not return to its previous heights. Britain prohibited American vessels from trading with its West Indian territories and taxed all shipments from there to the United States as foreign exports. However, most of the islands could not provide enough food for their growing slave and planter population, increasing the need for American food and lumber, especially oak staves, which were needed to make barrels for molasses. In 1784, the British Council authorized the importation of lumber, flour, grain, and livestock and the exportation of coffee, rum, sugar, molasses, cocoa nuts, and ginger with the stipulation that it had to be shipped on British vessels. These restrictions pushed American merchants to pursue trade with the

146 See M. Craig McDonald, 'The Chance of the Moment: Coffee and the New West Indies Commodities Trade', *William & Mary Quarterly*, Third Series, vol. 62, no. 3, July 2005, p. 445.

Dutch, Swedish, and Danish ports that were open to them.[147] Bad harvests in Europe as well as several hurricanes in the Caribbean had made it impossible for the European countries to meet flour demands in the colonies and, as a result, France opened five West Indies ports to American merchants in 1784 and 1785, three in Saint-Dominique. It abolished bans on American flour and food staples and allowed Americans to start bringing provisions to the island in exchange for colonial produce. Saint-Dominique, the world's leader in sugar and coffee production, took on the role of the United States' main supplier. Imports to Saint-Dominique surpassed all other American West Indies exports combined.[148]

In the late 1780s, the United States started to recover from its post-revolution recession and large parts of the country were engaged in the West Indies trade again, but now the trade with the French West Indies accounted for the largest share. That trend accelerated with the onset of the European Wars in 1793: the West Indies trade became one of the United States' main branches of foreign trade constituting nearly one-third of the total exports between 1790 and 1814.[149] In 1793, the French Council opened all French West Indian ports to American traders and in the decade after, half to four-fifths of all coffee imports in the United States came from the French Antilles.[150]

The war undermined European monopolies on trade with their colonies, opening up new trade opportunities as the belligerent powers turned to neutral American shippers. For example, during the European Wars high demands for American flour came from the West Indies. In 1790, more than half of America's flour went there.[151] The newly won freedom to trade, however, did not come without obstacles: the powers of war now tried to hinder and detain neutral vessels delivering provisions to their enemies, leaving American merchants in risk of detention and capture.

The Jay Treaty between the United States and Britain, although aimed to improve American commercial success, had the opposite effect. After learning of the new British-American alliance, France rejected American claims of neutrality and French seizure of American vessels sailing to England increased. After 1796, customs agents on the French Islands increasingly charged American vessels for illegal trading. In 1797, more than three hundred American ships

147 A detailed account on America's trade with the West Indies is found in J.H. Coatsworth, 'American Trade With European Colonies in the Caribbean and South America, 1790–1812', in *William & Mary Quarterly*, Third Series, vol. 24, no. 2, April 1967, pp. 243–266.

148 Coatsworth, 'American Trade with European Colonies', p. 245.

149 Coatsworth, 'American Trade with European Colonies', p. 243.

150 Craig McDonald, 'Coffee and the New West Indies Trade', p. 460.

151 Hunter, *Wheat*, p. 516.

were indicted by French customs in Saint-Dominique and Guadeloupe.[152] Likewise, the British authorized its naval forces to detain all ships going to and from the French West Indies in 1793, after the French opened all their ports to American traders.[153]

According to Coatsworth, the European powers viewed America's engagement with disagreement but had few options to prevent it. Although they tried to protect their commercial monopolies most legislations were undermined by the colonies. In 1798, Spain opened its ports to the United States and American merchants increasingly carried Caribbean products to Europe and South America. However, exports of gold and other goods remained prohibited for exportation to non-Spanish ports. When the colonies ignored the decree, 'systematically violating the ban,'[154] the crown saw itself forced to revoke the opening. However, the need for provisions and interest in trading with the United States remained too strong and the colonists conspired to ignore the evocation and keep most of the ports open. In 1798, U.S. imports reached $8 million a year. Cuba received the highest share of all American exports to Spanish colonies; as a result of the slave trade and the migration of French colonists from Saint-Dominique the island's population grew considerably between 1792 and 1817.[155] Trade to South American continental colonies also grew after 1807. Montevideo and Buenos Aires became important trading destinations for American merchants. Isaac Bell's business correspondence shows that he was trading with Buenos Aires in the early nineteenth century, continuing even after Argentinian independence from Spain.

The commodities that were shipped depended on the destination. While the British West Indies almost exclusively imported U.S.-American domestic products (from 1803 to 1812 they accounted for 89% of all imports) Spanish and French colonies relied much more on Americans as carriers.[156] In 1806, the United States 'was wholly in possession of the carrying trade between Mexico and Europe.'[157]

How profitable commerce with the West Indies was can be noticed in the fact that American merchants kept pursuing the trade although they constantly

152 Craig McDonald, 'Coffee and the New West Indies Trade', p. 462. Most of the ships were forced to sell their cargo before they left the ports. Craig McDonald points out that in most cases ships were stopped not for violating Caribbean export laws but because French Islands needed American food and staples. Craig McDonald, 'Coffee and the New West Indies Trade', p. 462.

153 Coatsworth, 'American Trade with European Colonies', p. 250.

154 Coatsworth, 'American Trade with European Colonies', p. 253.

155 Coatsworth, 'American Trade with European Colonies', pp. 253–254.

156 Coatsworth, 'American Trade with European Colonies', p. 257ff.

157 Liss, *Atlantic Empires*, p. 113.

had to take the seizure of a ship into account. The European conflicts in the West Indies presented great risks but even greater opportunities. That it was the Haitian Revolution that saved William Constable from bankruptcy is just one example of how much American merchants gained from these conflicts.

The Haitian Revolution

The Haitian Revolution began as a consequence of the French Revolution in 1791 when Saint-Dominique's 'free people of color' claimed full civil equality, which was opposed by the island's white planter elite. The claims added to the tense relations between slaves and plantation owners. The tension culminated in a massive slave revolt on 21 August 1791, drawing the colony in a civil war for thirteen years. Since Saint-Dominique was France's most valuable colony and producer of 40 percent of Europe's sugar and 60 percent of its coffee supplies,[158] the revolution constituted a major political and economic event in the Atlantic world. Not only were French troops involved in the fight, Britain and Spain also became immersed in the conflict. Hoping to secure Saint-Dominique for their own empire, Spanish colonial officials supported the revolting slaves by giving land and liberty to the soldiers. In 1793, Francois-Dominique Toussaint Louverture, leader of the revolting slaves, became a Spanish officer and remained such until 1794. Britain was interested in Saint-Dominique as well as in weakening France. First and foremost, it tried to hinder French ships from going to the Caribbean, but in September 1793, it deployed troops from Jamaica to Saint-Dominique. Fighting against Spanish and British forces, Léger Félicité Sonthonax, leader of the French commission to grand citizenship for 'the people of color', offered amnesty and freedom to the rebel slaves if they joined in the fight against the belligerents. In August 1793, he declared an end to slavery in the north, south, and west provinces of Saint-Dominique. The declaration was ratified by the French national convention on 4 February 1794, which ended slavery throughout France's West Indian territories. Toussaint Louverture deserted from the Spanish forces and became one of the island's most important French officers fighting Britain and Spain. In 1795, Spain signed a peace treaty with France. Toussaint was promoted to commander of the west provinces and negotiated treaties with Britains and the U.S., opening ports for trade despite the ongoing war between France and Britain. Within a few years, Toussaint managed to rebuild most of the island's economy, trading sugar and coffee to

158 L. Dubois, and J.D. Garrigus, *Slave Revolution in the Caribbean, 1789–1804: A Brief History With Documents*, Boston, Bedford/St. Martins, 2006, p. 8. The book provides a detailed account of the events of the Haitian Revolution.

American merchants. But Toussaint came into conflict with André Rigaud, general of the southern provinces and representative of the 'free people of color' whom Toussaint accused of continuing white racist politics. The conflict resulted in another thirteen months of brutal civil war and ended in Toussaint's victory stabilizing his rule over the island in 1800. But politics in Europe put the newly won freedom of Saint-Dominique's former slaves at risk. In 1804 Napoleon Bonaparte became emperor and many feared a return to slavery because his aspirational plans for France's empire relied on a restoration of its Atlantic economy. Hearing of the news from Paris, Toussaint 'made a bold move.'[159] He decided to write a new constitution for Saint-Dominique, which confirmed the abolition of slavery. The French government then sent expeditions to the Caribbean with the order to reinstate slavery. An excursion guided by Napoleon's brother-in-law, Charles-Victor-Emmanuel Leclerc arrived in Saint-Dominique arresting Toussaint and sending him to France where he was imprisoned until his death in 1803. When Leclerc tried to disarm the former slaves, fighting broke out again. Napoleon, getting closer to losing the island, gave up his American ambitions and sold Louisiana to the United States. On 1 January 1804, Jean-Jaques Dessaline declared independence from France and Saint-Dominique became Haiti, the first independent state in Latin America.

The United States' reaction towards the slave revolt were mixed. Especially in the Southern states, the revolt was seen as setting a terrible example which had to be stopped before revolutionary sentiments could spread among American slaves. The Northern states, on the other hand, welcomed the opportunity to establish trade with the former French colony. The Adams administration wavered between helping to stop slave unrest or using it as an opportunity to increase trade with the island and weaken France. While Adams was at first hesitant to support the revolutionists, the Quasi War with France during 1798 and 1800 caused a shift in his geopolitical strategy. During that time commercial and diplomatic ties were established between Saint-Dominique and the United States that were crucial for Saint-Dominique as it provided the island with much-needed supplies.

Historian Ronald A. Johnson argues that it was because of those ties that the Haitian Revolution succeeded, as American provisions and arms helped the island prepare for the French invasion. Americans in return benefited from open ports to the 'Pearl of the Antilles.' Adams and Louverture reached out to each other in 1798, when Louverture offered Adams closer commercial and political ties, which the Adams administration readily accepted. Diplomatic relationships to Saint-Dominique were established in the Intercourse Act of 1799 and Edward Stevens of Philadelphia was sent to Cap Français as Consul

159 Dubois and Garrigus, *Slave Revolution*, p. 35.

General. Great Britain, seeing a chance to interfere with France's Atlantic trade, supported the relationship. Fear that Stevens might negotiate an inclusive trade agreement with Toussaint, however, caused Britain to broker a tripartite trade accord, which tied the direct trade to Saint-Dominique exclusively to British and American ships. In the next two years, American merchants kept vivid trade relations with Saint-Dominique and the Adams administration provided military help to the rebels.[160]

When Jefferson came into power in 1801 the attitude to Saint-Dominique changed as the new president took a more ambivalent stance towards the slave revolt. A Francophile, Jefferson was tempted at first to support France's attempt to regain control of the island. He perceived Great Britain's rising dominance in the Caribbean as a threat and encouraged France to restore its commercial and naval presence to keep a balance of power in the Caribbean. But in 1802, when he heard about the size of the troops Napoleon had sent to the Caribbean with the Leclerc expedition, Jefferson hesitated. Suspicious of a greater plan by the French emperor that included the occupation of New Orleans, the president shifted his sympathies towards Louverture and the British. His administration took a neutral stance in the conflict and rejected France's wish to embargo Saint-Dominique and starve the revolutionists. They left the decision to continue trade with the island at the risk of French seizure to the merchants. That decision allowed American trade channels to Saint-Dominique to remain open, which maintained the supply of goods to the revolting slaves. That policy as well as Jefferson's refusal to supply the French expedition with loans or credits was directly helpful to Saint-Dominique's revolutionists and thus supported the island's independence. It also set an end to Napoleon's Caribbean aspirations and allowed Jefferson to purchase Louisiana from the French. After Haitian independence, Jefferson shifted his policies towards the island again, and like most European countries, refused to recognize Haiti's independence, rejecting any cordial bonds. That refusal and rejection resulted in tremendous economic hardship for the young republic and kept it diplomatically and socially isolated for decades.[161]

New York's merchants observed the slave revolt critically. For one, they shared a common European ethnocentrism where they regarded a slave revolution as

160 R.A. Johnson, *Diplomacy in Black and White: John Adams, Toussaint Louverture, and their Atlantic World Alliance*, Athens, GA, University of Georgia Press, 2014. Johnson inquires into the relationship between the United States and Saint-Dominique during the Adams administration and details the political debates about concepts of slavery and race that accompanied those discussions.

161 Tim Matthewson, 'Jefferson and Haiti', *The Journal of Southern History*, vol. 61, no. 2, May, 1995, pp. 209–248. Matthewson details Jefferson's motives and his weighing of reasons in the conflict.

something 'unthinkable'[162] and feared the economic consequences that would result from the loss of one of their main suppliers of colonial goods. In 1796, Gouverneur & Kemble wrote about the situation in Saint-Dominique:

> We are persuaded while the War continues the prices of West India produce must keep up both here and in Europe even if a peace should take place (which we are inclined to think is not very distant) the supply of those articles will be short for a considerable time. That valuable Island of St. Domingo is so desolated and laid waste by the emancipating of the Negroes it will produce very little for a length of time and attended with some difficulty to bring them into tolerable order again. Our trade with these colonies is much interrupted at present—the British capture our vessels going to the French ports and the French capture going to the British ports so that between the policy of the two they will ultimately injure each other, and cut off their supplies which has been considered requisite to arrive from this country.[163]

William Bayard made a similar statement six years later in a letter to Hottinguer & Co. of Amsterdam:

> Your house writes us that the accounts from St. Domingo were of the most melancholy & dreadful nature—it was apprehended the Whites would be compelled to evacuate that unfortunate Island, as the Insurgent Negroes were hemming them in on every quarter— nothing would save the Island but a fresh supply of troops, those already there were dying rapidly—The Crops both of Coffees & Sugars were destroyed—These most distressing Events to the feelings of humanity, will have an unfortunate influence in the neighboring Islands & Colonies, & must no doubt enhance the prices of their Produce.[164]

162 M.R. Trouillot, *Silencing the Past: Power and the Production of History*, Boston, Beacon Press, 1995, p. 73. The chapter on the Haitian Revolution is an interesting read on how the slave revolution became an unacknowledged event in historical scholarship. He points out that Western contemporaries were incapable of understanding what was happening as their 'categories were incompatible with the idea of a slave revolution.'

163 'Gouverneur & Kemble to Texier, Angely & Massac, 3 October 1796', Gouverneur & Kemble letter book 1796–1798. Manuscripts and Archives. The New York Public Library. Astor, Lenox, and Tilden Foundations.

164 'William Bayard to Hottinguer & Co., 24 December 1802', Bayard Correspondence 1751–1832, 1800–1802, Bayard-Campbell-Pearsall families papers. Manuscripts and Archives. The New York Public Library. Astor, Lenox, and Tilden Foundations.

American merchants were affected by a shortage of sugar and coffee that came with the slowdown of Saint-Dominique's plantation economy. Prices for these two commodities surged. In the letter William Bayard continued to lament how the crisis in the Caribbean had almost doubled prices in just eight days.[165] But soon merchants recognized that the conflict in Saint-Dominique offered them great economic prospects, as they could increase their carrying trade. As large numbers of French and British ships were involved in the conflict, the colonies became dependent on American merchants more than ever.[166]

A trade scheme by William Constable is a great example of how merchant houses profited from the Haitian Revolution.[167] In 1795, William Constable had returned from London to New York just in time to save his firm, which had been mismanaged during his absence by his brother James. James, with little sense for business, had driven the company into almost $300,000 of debt.[168] Constable had concentrated all his efforts into reorganizing the business when he learned of the opportunity that eventually saved his house. Phyn, Ellice & Inglis in London heard in summer 1795 that more British troops were to be sent to the Caribbean and sensed that great money could be made in the supply of their provisions. As John Inglis wrote to Constable on 21 August 1795:

> There are 2000 men going to the West Indies all to be fed from your country and I believe dependence will be placed upon open markets & no contracts made. If you can persuade any smart Yankee to set immediately about procuring proper means to carry cattle to the army … he will do well.[169]

In September 1795, another letter to Constable followed: 'Horses and Mules will be wanted in great numbers. Live cattle as they mean to give the army

165 'William Bayard to Hottinguer & Co., 24 December 1802', Bayard Correspondence 1751–1832, 1800–1802, Bayard-Campbell-Pearsall families papers. Manuscripts and Archives. The New York Public Library. Astor, Lenox, and Tilden Foundations.

166 Dubois and Garrigus, *Slave Revolution*, p. 34.

167 For a discussion of Philadelphia merchants' involvement with the revolution in Haiti see J.A. Dun, '"What Avenues of Commerce Will You Americans Not Explore!" Commercial Philadelphia's Vantage Onto the Early Haitian Revolution', *The William & Mary Quarterly*, Third Series, vol. 62, no. 3, July 2005, pp. 473–504.

168 Davis, *William Constable*, p. 231.

169 'John Inglis to William Constable, 21 August 1795', William Constable Correspondence, Constable Papers, Constable-Pierrepont family papers. Manuscripts and Archives. The New York Public Library. Astor, Lenox, and Tilden Foundations.

fresh meat & negroe provisions for five or six thousand pioneers.'[170] Just a week later, another letter arrived, advising Constable to get

> ... some active and fit persons to go to New London and buy up all the good fat cattle you think shipping can be procured to carry and engage all the shipping that can be got at the same time whether for them or fit to carry horses or Mules and any number of Horses or good mules may be purchased.[171]

Phyn, Ellice & Inglis managed to render a deal with George Cruden, a Martinique based merchant and member of a well-known London merchant house. Cruden, along with his partners Francis Pollard and Mr. Stuart, held a contract for supplying the British troops in the West Indies. Phyn, Ellice & Inglis acted as surety for them and recommended William Constable as a supplier of live cattle to Martinique and Barbados.[172] On December 12, 1795, Constable wrote that the sloop *Betsy* would leave for the Caribbean the following day loaded with thirty oxen and thirty hogs. Six days later, two other ships carrying 36 oxen, 50 hogs, and 50 sheep were dispatched as well as the ship *Sally* that carried 100 oxen and as many hogs.[173] Constable engaged Jeremiah Wadsworth of Hartford, Connecticut, and Joseph Howland of New London to organize the acquisition of cattle mainly from New Haven and Connecticut. In 1796, Cruden decided to give the entirety of his army contract business to Constable and partners, making it a business operation of considerable magnitude. In February 1795, more British troops were deployed to the West Indies increasing the number to 70,000.[174]

Accounts of Jeremiah Wadsworth and William Constable illustrate the extent of the venture. From May 1796 to February 1797 an account by Elias Shipman of New Haven lists the following shipments from New Haven:

170 'John Inglis to William Constable, 10 September 1795', William Constable Correspondence, Constable Papers, Constable-Pierrepont family papers. Manuscripts and Archives. The New York Public Library. Astor, Lenox, and Tilden Foundations.

171 'John Inglis to William Constable, 19 September 1795', William Constable Correspondence, Constable Papers, Constable-Pierrepont family papers. Manuscripts and Archives. The New York Public Library. Astor, Lenox, and Tilden Foundations.

172 R.J.B. Knight, and M.H. Wilcox, *Sustaining the Fleet, 1793–1815: War, the British Navy and the Contractor State*, Woodbridge, Boydell Press, 2010, p. 140.

173 'Constable to John Inglis, 12 December 1795', William Constable Correspondence, Constable Papers, Constable-Pierrepont family papers. Manuscripts and Archives. The New York Public Library. Astor, Lenox, and Tilden Foundations.

174 Davis, *William Constable*, p. 246.

1796:	
May 16:	34 oxen shipped on sloop *Dove*
May 21:	36 oxen shipped on brig *James*
May 23:	34 oxen shipped on ship *Two Brothers*
June 14:	34 oxen on brig *Friendship*
	34 oxen on brig *Eliza*
June 16:	32 oxen on brig *Susan*
September 20:	34 oxen on schooner *Iris*
October 5:	36 oxen on sloop *Dove*
	28 oxen on schooner *Amelia*
1797:	
January 19:	28 oxen in schooner *Amelia*
January 30:	30 oxen in schooner *Iris*
February 8:	34 oxen in sloop Captain Brown[175]

A business account between Jeremiah Wadsworth and James & William Constable shows that in May 1796, Wadsworth shipped an additional 388 oxen in shipments of 30 to 45 animals from New London on the ships *Friendship, Iris, Samuel, Four Sisters, Michael, James, Hannah, Lucy,* and *Polly,* as well as 18 sheep and 25 hogs. The shipments were valued at almost $30,000.[176] From these remaining accounts it can be estimated that Constable and his partners sent livestock at about 500 animals a month to the Caribbean with a value of around $50,000 monthly.[177] By 1797, French seizures and plundering of American ships increased drastically, leading up to the Quasi War of 1798–1800 between the United States and France. In view of the higher risks for American ships, Constable and his partners saw themselves forced to cancel the contract with Cruden.[178]

175 'Account of Jeremiah Wadsworth with Elias Shipman', Box 7, William & James Constable Shipping Papers, Cruden's Contract, William Constable Papers, Constable-Pierrepont papers. Manuscripts and Archives. The New York Public Library. Astor, Lenox, and Tilden Foundations.

176 'Abstract of Jeremiah Wadsworth's Account with William and James Constable', Box 7, William & James Constable Shipping Papers, Cruden's Contract, William Constable Papers, Constable-Pierrepont papers. Manuscripts and Archives. The New York Public Library. Astor, Lenox, and Tilden Foundations.

177 These numbers correlate with Davis's estimate that livestock for more than 5000 people was shipped per month at a value of $50,000 each month. Davis, William Constable, p. 246f.

178 Davis, *William Constable*, p. 248.

Interestingly enough, Cruden is also mentioned in Oliver Wolcott's correspondence from 1805. From Wolcott's remaining letters it appears that Jesse Hopkins & Co. of Hartford continued to deliver livestock for Cruden.[179] The letters revolve around a dispute with Cruden over three cargoes of livestock and flour that were shipped in spring 1803 to Barbados, which Cruden had considered unacceptable and for which he refused to pay.[180] Additionally, John M. Vickar of New York sued Hopkins & Co. for reimbursement of $4000 for goods shipped on these cargoes.[181] The records do not mention how the dispute with Cruden was resolved. They make clear, however, that New York's merchants were great profiteers of the lasting conflicts in the Caribbean. Haiti is also a great example of how federal politics supported American merchants in their international trade, which will be explored further in the next chapter.

Commercial Politics

American politicians faced a variety of challenging problems after independence. Besides establishing a new machinery of government they were confronted with the European wars and Atlantic conflicts in which they had to take a diplomatic stance. The protection of global interests (mostly economic) quickly became a leading norm in the new republic's foreign policy common to both Federalists and Republicans. Adams's and Jefferson's handling of Saint-Dominique are examples that show how foreign policy was driven by a pragmatic approach to guarantee the country's commercial interests. In fact, between 1784 to about 1815 international and global economic considerations were at least as important as domestic ones. American merchants profited enormously from these politics as it created a framework in which they could carry out free and unfettered trade.

Global factors already played a large role in the constitution-building process. After the revolution, the United States found itself in a commercially grim

179 'Oliver Wolcott to George Cruden New York 29 February 1804', Oliver Wolcott letterbook. Manuscripts and Archives. The New York Public Library. Astor, Lenox, and Tilden Foundations.

180 'Oliver Wolcott to Theodore Dwight, New York 29 January 1805', Oliver Wolcott letterbook. Manuscripts and Archives. The New York Public Library. Astor, Lenox, and Tilden Foundations.

181 'Oliver Wolcott to Theodore Dwight, New York 29 January 1805', Oliver Wolcott letterbook. Manuscripts and Archives. The New York Public Library. Astor, Lenox, and Tilden Foundations.

position. Great Britain, although it had ceased its hostilities, was still not friendly towards the young nation and remained in control of the northern frontier and parts of northwestern backcountry. The British also controlled large parts of the Atlantic trade and had refused to allow American merchants access to its ports. Similarly, Spain had imposed restrictions on its West Indies colonies and was involved with the United States in conflicts over the Mississippi River and New Orleans. The Congress of Confederation quickly sent diplomats to Europe to negotiate trade agreements with the European powers. John Adams, Benjamin Franklin, and Thomas Jefferson were sent to get the United States out of its desperate commercial position. Their success was slim. After two years they had only managed to carve out a trade agreement with Prussia, while the other European countries, committed to their protectionist policies, remained uninterested in trade agreements with the young republic.[182] They reasoned that America's decentralized system, in which each state could negotiate its own trade agreements, made negotiations too complicated and not worth the hassle. Consequently, the question of whether Congress or the president should have authority in foreign commerce was debated heavily in the next years between Republicans and Federalists.[183]

One of the battlegrounds at the Constitutional Convention was the Commerce Clause, centering on corporations and trade. In it, James Madison, author of the clause, addressed not only the regulation of foreign commerce, but also the permission of granting federal corporate charters, which was understood by opponents as the granting of monopolies. People's memories of trade monopolies were still fresh and repulsion towards them was high. Hence, in many state debates over ratification, the question of monopolies was a strongly disputed topic. Massachusetts, Rhode Island, New York, New Hampshire, and North Carolina approved the Constitution but voted for a ban on monopolies.[184]

Most merchants, too, feared monopolies, yet favored federal support of foreign trade matters. Their hopes were high for the federal government to facilitate international commerce. One of the measures was the introduction of tariffs and duties. Some of the port cities had already introduced tariffs but most merchants hoped for a uniform tariff regulation. The Tariff Act from 1789

182 On diplomacy of that time, read F.J. Merli and T.A. Wilson. *Makers of American Diplomacy, From Benjamin Franklin to Henry Kissinger*, New York, Scribner, 1974.

183 Ferling, *Jefferson and Hamilton* p. 154. Ferling argues that it was because of the problems he encountered in formulating trade agreements with the European powers that Jefferson changed his opinion on the nation's foreign commerce.

184 Fichter, *So Great a Proffit*, p. 40ff.

was such legislation. It was intended to stimulate trade, protect local industries, and generate federal revenue. It introduced a general duty on all goods imported to the United States. Alexander Hamilton, by then Secretary of the Treasury, had suggested the Tariff Act would encourage domestic industries. The extent of the tariffs was debated by two competing positions: advocates of a truly protective tariff and advocates of a tariff for revenue only. The introduced tariff taxed rates from 5 to 15 percent only, which was a moderate rate. Alexander Hamilton, for instance, argued for a much higher rate to expedite domestic industrialization.

The act also claimed higher duties for teas imported by the British East India Company and other European traders, compared to teas imported from China or India directly by American merchants, highlighting the importance attributed to that sector of trade. The East Indies merchants had lobbied successfully for the protection of their profitable business.

From a letter written by William Constable to William Chalmers in December 1787, it becomes apparent that Constable was a supporter of the Tariff Act. Constable had just made impressive profits on the sales of the cargo of the *Empress of China* and he informed his correspondent that though he had already made $150,000 with the sales, he feared competition from Dutch Bohea tea on the market. For this reason, he favored a uniform legislation on higher duties on foreigners for China goods.

> We are in hopes of getting the duties considerably augmented on China Goods not imported direct from the place of their growth. Which is at present the Case in several of the States. Should the New Confederation take place, one uniform Code of Commercial Laws will be adopted which must be attended with very great advantages to the Union at large, indeed this appears to be one of the principal points aimed at by the New Constitution, as it is the only real inconvenience which We labour under.[185]

Another political debate over the mingling of trade and foreign politics was the discussions on the Foreign Intercourse Bill of 1798.[186] South Carolina Federalist Robert Goodloe Harper had sent the bill, which asked for a budget for the

185 'William Constable to William Chalmers, 10 December 1787', William Constable Letterbooks 1782–1790, Volumes, Constable-Pierrepont families papers. Manuscripts and Archives. The New York Public Library. Astor, Lenox, and Tilden Foundations.

186 Historian Robert W. Smith covers the debate in detail. R.W. Smith, 'The Foreign Intercourse Bill of 1798 and the Debate over Early American Foreign Relations' in *Journal of the Early Republic*, vol. 36, no. 1, Spring 2016, pp. 125–149.

diplomatic corps for the next two years, to the House of Representatives. When Republican John Nicholas disapproved of the bill, arguing that the size of the diplomatic corps should be reduced, a debate over the fundamental nature of American foreign commerce began. According to the Republicans, trade was to be separated from politics. There was no need for diplomats as trade was to regulate itself and foreign ministers had no means to protect American trade. The disappointing results of the commercial treaties—most prominently the Jay Treaty—were used to justify that reasoning. Since European powers relied on trade with the United States, trade could be used as substitute for diplomacy and there was no need for any further involvement by diplomats into European politics. Republicans favored a policy that strictly avoided any entanglements with politics and prefered a commercial diplomacy that was conducted by consuls instead of public ministers (compared to public ministers, consuls were private non-salaried men). Federalists dismissed the strict separation of politics and trades, arguing that consuls could not substitute diplomats. As non-salaried private merchants, they were always to put their own interests first and were not protected under the law of nations. For Federalists, political contact between the United States and the European countries was important and diplomats were influential for the protection and pursuit of American interests abroad.[187]

Consuls took a leading role in the promotion of American business interests abroad. In the two decades after the revolution, American consuls rose from three in 1781 to ten in 1790 and 52 consular posts in 1800. The map below (Fig. 1) illustrates the concentrations of consuls along the most important trading hubs and shows how Americans had expanded their trade network around the world.[188]

Most of the consuls were businessmen who conducted their own enterprises while simultaneously offering consular services like assisting American seamen and captains; taking charge of stranded American ships; receiving protests and declarations against American shipping matters; inventorying ships or estates of Americans abroad; and providing information to captain and crew members. They were also supposed to report the number of American vessels arriving at their ports and the military and political situations in their cities to

187 Smith, 'The Foreign Intercourse Bill of 1798 and the Debate over Early American Foreign Relations', p. 136.

188 Department of State, Historian's Office, 'American Consular Officers, 1789–1800' (Unpublished Paper, 1964) cited by C.S. Kennedy, 'The American Consul: A History of the United States Consular Service, 1776–1914', *Contributions in American History*, No. 139, New York, Greenwood Press, 1990, p. 20.

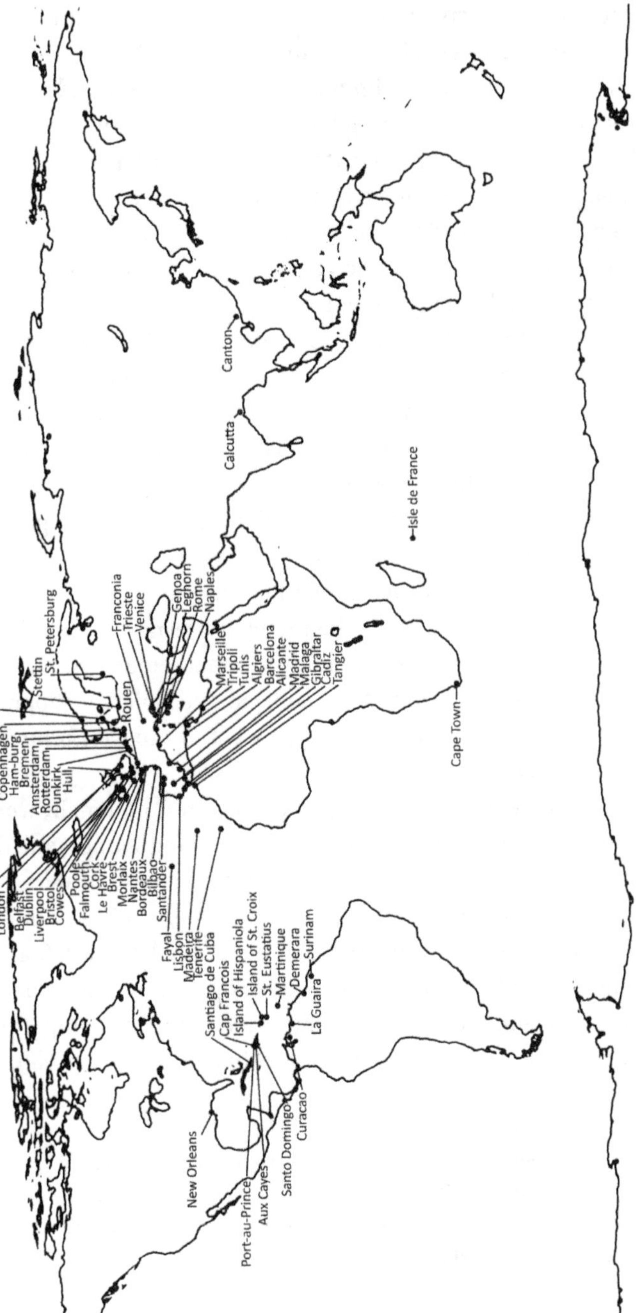

FIGURE 1 *American consular officers 1789–1800*
SOURCE: DEPARTMENT OF STATE, HISTORIAN'S OFFICE, 'AMERICAN CONSULAR OFFICERS, 1789–1800,' (UNPUBLISHED PAPER, 1964).

the Secretary of State every six months.[189] Especially in the relationship with the Barbary States, consuls were given an important role.[190]

Consul services were especially important between 1790 and 1815, when neutral American vessels often fell victim to capture and blockade by the French and British. A neutral ship that was stopped by naval vessels or privateers would usually be examined and when found guilty of carrying cargo from or going to an enemy port, would be taken as a prize. It was then brought to a friendly port where a tribunal would determine if the ship had been taken legally. If so, the cargo would usually be sold to the highest bidder and the money split between the capturers. The seamen and captain of the seized ships were left penniless. Consuls were important negotiators in these issues. They helped with legal matters and tried to get the ship back and attend to the distressed crewmembers.[191] Consuls were also often business partners and correspondents to mercantile firms. They were important in disseminating news about their home markets, and were often used to update captains and supercargoes who after months on sea, needed to be provided with detailed information. Their reports were especially crucial during the European wars, when political landscapes were constantly changing. The merchant firms at home thus benefited greatly from the consuls' market knowledge and credit establishments, their information of war and piracy and the legal and political support they provided in the ports. It is not surprising that most of *the merchants* kept in close contact with consuls in their trading networks.[192]

Government initiatives to protect private business internationally were welcomed by the merchant community as long as they offered support and did not regulate or shut off international trade like the Embargo Act of 1807. Among both Republicans and Federalists, international commerce was considered an important factor of the nation's well-being and of national interest. In his book *Jealousy of Trade*, Istavan Hont describes the development of that understanding of commerce as one of the reasons for the fierce European competition for global market. He shows how Enlightenment thinkers re-conceptualized the

---

189 Kennedy, 'American Consul', p. 21f.

190 J. Black, *British Diplomats and Diplomacy 1688–1800*, Exeter, University of Exeter Press, 2001, p. 11. According to Black, Britain's diplomacy at the time remained mainly centered on Europe. In non-European countries diplomatic matters often were in the hands of the military or British commercial companies.

191 Kennedy, 'American Consul', p. 23.

192 One of them was John Parish, American consul to Hamburg from 1793 to 1796. He was a close business partner of Gouverneur & Kemble in 1796. Parish was also a contact of William Constable.

role of the states within the context of a growing eighteenth-century global integration in the debates on political economy as domestic economies were increasingly related to international commerce.[193] James Sofka claims that Jefferson's decisions in the Barbary Wars were driven by a similar understanding of eighteenth-century international relations that regarded commerce as 'a measure and medium of state power.'[194] The Barbary Wars were thus a means to protect American commercial interests and undermine the power of the British and French trade networks in the region. Sofka points to the fact that three of Jefferson's principal goals for foreign policies found their implementation in the Barbary Wars: the securement of the country's international commerce; the protection of its neutral rights; and the building of a navy to secure those interests. The decision to stay neutral in the European conflicts was also based on such foreign policy considerations, which Sofka describes as '"new diplomacy" based on the liberal thought of the Enlightenment.'[195] Staying away from alliances with dominant powers allowed the United States to remain flexible in its choices and enter into agreements only if they offered advantages for the country. Commerce had become an instrument of foreign policy, which was based on the understanding of power and wealth as constituent for a nation's well-being.

Another example of extended government support for mercantile business were the French Spoliation Claims. They were one of the longest continuing claims entertained by the U.S. Congress against France, resulting from

193 I. Hont, *Jealousy of Trade: International Competition and the Nation State in Historical Perspective*, Cambridge: Belknap Press of Harvard University Press, 2005.The Embargo of 1807 and the War of 1812 are further examples highlighting the importance the government gave to global commerce. The war was officially declared as a response to British violations of the United States' neutral rights and the impressment of American merchant sailors. Surprisingly, most of the Congressional votes for the war were made by Congressmen from the south and the west and only few by Congressmen from the seaport areas. Since it was the northern states that profited most from sea trade, common explanations for the war seem insufficient. Additionally, research on domestic politics has shown that the reasoning to go to war was even more influenced by partisan considerations than by regional division, with Republicans voting for and Federalists against it. Jasper Trautsch points to the role that cultural factors could have played such as nationalism and the rise of liberalist capitalism that threatened republican traditions. J.M. Trautsch, 'The Causes of the War of 1812: 200 Years of Debate', *The Journal of Military History* vol. 77, 2013, pp. 273–293.

194 Sofka, *Jeffersonian Idea*, p. 163.

195 Sofka, *Jeffersonian Idea*, p. 166.

numerous attacks and seizures of American ships by French privateers and naval forces during the French Wars. France's navy at the time was small and the country commissioned a large number of privateers.[196] Since France was never officially at war with the United States, its privateering could be considered acts of piracy. A report for Congress, submitted by Secretary of State Henry Clay, listed 444 vessels that were seized between 1793 and 1800, grossing a value of more than $6 million.[197] To regain the value of their destroyed property, the United States urged claims against France. Those claims were one of the longest-running congressional matters, and from 1802 to 1862, 40 different committee reports were filed to Congress and its legal standings heavily discussed by members.[198] In the French Spoliation Act of 20 January 1885, Congress addressed the issue and the suits filed by heirs and descendants of the original petitioners for the last time. The last claim was decided in 1914 and many of the claims remain unpaid today.[199]

French privateers were not the only danger to American shipping. Pirates and privateers from Britain, Spain, and Naples as well as the Barbary Pirates also captured many vessels. Claims were filed against these countries. Some of the declarations, mainly those affected by the embargo of Bordeaux in 1793 and 1794, were settled in 1797 by Fulwar Skipwith, the American commercial agent in Paris. Other claims were settled in the treaty with France of 1800, the Louisiana Purchase Treaty in 1803, the Florida Treaty with Spain in 1819, and the convention with France in 4 July 1831.[200]

One of the ships listed in the Spoliation claims, which was caught by French privateers in 1797, was the *Confederacy* from the New York firm Leffingwell & Pierrepont. Hezekiah B. Pierrepont was one of the owners and supercargo of the ship. The *Confederacy* was on its way from Canton to Hamburg via Copenhagen, with 'liberty to touch and trade at all ports,' when it was captured by a French privateer and carried to Nantes where it was brought in front of a prize tribunal. Although the ship carried a license for trade annexed to the treaty of commerce between France and the United States, it was still held at Nantes

196 A.S. Lanier, 'The French Spoliation Claims', *The Virginia Law Register, New Series,* vol. 10, no. 1, 1924, p. 14.

197 G.H. Williams, *The French Assault on American Shipping, 1793–1813: A History and Comprehensive Record of Merchant Marine Losses*, Jefferson, McFarland & Co., 2009, p. 3.

198 Many people opposed the claims, arguing they had no legal justification. Supporters argued that since France was not technically at war with the United States the spoliations were in contravention of law and existing treaties. Lanier, 'French Spoliation', pp. 14–15.

199 Williams, *French assault*, p. 3f.

200 Williams, *French assault*, p. 3f.

and its capture was judged lawful. The French argued that the ship did not carry a list with all the crewmembers required by the Ordinances of Marine of 1681, 1744 and 1745.[201]

The Constable Pierrepont Papers contain records of the trial held at a British court between the firm and its insurance company. The *Confederacy* had sailed from London to Madeira from where it proceeded to the Isle of Bourbon and Mauritius where a great part of the cargo was disposed of. From Mauritius, it went to Bombay where the rest of the goods were sold and a cargo of cotton for Canton was obtained. It further stopped at Pulo Penang for a load of tin and then arrived in Canton in October 1796, where the cotton and tin were sold and the cargo for Hamburg was taken aboard. The insurance company refused to bear the costs, arguing the ship violated navigation acts by participating in the country trade. Citing the Jay Treaty, the insurer contended that trade with British possessions was only legal if a ship directly returned to an American port. The *Confederacy's* voyage from Bombay to Canton was thus considered illegal, which released the insurer from their duty to pay. Leffingwell & Pierrepont disagreed, insisting that the insurance was specifically obtained for the voyage from Canton to Hamburg. They cited other court decisions, which had determined such a trip as two distinctive voyages: one from London to Canton and one from Canton to Hamburg. In this sense the homeward cargo was not affected by any form of illegality. Furthermore, they argued that it was not the insurance company's business to consider how the funds for the insured cargoes were acquired and the cargo purchased. They stated that foreign ships had been participating in the country trade from Bombay to China for a long time and that the India House at Bombay had been aware of the practice and never considered it problematic. Judgment came in favor of Leffingwell & Pierrepont with respect to the lost cargo. The judge rejected the argument that the cargo was obtained by illegal funds and thus ineligible for coverage by the insurance company. He agreed that it was not the task of the insurer to prove the origin of the money used to fund cargo. But he rejected Leffingwell & Pierreponts claim for recovery of the lost vessel, arguing that it was a violation of French ordinance and thus could not be claimed from the insurance company.[202]

201 'French Spoliation Claims', Pierrepont Papers, Constable-Pierrepont family papers. Manuscripts and Archives. The New York Public Library. Astor, Lenox, and Tilden Foundations.

202 'Report Cases argued and determined in the Court of King's Bench in Easter Term in the 40th Year of Geo. III 1800, 'French Spoliation Claims', Pierrepont Papers, Constable-Pierrepont family papers. Manuscripts and Archives. The New York Public Library. Astor, Lenox, and Tilden Foundations.

The trial in front of a British court is a great example of how complex global trade had become. A similar case was a series of lawsuits with the French businessman, Louis Le Guen with whom the firm Gouverneur & Kemble was involved in the late 1790s. The case went through numerous New York courts from 1796 to 1800 and involved prominent lawyers like Alexander Hamilton and Gouverneur Morris. It dealt with important commercial issues like 'factor's liens, the misconduct of agents, the existence of special agreements and general contract law'[203] and was many times cited in other trials afterwards. It is detailed in Julius Goebel's work on the law practice of Alexander Hamilton. According to Goebel, Le Guen had come to New York in 1794 from the Isle of France, bringing a cargo of cotton and indigo, which he left with Gouverneur & Kemble. The firm acted as local agents and advertised Le Guen's goods for sale at their store. When the goods had not sold in more than a year, Le Guen convinced Gouverneur & Kemble to send them on a ship to France on his account. Arnold Henry Dorman, a New York merchant and middleman to Gouverneur & Kemble made plans to charter the *White Fox* to bring Le Guen's goods from New York to Le Havre. However, a third party expressed interest in the cargo in 1795 and made an offer. Le Guen refused the first offer but started negotiating other offers from Isaac Gomez Jr,. Moses Lopez, and Abraham Rods Rivera. On 13 April 1795, a contract for sale was signed for £48,996.6 payable in twelve months with ten months of interest at six percent. The sale came with four conditions, of which the fourth point was the cause for the action of law between Le Guen and Gouverneur & Kemble, which charged that Gomez, Lopez and Riviera had to pay the earnings out of the sale of cotton or indigo to Gouverneur & Kemble to abate the interest along with a premium of five percent for receiving it in Europe. It was up to Gouverneur & Kemble to decide whether to receive it in part or whole and at which port in Europe.[204] In their actions as agents, Gouverneur & Kemble arranged the voyage of the ship and ordered insurance and custom clearings. Summing up the advances, insurance bonds, and other expenses, Gouverneur & Kemble made a claim to Le Guen of more than £28,700, more than half of what was expected, which was the reason for the dispute. On 30 May 1795, Le Guen requested that adequate insurance be received and that he was provided with a copy of the contract and authorization to receive the profits in Europe. One day later, the ship set sail without assuring Le Guen a means to receive the proceeds. Gouverneur & Kemble, who

203 J. Goebel Jr., *The Law Practice of Alexander Hamilton. Documents and Commentary Vol. II*, New York, Columbia University Press, 1969, p. 49.

204 Goebel, *The Law Practice of Alexander Hamilton*, pp. 50–55.

feared that they would not get their money if Le Guen received the returns in Europe, did not comply with his requests and delayed the transactions. As Gouverneur & Kemble had worried, the voyage was not successful. Gomez, Lopez and Rivera accused the firm of fraud and left the cargo in the hands of Gouverneur & Kemble's London-based partners Smith & Atkinson. Protesting against the change of contract that came with the discharge of the goods in London instead of Hamburg, Le Guen hired lawyers in New York to object the contract and sue Gouverneur & Kemble. His legal team consisted of Alexander Hamilton, Richard Harison, and Aaron Burr. Gouverneur & Kemble's attorneys were Brockholst Livingston and John Cozine. A long and complicated lawsuit followed in New York's courts. Gouverneur & Kemble were also sued by Gomez, Lopez, and Riviera in London who complained that the New York firm had deceived them and the goods on board the ship had not been of the same quality as the samples first shown to them. Gouverneur & Kemble dismissed the trial as ridiculous at first, but soon realized that they were confronted with a more serious matter, due to the judicial skillfulness of Alexander Hamilton. Julius Goebels quotes a letter by Brockhold Livingston to Gouverneur & Kemble, in which the former calls them 'a victim of the reputation of Alexander Hamilton.'[205] Alarmed, Gouverneur & Kemble hired three more lawyers, among them Gouverneur Morris, and tried to channel the accusations of fraud against Le Guen. The trial reached a climactic final hearing at the Supreme Court in Albany in which Morris and Hamilton delivered eloquent speeches. It ended with a win for Le Guen, who was adjudged $119,915, the largest settlement in American history to that date.[206] These legal cases show the complexity of international commercial law whose realization was often difficult and long juridical disputes were common.

Merchants in the new republic enjoyed a high degree of commercial freedom that was fostered but not regulated by the government. This form of free, unfettered trade was a clear advantage over the European countries, where large parts of commerce were still controlled by government-chartered trade companies. Most American businessmen opposed state-organized commerce, believing the government was needed to protect commercial interests but should not pursue its own commerce. Treaties, tariffs, and consular services were regarded as useful government practices that served to protect private enterprises, the main source for wealth creation. However, the government regulations could not be so strict that they interfered with private business

205 Goebel, *The Law Practice of Alexander Hamilton*, p. 73.

206 Goebel, *The Law Practice of Alexander Hamilton*, pp. 44–78.

interests. After welcoming the introduction of minor tariffs in a letter to Chalmers, Constable argued, 'We must however use a degree of prudence in not raising the prices so high as to make it an object with Europeans to ship to this Country.'[207] The quote shows that Constable clearly favoured international commerce based on the principles of free trade.

207 'William Constable to William Chalmers, 10 December 1787', William Constable Letterbooks 1782–1790, Volumes, Constable-Pierrepont families papers. Manuscripts and Archives. The New York Public Library. Astor, Lenox, and Tilden Foundations.

CHAPTER 3

Local Spaces

The previous section analyzed *the merchants*' global relations, which connected New York to the world market. They were managers of flows of commodities, information, and capital across oceans and geographic regions. They were, however, also very involved with their local environment, influencing it in several ways. The following chapters examine how they contributed to the development of land and city space, their impact on finance, industry, and community leadership as well as the promotion of consumerism.

New York City after Independence

After the United States gained independence, New York was a small town, encompassing about four square miles and hosting a population of 12,000 people. The war had shaken the city politically and economically and its remaining population was confronted by a variety of new tasks and obstacles. The transformation of the colonial institutions into an independent government was one of the main challenges the city had to face in the coming years. Quarrels between radical and moderate Whigs still dominated large parts of the political discussion after 1784. Traders and artisans were especially disappointed with the leadership of Governor George Clinton and his congress, which was formed by radical Whigs shortly after independence. New import laws and taxes hindered the city's commerce. The British overloaded the city with cheap products, bringing in twice as much tonnage as all other countries combined and exhausting local markets, which antagonized New York's merchants and artisans, who saw it as a downturn in their revolutionary gains.[1] However, under Alexander Hamilton's lead, moderate Whigs soon gained more influence. Hamilton and his supporters were convinced that the attacks by radicals on loyalists and their property hindered the city's ability to build a 'climate of confidence,' which they believed was essential for international business.[2] Hamilton argued that a commercial elite was necessary for the growth of a prosperous commercial society. In the 1785 state assembly elections, the city's

1 E.G. Burrows and M. Wallace, *Gotham: A History of New York City to 1898*, Oxford, Oxford University Press, 1999, p. 279.

2 Burrows and Wallace, *Gotham*, p. 279.

 | DOI 10.1163/9789004356412_005

artisans, merchants, and most working people fully endorsed the conservative and moderate candidates tied to Hamilton. The General Society of Mechanics and Tradesmen supported three merchants who were also Hamilton supporters: William Duer, Robert Troup, and Evert Bancker. In 1786, Hamilton's alliance gained power and many former Tories returned to New York.[3]

In 1787, when the ratification of the Constitution was a central point of political concern, the city's commercial circles predominantly supported Hamilton and the Federalists, who emphasized the importance of a stable central government to benefit foreign commerce. The city's leading Federalists pressured delegates to ratify, threatening to separate from the state if the Constitution was not embraced. They organized a Grand Federal Procession to celebrate the Constitution after its signing in New Hampshire and Virginia, thus bringing enough votes for ratification.[4] The parade consisted of five thousand men representing different trades and professions, passing through Broadway, the Great Dock Street, and Hanover Square with colorful banners. From there it continued through Pearl, Chatham, and Division Streets to Arundel and Bullock Street.[5] At the center of the parade was the ship *Hamilton*, a frigate towed by horses, which showed the significance of foreign trade in maintaining the city's well-being.[6] One banner read: 'This Federal Ship Will Pour Commerce Revive/And Merchants and Shipwrights and Joiners Will Thrive.'[7] When the ship passed Bowling Greene salutes were fired to the President and members of Congress who were gathered there. On Pearl Street, the Constable and Edgar families were among the celebrants. It is said that when the ship passed Constable's house, Mrs. Edgar rushed to the window and waived a colorful flag.[8] The procession signified a great moment in New York's history. For one, it demonstrated the great support for the Federalists in the city. Second, it showed the expanding artisanal presence in New York, 'altering the course of municipal affairs.'[9] The city's artisans, mechanics, and tradesmen thought of themselves as equal citizens and laid the foundation for an active commercial society based on these principles. Forced by public pressure, the delegates in Poughkeepsie ratified the Constitution.

---

3 Burrows and Wallace, *Gotham*, p. 279.
4 Burrows and Wallace, *Gotham*, pp. 292–293.
5 Murphy and Mannion, *Friendly Sons*, p. 104.
6 Burrows and Wallace, *Gotham*, p. 293.
7 Burrows and Wallace, *Gotham*, p. 293.
8 Murphy and Mannion, *Friendly Sons*, p. 104.
9 Burrows and Wallace, *Gotham*, p. 293.

In 1788, the Confederation Congress temporarily declared New York City the nation's capital. City Hall was redecorated and furbished to host the city, state, and federal governments. George Washington was elected president and inaugurated in Manhattan.[10] Under its newly gained status, the city was revived. Men of power strolled around the streets of New York and several prominent New Yorkers gained positions in the new administration. Alexander Hamilton became Secretary of the Treasury; William Duer assistant to the Secretary of Treasury; Gouverneur Morris ambassador to France; and John Jay was declared Chief Justice of the Supreme Court.[11] In the short time that New York hosted the national government before the capital was moved to Philadelphia in 1790 the city was at the center of federal politics, providing ample space and resources for its commercial elite to consolidate its political networks and influence.

New York's merchant class was eager to rebuild the city's financial and commercial institutions. In 1784, a group of merchants met at the coffee house to organize the city's first bank under the lead of Alexander Hamilton. Alexander McDougall became the bank's first president, which began operating in June 1784.[12] The Chamber of Commerce was also resuscitated in 1784, concerning itself with the commercial progress of the city. Speculation with national debts and securities became a common routine for New Yorkers of all occupations. The wealthy classes, often supplied with inside information, bought large stocks of national and state securities. New York City quickly became a city of money. The increasing population attracted new people with capital eager to invest. The speculation bubble soon burst, hitting New York with a severe financial crisis. A group of prominent speculators, among them William Duer, Alexander Macomb, John Pintard, William Livingston, and Royal Flint were arrested and jailed. Their speculations had bankrupted large parts of New York's society, from 'the richest merchants to even the poorest women and the little shopkeepers.'[13]

Constable & Rucker were also involved in schemes with William Duer. In 1785, they developed a plan in which the merchant house applied to the Treasury to borrow money for payments to Nicholas and Jacob Van Staphorst in Amsterdam as well as merchants in France. Constable & Rucker obtained paper money and specie worth almost $100,000 from the government to make the payments in France and Holland. The time between receipt and payment could be prolonged up to eighteen months. In the meantime, the firm was free

10 Burrows and Wallace, *Gotham*, p. 296.
11 Burrows and Wallace, *Gotham*, p. 299.
12 Burrows and Wallace, *Gotham*, p. 277.
13 Burrows and Wallace, *Gotham*, p. 309.

to use the money for other enterprises. Duer had provided Constable with an immense interest-free loan.[14] As a response to the bubble, New York's wealthy elite laid a plan to create a new securities market that worked without questionable auctions and could be less easily manipulated. Known as the Buttonwood Agreement, the plan created the first stock exchange in 1792.

The city's commercial success brought on by the revival of foreign trade caused a tremendous increase in population. Eager to profit from New York's opportunities, Irish, Scottish, French, Caribbean, and German immigrants entered the city as well as New Englanders. Most of the immigrants were young men and women searching for new opportunities, which bestowed a youthful and energetic atmosphere on the city. New York's harbor was the center of life. Numerous ships lay ashore and wharves and warehouses distinguished its townscape. Busy people filled the streets unloading the many carts that brought and sold goods and loading ships.

John Lambert, an Englishmen who traveled throughout the United States from 1806 to 1808, described New York City's harbor the following way:

> When I arrive at New York in November, the port was filled with shipping, and the wharfs were crowded with commodities of every description. Bales of cotton, wool, and merchandize; barrels of pot ash, rice, flour, and salt provisions; hogsheads of sugar, chests of tea, puncheons of rum, and piles of wine; boxes, cases packs and packages of all sizes and denominations, were strewed upon the wharfs and landing places, or upon the decks of the shipping. All was noise and bustle. The carters were driving in every direction; and the sailors and labourers upon the wharfs, and on board the vessels, were moving their ponderous burthens from place to place. The merchants and their clerks were busily engaged in the counting-houses, or upon the piers. The Tontine coffee-house was filled with underwriters, brokers, merchants, traders, and politicians; selling, purchasing, trafficking, or insuring; some reading, others eagerly inquiring the news. The steps and balcony of the coffee house were crowded with people bidding, or listening to the several auctioneers, who had elevated themselves upon a hogshead of sugar, a puncheon of rum, or a bale of cotton; and with Stentorian voices were exclaiming, 'Once, twice. Once, twice.' 'Another cent.' 'Thank ye, gentlemen ….' The coffee-house slip, and the corners of Wall and Pearl-streets were jammed up with carts, drays, and wheelbarrows; horses and men were huddled promiscuously together, leaving little or no room for passengers to pass…Everything was in motion; all was life, bustle, and activity. The people were scampering

14 Tailby, *Business Career*, p. 206ff.

> in all directions to trade with each other, and to ship off their purchases for the European, Asian, African, and West Indian markets. Every thought, word, look, and action of the multitude seemed to be absorbed by commerce; the Welkin rang with its busy hum, and all were eager in the pursuit of its riches.[15]

New York's rapid growth demanded an expansion of city space. The city invested in developing Manhattan's waterfront. Wharves were built along the East River stretching almost a mile north; new warehouses were erected and new shops emerged. Front Street and Pearl Street evolved into wholesale roads. Water and Wall Street were the central points of commerce and the Tontine Coffee House, established in 1793, was situated at the corner. By the late eighteenth century new houses were erected with beautiful three- and four-story brick stone facades. Coffeehouses and taverns emerged, serving as a center for business and news exchange.[16] In 1794, the City Hotel opened. From the harbor one could also see the spires of Trinity Church and Saint Paul's Church, Manhattan's landmarks. In 1791, New York Hospital reopened and the Bellevue Hospital for the treatment of contagious diseases followed in 1794.[17] Diseases were common in the city and yellow fever frequently plagued its inhabitants. Many of the disease outbreaks were caused by bad drinking water.

Besides becoming the nation's main commercial hub, New York also became a nucleus of intellectual life. The number of newspapers available to readers in the city increased from 9 to more than 20 between the years 1790 and 1807, making New York an important news center. Simultaneously, there came an expansion of libraries and bookstores, catapulting New York to the nation's literary capital by 1820, ahead of Boston and Philadelphia. The same period also saw a rise in arts and theater, and the emergence of new societies, all forming new platforms for social encounters.[18]

Land Development

In 1810, John Lambert wrote the following description of New York City in his travel report:

15 John Lambert, *Travels through lower Canada, and the United States of North America in the years 1806, 1807 and 1808*, London: Printed for Richard Phillips, 1810, vol. 2, pp. 155–157.

16 Burrows and Wallace, *Gotham*, p. 338.

17 G.J. Lankevich, *American Metropolis: A History of New York City*, New York, New York University Press, 1998, p. 54.

18 Lankevich, *American Metropolis*, p. 54.

> New York has rapidly improved within the last twenty years, and land which then sold in that city for fifty dollars, is now worth 1,500.
>
> The Broadway and Bowery Road, are the two finest avenues in the city, and nearly of the same width as Oxford-street in London. The first commences from the Grand Battery situated at the extreme point of the Town, and divides it into two unequal parts. It is upwards of two miles in lengths, though the pavement does not extend above a mile and a quarter; the remainder of the road consist of straggling houses which are the commencement of new streets, already planned out. The Bowery road commences from Chatham street which branches off from the Broadway to the right, by the side of the park. After proceeding about a mile and a half it joins the Broadway, and terminates the plan which is intended to be carried into effect for the enlargement of the city. Much of the intermediate spaces between these large streets, and from thence to the Hudson and East rivers, is yet unbuilt upon, or consists only of unfinished streets and detached buildings.
>
> The houses in the Broadway are lofty and well built. They are constructed in the English style, and differ but little from those of London at the west end of the town; except, that they are universally built of *red* brick. In the vicinity of the Battery, and for some distances up the Broadway, they are nearly all private houses, and occupied by the principal merchants and gentry of New York; after which, the Broadway is lined with large commodious shops of every description, well stocked with European and India goods; and exhibiting as splendid and varied a show in their windows, as can be met with in London. There are several extensive book stores, print-shops, music-shops, jewellers, and silversmiths; hatters, linen-drapers, milliners, pastry cooks, coach makers, hotels, and coffee-houses.[19]

The rise of shipping and the increase in population changed the urban landscape of New York City. New York's harbor expanded (see fig. 2). Merchants and artisans who sold their goods in their shops demanded strategic locations for wholesale and retail. The number of business establishments grew and elites became increasingly interested in the city's geography. The city's merchant class invested into the development of new buildings, stores, and wharves along the harbor. In 1791, eight merchants owned 75 percent of the property between Wall Street and the Old Slip.[20] Most merchants had their businesses

19 Lambert, *Travels, Volume II*, pp. 147–148.

20 Blackmar, *Manhattan for Rent*, p. 78.

FIGURE 2 *Plan of the city of New York 1804*
SOURCE: NEW YORK CITY MAP 1804, HOLLAND SOCIETY NEW YORK.

and counting houses close to the East side harbor, at Pearl, Water, and Wall Street with warehouses at the docks. Being located in the center of New York's commercial area and close to the port was a great benefit for the management of their business transactions. Filled with banks, insurance companies, auction houses, merchant firms, and coffee shops, New York's harbor was a buzzing environment where news and information spread rapidly.

The 1786 city directory lists Constable & Rucker on Mill Street (now South William Street); William Constable lived on Pearl Street. William Edgar's business is listed as 7 Wall Street and later, after 1799, at 39 Broadway.[21] The Gouverneur family possessed numerous real estate holdings in south Manhattan. In the assessment of real and personal property of the East Ward in 1791, they were listed with the following buildings: House at 27 Front Street; House and Store in the alley of 26 Front Street; Wharf at Front Street; Coopers House in Front Street; Double Store in Front Street; House at 13 Water Street. Nicholas Cruger is listed with a store at Front Street. The same assessment lists property owned by William Bayard at 43 Wall Street and the firm of Le Roy, Bayard

21 *New York City Directory 1786*, New York Public Library.

& Co. at 201 Water Street.[22] At his death, Isaac Gouverneur left a brick store in Gouverneur Alley, his house, and a lot in Smith Street and property on Mount Pleasant.[23]

When Samuel Ferguson moved to New York in 1802, he and Jonathan Day rented a house on Wall Street, next to the Bank of the United States of America before they moved the business to 94 Greenwich Street.[24] They paid $750 a year in rent but subleased the front room as a broker's office for $200. The house consisted of a small room used as a counting room, two parlors and several lodging rooms as well as a dry cellar, which was used as storage.[25]

That Ferguson & Day relocated to Greenwich Street after 1800 elucidates their success. As they became more prosperous, most merchants moved to better and more residential neighborhoods. The area near the Battery close to the Hudson, including State Street, Whitehall, Greenwich Street, and lower Broadway, became known as one of New York's better neighborhoods. Elizur Yale Smith called it 'The Gold Coast of old New York' and emphasized that Greenwich Street, also known as 'Millionaires Row,' was home to the city's most affluent circles.[26]

When the city made plans to extend Manhattan in the 1790s, they developed the West side of Manhattan's shore at the Hudson River. First Street, later named Greenwich Street, became a lively commercial area with wharves, docks, and warehouses built close to the mansions. Many of the houses had gardens that reached the water. Between 1790 and 1840, it was a mostly residential neighborhood and home to many prominent New Yorkers. It was also home to William Edgar in his later life and Isaac Bell. Le Roy lived close at 7 Broadway in his white marble house and his daughter Cornelia at 7 Greenwich Street with Edgar's son. Most of that area's residents were successful merchants, ship

22 *'Assessment of the real and personal property of the East Ward of the city of New York as made up June 24, 1791; with order from the mayor, recorder & to collect the same, and receipts from the city treasurer for amounts paid in by the collector. New York (City) Assessors'*, The New York Historical Society, The John Watts DePeyster Publication Fund Series, New York: Printed for the New York Historical Society, 1911. William Edgars house at 7 Wall Street was listed with a value of £2200.

23 'Isaac Gouverneur's Will', Will and Family Papers, Gouverneur & Kemble Family Collection, New York Historical Society Mss Collection.

24 New York City Directory 1804–05, New York Public Library.

25 Jonathan Day to Samuel Ferguson, 9 February 1802, Series 1: Correspondence, To Samuel and John Ferguson 1802, 1806, 1825–1827, Ferguson family papers. Manuscripts and Archives. The New York Public Library. Astor, Lenox, and Tilden Foundations.

26 E.Y. Smith, 'The Old Merchants of Greenwich Street', Article from 1940. Isaac Bell Papers 1787–1940, Rare Book & Manuscript Library, Columbia University in the City of New York.

builders, and bankers, who profited from living close to the river. Some of them had separate counting houses on Pearl and Wall Street.

To have counting rooms and offices in the front of one's home was very common for merchants at the time. Usually business was conducted on the ground floor while the family lived on the stories above. Only wealthier merchants had their living and workspaces separated like Gouverneur & Kemble, Le Roy, Bayard & Co., and Constable & Rucker. The trend of separating office and home gained ground in the early nineteenth century with the increasing specialization of commerce. Analyzing New York City directories, Diana diZerega Wall observes that the percentage of New York's commercial elite listed with two addresses rose sharply from almost zero percent in 1790 to 70 percent in 1840. This exemplifies the immense changes in social and household environments that detached the house from the public space and marked the 'development of an increasingly impersonal marketplace.'[27]

Elizabeth Blackmar points out that between 1790 and 1820 significant shifts in Manhattan's housing market took place. It was a period of geographic displacement that forced poor and lower-middling people to leave the port area. Wealthy merchants and professionals involved in the shipping industry occupied lower Manhattan's houses. Leases in those areas often contained stipulations to build brick stone fronts which only rich occupants could afford. Constructions of dwellings and multiple tenant homes were common, producing a decline in smaller one and two family homes. The traditional integrated house and shop constellations of mixed trade streets slowly disappeared from lower Manhattan.[28]

With the expansion of New York's geography, new streets had to be built. In 1807, a commission was established to lay out a street plan above Chambers Street (see fig. 3). The 1811 plan regulated Manhattan's future development to

27 According to diZerega Wall the trend mirrored the manifestation of a changed ideology where economics were isolated from morals and the legitimacy of economic activities was no longer measured by social value. 'The traditional image of the "merchant prince", with its connotations of statesmanship and benevolence, gave way to a modern image of the parvenu businessman directed by the profit motive.' A similar trend was reflected in the changing role of clerks around 1840. While clerks commonly were apprentices of the merchants and usually the sons of friends and business partners their social status changed in the mid-nineteenth century when merchants and clerks were considered a part of different social class. D. diZerega Wall, 'At Home in New York: Changing Family Life Among the Propertied in the Late Eighteenth and Early Nineteenth Centuries', PhD Thesis, New York University, 1987, p. 44.

28 E. Blackmar, *Manhattan for Rent*, 1785–1850, Ithaca, Cornell University Press, 1989, pp. 92–95.

FIGURE 3
The commissoners map of the city of New York 1807
SOURCE: THE COMMISSIONERS' PLAN OF 1811. PROVISIONAL MAP RELEASED IN 1807.

a grid pattern. Twelve avenues ran north to south and numerous cross streets ran east to west, creating rectangular city blocks which accommodated 50 to 60 town lots.[29]

Artisans and craftsmen started to move north of the port and new trade neighborhoods were established. The Lower East Side, for instance, developed into a shipbuilding and maritime craft center.[30] By 1820, the foundation for neighborhood social differentiation was laid, defining New York's cityscape in the nineteenth and early twentieth centuries.

Manhattan's landholding families profited enormously from the city's expansion and many turned to real estate speculation. The city's property holders, mostly merchants and entrepreneurs, were able to control land supply and raise the prices for sales and rents.[31] One of Manhattan's most well-known property speculators was John Jacob Astor. In the early years, Astor bought large amounts of Manhattan land that he resold for profit. Porter estimates that between 1800 and 1819, Astor invested more than $715,000 in land property. Most of the investments were made before 1812 and large parts of the capital came from profits from the China trade. Astor quickly resold his property and applied the gains for reinvestments.[32] In 1805, he bought 243 lots of George Clinton's Greenwich Village land for $75,000, paying $300 a piece, which he resold for $1000 each between 1806 and 1814. Astor proved to have good foresight of Manhattan's quick expansion and the returns on his investments usually came back quickly.

Another real estate developer with great vision was Hezekiah Pierrepont, who invested heavily in Brooklyn property. In the late eighteenth century, Brooklyn was mostly used as farmland and was sparsely populated. That changed quickly with the rise of population in the nineteenth century. In 1802, Pierrepont acquired the old Livingston Brewery at the foot of Joralemon Street, opposite of Lower Manhattan. In 1804, he bought the Benson farm, where he relocated to from his house at 68 Greenwich Street. He erected his homestead in today's Brooklyn Heights, at the junction of Pierrepont Place at Montague Terrace.[33] He also purchased the adjoining De Bevoise farm and parts of the

29 Blackmar, *Manhattan for Rent*, p. 95.

30 Blackmar, *Manhattan for Rent*, p. 101.

31 Blackmar, *Manhattan for Rent*, p. 105.

32 K.W. Porter, *John Jacob Astor, Business Man. Vol.* 2, Cambridge, Harvard University Press, 1931, p. 915.

33 Pierrepont family papers, ARC.263, Series 1: Mercantile, Farm and Distillery, 1802–1824, Accounts of cow and cattle establishment and of persons indebted to H.B. Pierpont Brooklyn Historical Society.

Remsen farm. His land extended from the river to today's Love Lane in the north, Fulton Street in the west, and Joralemon Street in the south. Pierrepont paid a surveyor to measure his land and laid out a plan for streets and lots, which is still preserved in today's Brooklyn Heights. He sold the lots with the stipulation that brick houses be built and laid out restrictions for stables and similar buildings to guarantee an upper-class residential area.

When Pierrepont died, his estate, which was divided in 1844, listed these remaining lots; one lot was usually 20 to 25 by 100 feet (as listed in the original document):

> 8 vacant lots in Willow Street,
> 15,5 lots at Columbus Street,
> 24 lots on Furman Street
> 68 1/3 lots and mansion on Pierrepont Street (homestead plot)
> 2 lots and house at College Place
> 2 vacant lots on Court Street corner of Montague Place
> 9 vacant lots and whole Estate front from Joralemon to Livingston
> 1 house and lot on Henry Street between Remsen & Joralemon
> 4 lots South East Corner of Sidney Place
> 4 vacant lots North East Corner of Sidney Place
> 10 vacant lots on North Side of Montague Place between Hicks and Henry Streets
> 33 vacant lots on South Side of Montague Place
> 8 vacant lots on North Side Montague Place
> 14 vacant lots at North East Corner of Clinton Street
> 16 vacant lots at South East Corner of Clinton Street
> 1 House and Lot at Pierrepont Street between Hicks and Henry Street
> 1 vacant lot North East of the above
> 8 lots on Pierrepont Street between Henry and Clinton Street
> 1 vacant lot on Pierrepont Street next to Church
> 4 1/2 Lots on South Side of Pierrepont Street
> 2 1/3 vacant lots East of Church of the Pilgriming on Remsen Street
> 24 Lots on Remsen Street between Henry and Clinton Street[34]

34 'Brooklyn Heights property conveyances', Series 3: Brooklyn Real Estate, 1761–1873, Pierrepont family papers, ARC.263, Series 1: Mercantile, Farm and Distillery, 1802–1824, Accounts of cow and cattle establishment and of persons indebted to H.B. Pierpont Brooklyn Historical Society.

The combined value of those parcels of land was listed as $483,510 and brought a fortune to Pierrepont's family.[35] In 1823, Pierrepont advertised his lots in a local newspaper:

> Lots on Brooklyn Heights
>
> Situated directly opposite the s-w part of the city, and being the nearest country retreat, and easiest of access from the centre of business that now remains unoccupied; the distance not exceeding an average fifteen to twenty-five minutes walk, including the passage of the river; the ground elevated and perfectly healthy at all seasons; views of water and landscape both extensive and beautiful; as a place of residence all the advantages of the country with most of the convenience of the city.
>
> Families who might desire to associate in forming a select neighborhood and circle of society, for a summer's residence, or a whole year, cannot anywhere obtain more desirable situations; and by securing to themselves an entire square or portion of a street may always remain detached, even when the whole space between the river and Fulton-street shall be occupied, which, from the rapid increase of respectable buildings in this quarter, it is evident will be the case in a very few years.
>
> Gentlemen whose business or profession require their daily attendance in the city, cannot better, or with less expense, secure the health and comfort of their families, than by uniting in such an association.
>
> Lots are 25 feet by 100—some fronting the city, others on spacious streets 60 feet wide. They will be sold in squares, or blocks of four or more lots, or separately, as may be desired.[36]

With the expansion of Manhattan, Brooklyn was promoted by many as a suburb of the thriving metropolis. It was seen as a healthy alternative to the city but still in close proximity. The Long Island newspaper, *The Star*, advertised Brooklyn in 1815 as, 'A favorite residence for gentlemen of taste and fortune,

35 'Brooklyn Heights property conveyances', Series 3: Brooklyn Real Estate, 1761–1873, Pierrepont family papers, ARC.263, Series 1: Mercantile, Farm and Distillery, 1802–1824, Accounts of cow and cattle establishment and of persons indebted to H.B. Pierpont Brooklyn Historical Society.

36 *The Star*, Long Island newspaper, 1 September 1825. Cited in R.F. Weld, *Brooklyn Village, 1816–1834*, New York, Columbia University Press, 1938, p. 28.

for merchants and shopkeepers of every description, for artists, artisans, mechanics, laborers, and persons of trade in society.'[37]

The need for a Brooklyn corporate body increased as the establishment of a ferry system became realistic. In 1808, Robert Fulton and Robert Livingston managed to get a lease for building a ferry, granted by the city of New York, which was by then in control of the Brooklyn shoreline. The New York and Brooklyn Steam Boat Ferry Association was founded, which initiated a proposal for incorporating Brooklyn as a village. Pierrepont was a member of the committee drafting a charter for incorporation of the village and a friend and counselor to Fulton. On 8 May 1814, the Fulton Ferry Company sent its first steamboat, the *Nassau*, from Brooklyn to Manhattan. In 1816, the Village of Brooklyn was politically established with a population of 4000. By 1834, it was home to 18,000 people. Large factories and warehouses were built and rope walks established.

A further means of investment for New York's wealthy merchants was the purchase of land and the development of settlements in New York state's 'wild land.' In 1786, the New York state legislature made plans to give away large parts of un-surveyed and unexplored land in northern New York. The land was exempt from taxes for seven years but had to be settled within that period. The commissioners directed a surveyor to lay out ten towns of 100 square miles each developed in the northwestern parts of what is today Lawrence County: Cambray, Canton, DeKalb, Hague, Lisbon, Louisville, Madrid, Oswegatchie, Potsdam, Stockholm. They were sold in public auction at the Coffee House in New York City on 19 July 1787. Alexander Macomb, friend of William Constable, became the main buyer. He was probably familiar with the land from his former business in the fur trade. Although Macomb quickly sold some lots, the majority of the land was not sold fast enough and he was never able to pay back his debt and was put into debtor's prison as a result.[38] It is unclear if William Constable had been involved with Macomb early on but in June 1792, Macomb sold Constable the towns of Madrid, Potsdam, and parts of Stockholm and Louisville. The towns of Lisbon and Canton were sold to William Edgar for £12,000.[39]

Macomb was also involved in a speculation venture known as the 'Macomb Purchase'. In June 1791, he acquired almost four million acres from the

37 *The Star*, Long Island newspaper, 1, 8, 15, 29 November 1815. Cited in R.F. Weld, *Brooklyn Village, 1816–1834*, New York, Columbia University Press, 1938, p. 16.

38 H.F. Landon, *The North Country; A History Embracing Jefferson, St. Lawrence, Oswego, Lewis and Franklin Counties, New York*, Indianapolis, Historical Pub. Co., 1932, p. 134ff.

39 Murphy, *Friendly Sons*, p. 135.

Commissioners of the Land Office, nearly one-tenth of all the land in the state, for eight pence per acre. The land was compromised of what is now known as Franklin, Jefferson, Lewis, and St. Lawrence Counties as well as parts of Oswego and Herkimer County. Macomb acted in company with William Constable and Daniel McCormick; although Macomb's name was the only one on the contract each man held one-third interest.[40] After his bankruptcy, Macomb's associates took over the management of his land and had it surveyed, subdivided, and settled. The developers of northern New York were Daniel McCormick, William Constable, John McVickar, Hezekiah B. Pierrepont, and Richard Harison.[41] Most of them were acquainted with Macomb through the Society of the Friendly Sons of Saint Patrick. Constable received 1,920,000 acres of land from Macomb for £50,000 in June 1792 and resold 1,200,000 acres of the land to Samuel Ward for £100,000 in December of the same year.[42] Constable also accepted more land from McCormick as well as six full townships and parts of two others. Janestown, Matildavale, and Emilyvale were named after Constable's daughters.[43] The towns Constableville in Lewis County and Constable in Franklin County hold Constable's name. The Constable Hall, a limestone mansion erected in 1819 by his son William Constable Jr. is still open to visitors in Constableville.[44]

Benjamin Wright, later famous for his work on the Erie Canal, served as Constable's land surveyor. He, as well as Constable's brother James, rode hundreds of miles through unexplored land in northern New York state.[45] Of McCormick's land, 15,200 acres were given to Herman Le Roy and William Bayard in a trust for the French writer Madame de Stael; Gouverneur Morris had recommended the investment to her. Le Roy, Bayard & McEvers also invested in North County lands.[46] Le Roy was in charge of two million acres of land, which he had bought in various operations from Robert Morris in 1792 and 1793.[47] The town Le Roy in Genesee County was named after him in 1813. In 1792, Le Roy and Bayard represented the Holland Land Company, which owned three

40 Murphy, *Friendly Sons*, p. 136.

41 Murphy, *Friendly Sons*, p. 137.

42 Murphy, *Friendly Sons*, p. 137.

43 Murphy, *Friendly Sons*, p. 138.

44 Landon, *Northern Country*, p. 101. In 1792, Constable went as an agent for Macomb to France to initiate sales of the land. French families soon arrived in the United States to settle the land, but many of them were unprepared for the wilderness that received them and the project ended in failure.

45 Murphy, *Friendly Sons*, p. 141.

46 Murphy, *Friendly Sons*, p. 139.

47 Steward, *Le Roy Family*, p. 22.

million acres of land in western New York.[48] Peter Kemble and Samuel Gouverneur also owned land and town lots in Delaware County.[49]

In his later years, Constable dedicated almost all of his entrepreneurial energy to land development. After his trip to Europe was cut short when he learned of his brother's mismanagement of the firm, Constable canceled most of the company's commercial involvements and focused on his estates some of which were discharged to his creditors. Constable died on a journey to Lewis County in Rome, New York in 1803.[50] His estate listed 600,000 acres of land in Oneida, Lawrence, and Clinton Counties and the townships of several towns, as well as shares of land in Georgia and Ohio. His last will called for an even division of the land among his children. When the will was settled in 1819, a great share of it went to Hezekiah B. Pierrepont, who was married to Constable's daughter Anna Maria. In 1806, Pierrepont had already purchased the town of Pierrepont and parts of Stockholm in Lawrence County. He continued to make additions to his land holdings until he eventually owned 500,000 acres of land in northern New York and 150,000 acres in Lewis County alone. Pierrepont was strongly devoted to the development of his lands and towns, which he visited annually. One of his main incentives in developing the land was to improve transportation. Pierrepont directed the erection of the St. Lawrence Turnpike, which led from the Black River to Franklin County and a turnpike from Rome to Constableville.[51]

Historian Paul Gilje calls the late eighteenth century and early nineteenth century the beginning of the 'transport revolution.'[52] That revolution started with the turnpike boom in the 1790s, followed by the expansion of canals and waterways in the 1820s, and the erection of the railroad system in the 1840s and 1850s. By 1811, New York had chartered 137 turnpikes and New England 180. They were erected by a combined capital of more than seven million dollars and spanned a distance of more than four thousand miles.[53] Turnpikes were

48 E.A. Le Roy, 'Genealogical Chart and History of the Le Roy Family', June 1993, New York Public Library.

49 'Family Papers', Gouverneur & Kemble Family Collection, New York Historical Society Mss Collection. In 1805 Samuel Gouverneur accused Kemble of deforcing him of his share of 20,000 acres, 10 barns, and 10 messuages. The Supreme Court of New York heard the case and Kemble was forced to relinquish the land.

50 Murphy, *Friendly Sons*, p. 142.

51 Murphy, *Friendly Sons*, pp. 142–143. Pierrepont also held shares in the first railroad in New York State.

52 P.A. Gilje, 'The Rise of Capitalism in the Early Republic', *Journal of the Early Republic*, vol. 16, no. 2, Special Issue on Capitalism in the Early Republic, 1996, p. 165.

53 North, *Economic Growth*, p. 49. Between 1799 and 1819, the charters for 353 corporations for the construction of turnpikes were granted in New York, and 70 for the construction

state of the art toll roads erected by companies and chartered by individuals interested in an area's expansion and reliable transportation. At the time, it was cheaper to move goods over the Atlantic than it was to bring them overland. Better roads facilitated the shipment of commodities from the hinterlands to the metropolis and integrated small farmers into the market economy. The demand for agricultural goods surged in the big cities, caused by population increases and the international shipments of provisions to Europe and the West Indies. Speedier transport also increased information supply and enhanced the value of land and settlements.

Turnpike development transformed New York's infrastructure. The Albany-Schenectady Turnpike was established in 1797 and by 1800, it was possible to use only turnpike roads to travel to western New York. The 157-mile Seneca Turnpike connected Utica to Canandaigua and was the longest Turnpike in the state. The Mohawk Turnpike connected Utica to Schenectady. The westward expansion via turnpikes to Buffalo connected the city to Lake Erie.[54]

Merchants were eager to facilitate the infrastructure of the hinterlands. Many of them invested in the development of roads and turnpikes. William Edgar was on the board of several turnpike corporations such as the Highland Turnpike Road, which aimed to connect New York to Philadelphia, the Maryland Turnpike and the Westchester Turnpike. He was also on the board of the Trenton Turnpike Company, which built a road from Trenton, New Jersey, to New Hope in Sussex County and had shares in a turnpike company in New Brunswick with the plan to connect New York to Philadelphia via turnpikes.[55] Throughout Northeastern America, turnpikes were the leading type of all business incorporations from 1800 to 1830. In New York they made for one-third of all incorporations.[56] They were 'embedded into the community,

of bridges. R.A. Davison, 'Comment: New York Foreign Trade' in D.T. Gilchrist (ed.), *The Growth of Seaport Cities 1790–1825. Proceedings of a Conference Sponsored By the Eleutherian Mills-Hagley Foundation March 17–19, 1966*, Charlottesville, University Press of Virginia, 1967, pp. 68–78.

54 Wheat brought from Buffalo to New York was three times its original price once it reached the city. It cost about $100 a ton and required 20 days to get there. Once the Erie Canal was erected, prices dropped to an average of $8.81 per ton between 1830 and 1850. C.E. MacGill, *History of Transportation in the United States Before 1860*, New York, P. Smith, 1948, p. 42.

55 'Furman to William Edgar, 29 May 1806', William Edgar Correspondence, Volume 6, William Edgar papers. Manuscripts and Archives. The New York Public Library. Astor, Lenox, and Tilden Foundations.

56 D.B. Klein, and J. Majewski, 'Economy, Community, and Law: The Turnpike Movement in New York, 1797–1845', *Law & Society Review*, vol. 26, no. 3, 1992, p. 470.

both figuratively and literally,'[57] offering access to all kinds of people and their businesses.

To avoid large costs and to secure supply, some merchants invested directly into agricultural production. When the war in Europe raised the price of wheat, Constable acquired the confiscated estate of Philipse Manor in Yonkers, which was comprised of 320 acres of land 19 miles from New York City. He erected a new stone mill, which produced flour that was then shipped to Europe.[58] Le Roy also possessed a flourmill at Old Buttermilk Falls close to the village of Le Roy, which produced Genesee Flour.[59] The supply of ginseng was another reason for land development. Merchants' great demand for it constituted a considerable income for many small rural towns in the mountain regions of upstate New York, Virginia, Massachusetts, and the Connecticut River Valley. The towns of Rochester, Paris, Utica, and Clinton in New York were all linked to the ginseng trade. David Hancock points out that by extending their enterprises to agricultural production, merchants were pursuing 'backward integration, meaning that large portions of the supply chain are managed by one company.'[60] Backward integration method guarantees a steady supply of the products needed and ensures consistent quality. It is especially helpful in markets with fluctuating supplies as it relieves the pressure of procurement and avoids price hikes. By applying more control to the production of flour, Constable and Le Roy increased their profit opportunities and eliminated market uncertainty.

Land speculations and transportation improvements were important to the expansion of the American frontier. That expansion was to a large part funded by mercantilist capital. With the liberation of lands from imperial control, merchants saw an opportunity to profit from and promote the growth and integration of markets. Improved transportation allowed farmers and artisans to sell their goods in larger markets ultimately enhancing production. Lengthy transportation was associated with high costs and therefore constituted a barrier difficult for small farmers and artisans to overcome. Road improvements lowered costs and allowed farmers to bring their products to the New York markets, encouraging them to produce larger quantities. Faster transport helped reduce the large amount of working capital required for many business transactions. The improvement of transportation thus stimulated processes of commercialization and industrious revolution in rural areas.[61]

57 Klein and Majewski, 'The Turnpike Movement in New York, 1797–1845', p. 470.

58 Moffat, *The Pierreponts*, p. 20.

59 Steward, *Le Roy Family*, p. 21.

60 Hancock, *Citizens of the World*, p. 81.

61 Improved transportation also helped to circulate information. See R.D. Brown, *Knowledge is Power: The Diffusion of Information in Early America, 1700–1865*, Oxford, Oxford University Press, 1989.

Finance and Industry

Merchant capital was also invested into the improvement of the financial and industrial sector of the young U.S. republic. In 1784, the Bank of North America organized by Robert Morris in 1781 was still the only bank in the whole country. In 1791 there were three banks in operation, by 1811 there were 90, and by 1820 there were more than 300.[62] Unlike the banks in Europe, the U.S. banks were established out of a necessity for capital rather than a surplus of it and most of the initiators were merchants who desired easier means to acquire credit.[63]

Encouraged by the success of the Bank of North America, New York merchants met at the Coffee House as early as 1784 to organize New York's first bank, which started its business out of the old Walton Mansion at Pearl Street in June 1784.[64] Upstate landholders had promoted a land bank, which would have composed two-thirds of its capital from mortgages and real estate. Such an institution was vividly opposed by the city's merchant class, prominently led by Alexander Hamilton, who made plans for a specie bank providing bank notes rather than bills of credits. They argued that a land bank would be insufficient in providing the necessary liquidity in times of economic distraction. Legislation denied charters to both banks but that did not stop its founders and the Bank of New York continued operating, albeit as an association.[65] On 23 February 1784, an announcement in the *New York Packet* read the following:

> Bank
> It appeared to be the disposition of the gentlemen in this city to establish a bank on liberal principles, the stock to consist of specie only, they are therefore hereby invited to meet tomorrow evening, at six o'clock,

62 B. Hammond, *Banks and Politics From the Revolution to the Civil War*, Princeton, Princeton University Press, 1957, p. 145.

63 Hammond, *Banks and Politics*, p. 75. Hammond identifies three different kind of banks that emerged after the Revolution and existed until the early nineteenth century. These were the 'money banks' in the commercial centers that paid capital in specie and gave short-term loans to merchants and businessmen. The banks in agricultural communities had less specie capital but were funded with state credit. And a third class that combined banking with other investment activities such as the building of infrastructure. In the long run, commercial banks with little government proprietary succeeded. pp. 170–171.

64 Burrows and Wallace, *Gotham*, p. 276.

65 R.E. Wright, *Origins of Commercial Banking in America, 1750–1800*, Lanham: Rowman & Littlefield, 2001, p. 82.

at the Merchants' Coffee House, where a plan will be submitted to their consideration.[66]

Henry W. Domett tells the history of the bank in detail: organized as a joint stock company, it had a capital of $500,000 in gold and silver, accumulated by 1000 shares of $500 each. Stockholders received one vote for each share with a seven-vote maximum. After one month, the first five hundred shares were sold and the president and board of directors were appointed.[67] The bank was successful enough that it paid semi-annual dividends of three percent until 1788 and three and a half percent afterwards. In 1791 the dividend was seven percent. By 1791, the bank discounted bills and notes amounting to more than $10 million and received more than $42 million in cash.[68]

Edgar and Constable were on the board of directors of the bank in 1789. In 1796, the bank bought Constable's house and lot at the corner of Wall Street and William Street, tearing down the existing house and erecting a bank building. Nicholas Gouverneur was on the committee supervising the construction. In 1799, he was elected president of the bank. He was the first president to experience competition by a rival bank, the Manhattan Company, founded by Aaron Burr in 1799. After Nicholas Gouverneur's death in 1802, Herman Le Roy became president.[69]

One of the bank's characteristics was, that, as a merchants' bank, it made advances on merchandise. A bank organized principally on bills of credits would have meant less liquidity and would therefore hindered business, especially since bills of credit were often not accepted in other countries, had high premiums, and generally contained deficits in the balance of payments.[70] In New York, there was a particularly high necessity for a stable credit system. Due to the constant fluctuation of people and the fragmentation of former elites, New York relied less on a personal credit system than other cities. The availability of specie was crucial for international transactions and New York's merchant class depended on its reliable supply. The bank provided the capital

66 New York Packet, 23 February 1784. Cited in H.W. Domett, *History of the Bank of New York*, New York, G.P. Putnam's Sons, 1884, p. 7.

67 The first president was General Alexander McDougal. The directors were: Samuel Franklin, Robert Browne, Comfort Sands, Alexander Hamilton, Joshua Waddington, Thomas Randall, William Maxwell, Nicholas Low, Daniel McCormick, Isaac Roosevelt, John Vanderbilt, and Thomas B. Stoughton. William Seton was Cashier. Domett, *Bank of New York*, p. 9.

68 Domett, *Bank of New York*, pp. 30–38.

69 Domett, *Bank of New York*, pp. 52–61.

70 Wright, *Origins*, p. 87.

individuals needed to make investments and thus impacted the social organization of the city.

The establishment of banks introduced a more impersonal and equal credit system. It became possible for individuals with few personal relationships to obtain credit from the bank, which guaranteed security and gave assurance that interactions with unknown business partners were no longer a hindrance. The banks created a system of liquidity and fostered entrepreneurial opportunities, which superseded the paternalistic and hierarchical credit system of the colonial society.[71] Cochran notes, that '[s]ince working capital was the largest credit requirement of most early business, these numerous competing banks, each making short-term but renewable loans, were a strong aid to expansion and growth.'[72]

Research on America's early bank customers shows that a high percentage of customers taking out banking credits were from the middling classes. They were less affluent merchants, craftsmen, artisans, and farmers who were in the need of short-term commercial credit.[73] From 1790 to 1791, twenty percent of the Bank of North America's customers were artisans, whereas in 1787, it was about ten percent.[74] By giving money to people who were short on cash, early American banks 'democratized banking'[75] and were motors of the expansion of commercial activities of the middling classes.

Insurance companies, organized like the banks as joint stock companies, also mushroomed in the decades after 1784.[76] Before 1793, marine insurance was mostly provided by private underwriters, usually wealthy citizens, who were guaranteed as individuals or in partnerships, and by underwriters abroad, mainly in England. The late eighteenth century marked the beginning of insurance companies as joint stock corporations. Different shareholders chartered the first marine insurance stock company, the Insurance Company of North America, in Philadelphia in 1794.[77] With the growth of overseas commerce, other seaport cities soon followed and marine insurance companies emerged

71 Wright, *Origins*, p. 25ff. and p. 112ff.

72 Cochran, *Business Revolution*, p. 1460.

73 Wright, *Origins*, p. 149.

74 Unfortunately there are not enough remaining records to study New York's bank clients but one can assume a similar trend. Wright, *Origins*, p. 152.

75 Gilje, *Rise of Capitalism*, p. 164.

76 On the emergence of American insurance companies see Christopher Kingston, 'Marine Insurance in Britain and America, 1720–1844: A Comparative Institutional Analysis', In *Journal of Economic History* vol. 67, no. 2, 2007, pp. 379–409; and S. Huebner, *Marine Insurance in the United States*, Philadelphia, University of Pennsylvania, 1905.

77 Huebner, *Marine Insurance*, p. 253.

in New York, Boston, Baltimore, and Charleston. The New York Insurance Company was established in 1796, followed by the Associated Underwriters in New York City in 1797 (New York already had a fire insurance company, the Knickerbocker Fire Insurance Company since 1787). Other insurance companies in New York were: the United Insurance Company (1797); the Columbian Insurance Company (1800); Washington Mutual Insurance Company (1802); Marine Insurance Company (1802); Commercial Insurance Company (1804); Phoenix Insurance Company (1807); Fireman's Insurance Company (1810); and Oceans Insurance Company (1810).[78] The New York Insurance Company had capital resources of $500,000 and after 1827, the combined capital New York's insurances possessed was $16 Million.[79]

The Napoleonic Wars increased the need for insurances as the numbers of captured vessels rose. Gouverneur & Kemble's anxiety when their ship *Diana* sailed from France to the West Indies without proper insurance exemplified the need. By 1800, thirty-two marine insurance companies facilitated the shipping boom of the new republic.[80] Many of the large insurance companies were 'general insurance companies' that in addition to maritime insurance services offered fire and life insurances. These general insurance companies were, according to Edwin J. Perkins, an American innovation, 'an organizational schema unduplicated in London or elsewhere.'[81]

In 1789, the New York Manufacturing Society was formed as a joint stock association with the 'purpose of establishing useful manufactures in the city of New York and furnishing employment for the honest industrious poor.'[82] There were 260 subscribers who purchased 380 shares at £10 each.[83] In 1790, 14 weavers and more than 130 spinners worked at the society, which operated out of a large brick building at Vesey Street. The business, however, was a disappointment and the property was sold in 1794.[84]

In 1791, Constable was engaged in an enterprise established to manufacture cotton cloths. He became stockholder of the New Jersey Society for Establishing Useful Manufactures (S.U.M.). The society was founded in 1791 by United States Assistant Secretary of the Treasury Tench Coxe and supported

78 Huebner, *Marine Insurance*, p. 254; Perkins, *Public Finance*, p. 300.

79 Davison, *Comment*, p. 70. Davison quotes Margaret Myers, et al., *The New York Money Market: Origins and Development*, New York, Columbia University Press, 1931.

80 Huebner, *Marine Insurance*, p. 254.

81 Perkins, *Public Finance*, p. 304.

82 J. Stancliffe Davis, *Essays in the Early History of American Corporations*, New York, Russel & Russel, 1965, p. 275.

83 Davis, *Essays*, p. 275.

84 Davis, *Essays*, p. 275.

by Alexander Hamilton. It was chartered in New Jersey as a state-sponsored enterprise to promote manufacturing. Hamilton envisioned an industrial site powered by the Great Falls of the Passaic River. Main stockholders and leaders of the joint-stock organization were the New Yorkers William Duer, Alexander Macomb, Walter Livingston, John Dewhurst, Royal Flint, and Benjamin Walker. The company's capital consisted of $500,000, to be divided into five thousand shares of $100 each.[85] One of the society's first activities was to establish the printing of cloths, for which Macomb suggested that Constable supply the corporation with plain white cloths imported from India.[86]

> I have engaged your house in one more speculation which is not perfected as yet. It is to purchase the *America* when she arrives and hold her between Duer, Walter Livingston, your house and keep her in the trade between this and Calcutta with a view particularly to supply the manufacturing society with white cloths for the printing business which it is intended shall be a primary object of the society.[87]

S.U.M.'s aim was to compete with British industry. The society's prospectus mentions the importance of promoting the U.S. manufacturing industry. 'It is an almost self-evident proposition that that community which can most completely supply its own wants is in a state of highest political perfection.'[88] The following articles were to be manufactured:

> ... paper and pasteboards, paper hangings, sail cloth and other coarse linen cloths, such as sheetings, shirtings, diaper, oznaburgs &ca. The printing of Cottons and linens; and as incident to this but on a smaller scale the manufacturing of the article to be printed. Women shoes of all kinds. Thread, Cotton and Worsted Stockings. Pottery and Earthen Ware. Chip Hats. Carpets, Blankets, Brass and Iron wire, Thread and Fringes.[89]

85 A. Hamilton, 'Prospectus of the Society for Establishing Useful Manufacture', August 1791, in H.C. Syrett and J.E. Cooke, *The Papers of Alexander Hamilton*. vol. IX, New York, Columbia University Press, 1965, p. 148.

86 'Alexander Macomb to William Constable, 3 December 1791', William Constable Correspondence, Constable Papers, Constable-Pierrepont family papers. Manuscripts and Archives. The New York Public Library. Astor, Lenox, and Tilden Foundations.

87 'Alexander Macom to William Constable, 1 January 1792', William Constable Correspondence, Constable Papers, Constable-Pierrepont family papers. Manuscripts and Archives. The New York Public Library. Astor, Lenox, and Tilden Foundations.

88 Hamilton, 'Papers', p. 144.

89 Hamilton, 'Papers', p. 147.

To fulfill its manufacturing promises the society hired an English mechanic familiar with Arkwright machinery.[90] Unfortunately the S.U.M. experienced monumental problems in the 1792 financial crisis caused by Duer's bankruptcy and most of the company's funds were lost. The works closed down in 1796.

The emergence of the Bank of New York, the rise of turnpike and insurance companies as well as the S.U.M. are part of a trend of joint stock corporations setting in after 1784. Economic historian Thomas Cochran has regarded the appearance of joint stock corporations as one of the most important developments of the 'business revolution'.[91] He argues that this form of business organization was one of the leading sectors responsible for economic growth, even more than the advancement of technology or capital accumulation. The evolution of business corporations in the United States is striking. Cochran states that '[i]n 1800, when neither Britain or France had more than about a score of the modern type of corporations, the United States, with only a small fraction of the population of the two European states, had incorporated over three hundred such private enterprises.'[92]

Different to France and England, American corporations were incorporated by the states rather than the national government, which granted them wide powers. This flexibility was crucial in ensuring a company's success. A corporation's main benefit was that it succeeded as a means to mobilize capital from small businessmen and allowed them to invest in businesses that were not under their own control and spread over a larger geographical area. These private corporations were organized at a high level of control, which was ensured by multiple directors and strict requirements for voting and record keeping. For this reason it was relatively safe to invest in a business enterprise even if it was geographically distant, such as a turnpike company.[93] It also allowed merchants and small entrepreneurs to invest in a number of business ventures which decreased their overall investment risk. The amount of par value varied significantly: for banks they were usually relatively high starting at around $250, but turnpike shares were lower, from $20 to $50, giving less affluent people access to investments.[94] According to James Hardie's special census of 1824, 'monied corporations' other than banks and insurance

90 D. Ben-Atar, 'Alexander Hamilton's Alternative: Technology Piracy and the Report on Manufactures' in *William & Mary Quarterly* vol. 52, 1995, p. 409.

91 Cochran, 'Business Revolution', p. 1461.

92 Cochran, 'Business Revolution', p. 1458.

93 Cochran, 'Business Revolution', pp. 1458–1461.

94 Davis, *Essays*, p. 299.

companies, possessed a capital of $2,179,250.[95] Merchants constituted the largest group of shareholders in these corporations, 'ranging from the small country store keeper to the wealthy metropolitan merchant importer.'[96] According to Cochran, they were also the largest group of subscribers of capital to the local banks.[97] The fact that merchants were among the main stakeholders in these new financial institutions shows how influential international trade was for the young republic's economic development.

Community Leadership

Most of New York's merchants who were active in international trade, especially in the East Indies, quickly moved up the social ladder, becoming part of the city's most influential financial, industrial, and political circles and serving on the boards of a variety of corporations.

Constable was well connected through the Society of the Friendly Sons of Saint Patrick, a charitable and social organization for natives and descendants of Ireland. Murphy and Mannion provide a detailed account of the Society's history: It was founded in Philadelphia in 1771 and listed many important members with political and military ranks. General George Washington, Thomas Jefferson, and Alexander Hamilton were regular guests at its St. Patrick Day's celebrations during the revolutionary years. Washington signed its rules in 1787. His signature appeared next to that of Constable. After 1790, the Philadelphia chapter disbanded, but Constable was a driving force behind the founding of the New York branch. The first meeting of the New York Society of the Friendly Sons of Saint Patrick was on 17 March 1784. The primary aim for founding the New York branch was to help poor and distressed Irishmen, many of whom were in dire financial situations shortly after the war. From 1789 to 1791, and again in 1795, Constable served as president of the Society. Constable and Edgar also served as counsel from 1785 to 1792 and 1788 to 1791, respectively. The Society's most important event, which drew the attention of the city's elites, was its yearly anniversary dinner held on St. Patrick's Day heavily covered by New York's press.[98]

Personal attachments with important public figures worked to the advantage of *the merchants*. John Jay worked together with Le Roy, Bayard & Co. in

95 Davison, *Comment*, p. 71.

96 Davis, *Corporations*, p. 298.

97 Cochran, 'Business Revolution', p. 1460.

98 Murphy and Mannion, *Friendly Sons*, pp. 141–150.

a trading enterprise with Dutch businessmen in 1794 and Gouverneur Morris was a silent partner in William Constable's firm.[99] Isaac Bell, William Bayard, and William Constable were all close to Alexander Hamilton. William Edgar was very acquainted with Gurdon S. Mumford, a United States Representative of the ninth, tenth and eleventh congress and Chairman to the Committee on Commerce and Manufactures. He was also friendly with Henry Remsen, a New York merchant who served in the Continental Congress and was secretary to John Jay.[100] The merchant class was directly involved in city politics. According to historian Frederic C. Jaher, 117 of New York officeholders between 1778 and 1815 were men who were or would become foreign traders, and of the 114 common councilors from 1783 to 1801, nearly one-third were merchants.[101]

Becoming a gentleman was important to *the merchants*. They were philanthropists interested in the betterment of themselves and society as evidenced by their dedication to social issues, preoccupation with arts and education, and participation in social associations. Education was crucial for a gentleman, especially in the topics of arts and literature. William Bayard was very interested in European architecture and created page-long descriptions of European churches and cities.[102] He and Le Roy sent their sons to Paris for schooling in 1806. There the teenagers studied Spanish, bookkeeping, and the calculation of exchanges. The boys also enjoyed Parisian social life, attended balls, and developed a taste for dancing, which became 'their favourite amusement.'[103]

As literature gained relevance as a means of cultural communication, the circle of readers grew continuously expanding to all ranks of society. The middling classes advocated reading not only newspapers and fashion magazine but also books, which they discussed in literary circles and social gatherings. William Constable's estate lists 960 books, of which 601 were English volumes and 359 French.[104] In his will he bequeathed all his French books to 'my friend

99 Jaher, *Urban Establishment*, p. 209.

100 'William Edgar Correspondence', William Edgar papers. Manuscripts and Archives. The New York Public Library. Astor, Lenox, and Tilden Foundation. Edgar received several letters from Mumford during 1806 to 1808.

101 Jaher, *Urban Establishment*, p. 210.

102 Bayard Accounts and Papers 1663–1848, Bayard Genealogy, Bayard-Campbell-Pearsall families papers. Manuscripts and Archives. The New York Public Library. Astor, Lenox, and Tilden Foundations.

103 William Bayard Correspondence, 1806 Jan-March, Bayard-Campbell-Pearsall families papers. Manuscripts and Archives. The New York Public Library. Astor, Lenox, and Tilden Foundations.

104 William Constable Estate, Constable Pierrepont Papers, Constable Papers, Constable-Pierrepont family papers. Manuscripts and Archives. The New York Public Library. Astor, Lenox, and Tilden Foundations.

General Alexander Hamilton.'[105] Samuel Ferguson often received letters with literature tips and was also supplied with new English publications from his aunt at Millhouse. In June 1799 she sent him a box from Liverpool with the books 'A tale of the times' by Arthur Fitz Albini', 'Letters to Literary Ladies' of the Monthly Magazine and Leeds Newspapers, and an article from the Magazine of March 1798 entitled—'What is Education?'[106]

Values, worldviews, and other social mores were communicated through literature and reached a large audience. Books and magazines were means for sharing experiences and expectations and built a common identity among those in the new middling classes. Similar to consumer goods, books were transmitters and providers of cultural identification for the growing social class. Apart from reading, another activity that played a central role in the lifestyle of upper and middling ranks culture was entertaining at home, dinner, coffee or tea parties. For example, the purpose of New York's Sub Rosa Dining Club, which held private dinners at the homes of its members, was to enjoy supper and pursue amusements such as card games. The club had at most thirty members who met every Saturday during the summer season. Each member had to pay a subscription fee that covered the cost of the dinners. Members could also bring guests and suggest new members. Dinner was usually served at three o'clock with amusement beginning at six. It was especially stated that, 'no motion on business of any kind shall be proposed or debated upon, at or after dinner.'[107] A favorite dinner item was green turtle, which was served six times in 1800.[108] In 1795, the subscribers were: William Bayard, Thomas Buchanon, John Charlton, Daniel Cornidle, Captain Crowninshield, Henry Cruger, Nicholas Cruger, Robert Dale, Edward Goold, Nicholas Gouverneur, Archibald Gracie, Peter Kemble, S. Kennan, William Laight, Robert Lenox, William Ludlow, John Marston, Thomas Maule, Samuel Nicoll, Capt. Philips, Thomas Roach, Cornelius Ray, Miles Sherbrooke, William Shudden, Charles Smith, Corn. Stevenson, Robert Waddell, J. Waddington, Girard Walton, Frank Winthrop, and William Winthrop. Governor Crawford, and William Odgen were also members and visitors from 1795 to 1800. Many of the men listed above were successful businessmen and other important members of

105 Will of William Constable, Constable Papers, Constable-Pierrepont family papers. Manuscripts and Archives. The New York Public Library. Astor, Lenox, and Tilden Foundations.

106 Letter from Elizabeth Rawson, 1 June 1799. Series 1: Correspondence, From Elizabeth Rawson 1795–1807, Ferguson family papers. Manuscripts and Archives. The New York Public Library. Astor, Lenox, and Tilden Foundations.

107 Rules for the Sub Rosa Dining Club 1795, Sub Rosa Club, Records 1795–1800, New York Historical Society Mss Collection.

108 Rules for the Sub Rosa Dining Club 1795, Sub Rosa Club, Records 1795–1800, New York Historical Society Mss Collection.

New York's society. An inventory of the club's property in December 1798 lists 20 gallons of wine, 22 bottles of wine, 13 bottles of port, 20 bottles brandy, 3 bottles spirits, 8 packs of cards and half a cheese.

Associations like the Sub Rosa Dining Club and the Friendly Sons of Saint Patrick were good places to network professionally. They also facilitated mobility as they helped migrants, merchants, traders, and other traveling professionals find new connections in foreign cities and places. Peter Clark, historian and professor of European urban history, has described those new social clubs as 'mixed space.'[109] They were 'centered around drinking premises, incorporating some of the conventions of both public institutional and private domestic space, but with a distinct character shaped by the commercial imperative.'[110] The clubs were important arenas for social interaction and dialogue that demanded the art of conversation and required the implementation of certain manners that illustrated one's belonging to an existing genteel culture. They were fields of social explorations and arenas for forming social and cultural identities whereby much of the social activity of the middling classes occurred.

Social and philanthropic engagements were important characteristics of a gentleman. By the last quarter of the eighteenth century an unprecedented number of intellectual, professional and charitable societies emerged in New York City designated to improve and cultivate civic culture. These included the Society for Encouraging Useful Knowledge (1784); the Calliopean Society (1788); the New York Society for Promoting Agriculture, Arts and Manufactures (1791); the Friendly Club (1793); the Horanian Literary Society (1796); the American Mineralogical Society (1798); Belles Lettres Club (1799).[111] Charitable institutions included the Humane Society (1787) (originally named the Society for the Relief of Distressed Debtors); the Society for the Relief of Poor Widows with Small Children (1797); the Female Association (1798); the Samaritan Society (1805); the Orphan Asylum Society (1806); and the Assistance Society (1808). Immigrant societies like the German Society (1784), the French Benevolent Society (1808), and the Society of the Friendly Sons of Saint Patrick, aimed to help distressed landsmen.[112] The added 'friendly' in the Friendly Sons of Saint Patrick illustrates the time's emphasis on politeness. Friendliness underlined the virtue of its members and their benevolence and generosity not only in humane and moral regards, but also through financial support. Most

---

109 P. Clark, *British Clubs and Societies 1580–1800: The Origins of an Associational World*, Oxford, Oxford University Press, 2000, p. 246.

110 Clark, *Clubs and Societies*, p. 246.

111 Bender, *New York Intellect*, p. 28.

112 R.A. Mohl, *Poverty in New York, 1783–1825*, Oxford, Oxford University Press, 1971, p. 137ff.

charitable institutions were organized in committee formats: annual subscribers elected a board of directors. The directors usually worked voluntarily while the subscribers provided the money through dues and donations. Further funds were organized through beneficial concerts, theatre shows, door-to-door collections, and appeals from newspapers. State or municipal governments usually provided partial funds.[113]

According to Jaher, the merchant class was paramount among the subscribers of those private charities. Of the 109 Humane Society trustees between 1787 and 1831, 58 of those trustees with identified occupations were merchants.[114] Many merchants had the financial capital to provide support for charitable societies. William Bayard was one of the founders of the New York Hospital and William Constable and William Edgar were among the founders of the society of the Friendly Sons of Saint Patrick in New York. According to Peter Clark the social significance of those societies was tremendous:

> They promoted ideas of national improvement, and encouraged collaboration and mutual trust among members, both through the convivial rites of fellowship, and by stressing the convergence of private and collective interests. But probably the most significant way in which societies contributed to political change was through the low-level but regular political experience they offered to their membership. For, in Alexander Hamilton's words, 'clubs…are civil governments in miniature.'[115]

Support of civic society institutions is just another example of *the merchants'* community leadership. Having achieved great wealth from their commercial activities, community commitment, and cultural accomplishments were part of a merchant's desire to leave a lasting legacy. It also illustrates the close linkage between civic and business life. While in prior times, sponsors of learning were usually the church or monarchical courts and institutions such as the Royal Academies, the late eighteenth century marked a shift towards private patronship of intellectual and scientific life.[116] Merchants' preoccupation with civic improvement fit with the time's enlightened virtue, generated from intellectual and scientific concerns rather than from theological convictions. They shared a general optimism about human progress through education and a utilitarian approach to society.

---

113 Mohl, *Poverty in New York*, p. 151.

114 Jaher, *Urban Establishment*, p. 241.

115 Clark, *Clubs and Societies*, p. 464.

116 Bender, *New York Intellect*, p. 10.

The fact that America's northeast and mid-Atlantic port cities competed with each other in international and regional markets was favorable for the blending of business and politics. The city's welfare and success depended in large part on commerce, which resulted in an eagerness among city and state officials to assist in its promotion and stimulation. The issuing of charters of corporations and the implementation of new laws and rights that happened on the municipal and state level are examples of how New York City and New York state oriented their policies after commerce. Supported by the policies of the federal government during the 1790s American local and national politicians managed to create an atmosphere in which capitalist development could prosper.[117]

By the late eighteenth century New York offered many cosmopolitan features similar to the centers of Europe where commercial success created a distinct conjunction of intellectual and practical affairs. David Hancock has described the merchants of his study as representative of the 'practical side of the enlightenment.'[118] This characterization also fits the merchants of New York. They were not progenitors of intellectual thought but they were practitioners of the enlightened realm, confident of the possibilities of human reason, and ambitious in the advancement and betterment of human communities. A letter from John Day to Samuel Ferguson illustrates that Day was aware of how his cosmopolitan experience had influenced his reasoning and approach. Day responded to Ferguson, who had written to him from England to tell him that Day's brother, a clergy member, had objected to Ferguson's marriage to Day's sister Elizabeth because Ferguson was not religious enough. Day replied:

> You and I perfectly understand one another on this point, & have both of us seen too much of the World not to be convinced, that provided a Man is an honest Man, that provided a Man does as he would be done by, and venerates & respects every Religion that tends to promote the true Spirit of Christianity, Morality & Virtue, it is but of little Consequence, whether he is high Church or low Church; at the same time we must not condemn those who do not exactly think as we do, but make allowances for people who have not had the Advantage of the extensive Sphere of Observation, we have, & who have had no Opportunity of guarding against Prejudices which have been instilled by Education and confirmed by Habit.[119]

117 On the benefits of this competition read also Cochran, *Business Revolution*, p. 1456 and Gilje, *Rise of Capitalism*, p. 177.

118 Hancock, *Citizens*, p. 396.

119 Jonathan Day to Samuel Ferguson, 24 May 1802, Series I: Correspondence, To Samuel and John Ferguson 1802, 1806, 1825–1827, Ferguson family papers. Manuscripts and Archives. The New York Public Library. Astor, Lenox, and Tilden Foundations.

As a port town, New York benefited from the expansion of global commerce economically and culturally. In *The Birth of the Modern World*, C.A. Bayly writes that the political revolutions between 1780 and 1830 were accompanied by a 'quieter revolution, the emergence of the commercial middle class and its values.'[120] The emergence of a commercial society manifested a transformation of social values. Expressing gentility, friendliness, and education through the refinement of houses and fashion and through new forms of sociability became important virtues of the new middling classes. How the merchant class contributed to this trend will be explored in the following.

Commercialization

Huzza for COMMERCE-NAVIGATION-
The LIFE and SOUL of every nation;
May no embargo's backward force
E'er put a stopper on their course.
Huzza for FARMERS and their trade,
(By which all commerce must be made),
Without whose noble enterprise
All TRADE and NAVIGATION dies.
Huzza for all MECHANIC arts,
By which the above perform their parts,
Which lend their expeditions aid
To AGRICULTURE, and to TRADE.
Huzza for SAILORS, ev'ry one
Who steer by chart of WASHINGTON.
Huzza for those whose fortitude
Can stem the torrent rough and rude,
Which threatens to o'erwhelm the ship,
And sink her in the boundless deep.
Huzza for ALL our PATRONS kind,
By whose support we raise the wind;
May they enabled be to keep
Their barks afloat upon the deep,
And meet no cross tempestuous gales
To check their way, or back their sails,
Till death's grim blast shall on them frown,
And bring their masts and rigging down,

120 Bayly, *Birth of the Modern World*, p. 114.

Then may they land on heav'n's shore,
To sail in pleasure evermore.
(*New York Gazette 1810*)

These lines, part of a poem published as a broadside in 1810 in the *New York Gazette*, reveal the connections between New York's world trade and local industries. The expansion of global commerce was not only a profitable enterprise for the merchants who organized it; in fact a variety of different people were connected to the trade industry and made a living from it. Farmers, artisans, tradesmen, shipbuilders, as well as day laborers all profited from the rising shipping industry.

An abstract written in 1786 by Friedrich Justin Bertuch, the publisher of the German *Journal des Luxus und der Moden*, a magazine on fashion and cultural and economic trends, gives a similar testimony to the socio-economic effects that came with the rise of commerce.[121] Bertuch argues that the growing consumption of coffee, which he called 'part of our European luxury,' had been of substantial benefit to Europe's economies. His estimates were based on a total European population of around 128 to 130 million people of which he calculated one fourth to enjoy one loth[122] of coffee daily, amounting the consumption of about 185,000 tons of coffee a year. Bertuch estimated that it required around 925 200-ton vessels to transport the coffee from the different world regions to Europe, costing about 130,000 florins per ship. The requisition of the materials needed to build the ships (wood, iron, rope, et cetera) employed around half a million people per year. Additionally, he counted the merchants engaged in the trade and those who produced the bags, boxes, and barrels used in transporting the coffee, as well as those involved in the production of the items used for its consumption like ceramics, cutlery, pots, milk. Bertuch remarked that if sugar, indispensable for the consumption of coffee, was added to the math, the number of people profiting even doubled. He concluded: 'What great number of rich, middle and poor people make a living from coffee in Europe alone, of the one daily loth that only every fourth consumes…and how many live from the enormous amount of tea that comes to us every year.'[123]

Bertuch's judgment is not unrealistic. William Constable's accounts contain a list ranking costs and disbursements of the ship *Canton* on a voyage to Bombay and China paid to Isaac Hazlehurst in Philadelphia. It lists 37 payments to all kinds of tradesmen like ship carpenters, sail makers, plumbers, blacksmiths,

121 Friedrich J. Bertuch, *Journal des Luxus und der Moden* vol 1., 1786, Teilnachdruck aus den Bänden 1–10, G.M. Kraus, Leipzig, Edition Leipzig, 1786, p. 37ff.

122 Loth is an old German unit of weight. 32 loth equaled one pound.

123 Bertuch, *Journal des Luxus und der Moden* p. 38.

painters, upholsterers, block makers, coopers, and gunsmiths. Additionally, 33 payments were made to provision providers for food (beans, cheese, beef, flour but also port wine, cinnamon, and vinegar) and 50 payments went to manufactured and semi-manufactured good providers for commodities like looking glasses, compasses, saltpeter, paper, pikes, and muskets. There were also reimbursements for porters, wood haulers, and seamen. The total sum of the money paid to local tradesmen, retailers and sailors amounted to £6426.15. The highest sums were paid to the shipbuilders: Snowder & North received £354.2; Joshua Humphreys, a ship carpenter, £441.10; the blacksmith William Clifton received £142.18; and John Dowers, a sail maker, £106.12. For canvas Constable paid £600 to three different providers. To James Bringhurst & Sons and Adam Foulke he paid £137.10 and £206.13, respectively, for stores. The bakers received more than £160. For sundry groceries, Constable paid £200.17, and for beef £188.8. Two months' advance of wages for officers and seamen cost £88.8.[124]

The expansion of trade increased the demand for ship carpenters, sail makers, ship chandlers, and other occupations related to the construction and equipment of ships. New York rose to become the United States' most important shipbuilding market, even though the city had not been an important center for shipbuilding before the revolution. The *Empress of China*, for example, was built in Baltimore.[125] In 1792, 30 ship carpenters lived in New York, but by 1805, the number had already risen to 117.[126] By 1830, 'shipbuilding had become a great industry, employing thousands of men and engaging the keenest businessmen of the city. Coming along the East River, one saw more fine vessels on the stocks and great piles of lumber, white oak, hackmatack, and locust for ribs, yellow pine for keelsons, and ceiling timbers, white pine for floors, live oak for "aprons."'[127]

The construction of ships created demand for a variety of assets from lumber to copper sheet. Abundant lumber resources enabled American shipbuilders to provide vessels at much lower costs than their French and British competitors.[128] While the United States could draw from plentiful wood resources, copper sheet was more difficult to acquire and had to be imported

124 'For amount of Cost and Disbursement of said Ship on a Voyage to Bombay and China, 12 December 1789', William Constable Shipping Papers 1788–1791, Constable Papers, Pierrepont papers. Manuscripts and Archives. The New York Public Library. Astor, Lenox, and Tilden Foundations.

125 J.H. Morrison, *History of New York Ship Yards*, New York, W.F. Sametz, 1909, p. 18.

126 Morrison, *Ship Yards*, p. 21 and p. 23.

127 *Ships and Shipping of Old New York*, p. 46.

128 Nettels, *National Economy*, p. 234. Nettels quotes Tench Coxe who estimated that French shipbuilders produced at a rate of $55 to $60 a ton, while Americans produced at $33 to $35 a ton.

from Great Britain. Many merchants had their vessels coppered in England during a trading voyage, like the *Sampson* in 1796. To boost the industry the federal government launched a variety of initiatives. For instance, a payment of $10,000 was made in 1798 by the Navy Department to the Boston firm Paul Revere & Son, for the promotion of cotton sheet manufacturing.[129]

Shipbuilders became some of the wealthiest artisans in New York.[130] The shipping industry 'ran vertically through all occupational groups from merchants, clerks, and shopkeepers to shipbuilders, dockworkers, and mariners.'[131] Sailors' wages rose from $8 to $30 a year.[132] When shipping came to a standstill during the embargo and the War of 1812, unemployment soared.[133]

Sean Wilentz details the changes in the labor structure that came with the expansion of trade in New York City. Tradesmen and artisans dominated the city's main labor landscape in the eighteenth century. Merchants and financiers constituted the upper rank and were usually large property owners. At the lower end of the laboring class stood immigrants, sailors, free Blacks, day laborers, and transients who did not own property. Between the very rich and the poor were the artisans and academic professionals with smaller amounts of property. Wilentz analyzed the New York City directory from 1796 according to which about half of the city's workers were artisans. These numbers are not very unusual, as artisans such as masters and journeymen had represented the typical urban labor force for centuries. However, at the end of the eighteenth century a new group of craftsmen emerged, propelled by the expansion of trade and market integration. To make more money, many artisans increased their output, expanded to larger markets, and hired more workers. Wilentz identifies that group of artisans as 'craft entrepreneurs.'[134] They were mostly from industries like leather tanning, shipbuilding, consumer finishing, construction, and printing trades.[135]

A growing population as well as expansion into local and international markets created an incentive for large-scale supply and fostered the rise of

---

129 Morrison, *Ship Yards*, p. 19.

130 Henry Eckford, Christian Bergh, the Adam brothers, and Noah Brown were some shipbuilders of wealth and good name. The sailmaker Stephen Allen was also a rich and influential man who was engaged in politics and on the board of various financial institutions. See S. Wilentz, *Chants Democratic: New York City and the Rise of the American Working Class, 1788–1850*, Oxford, Oxford University Press, 2004, p. 37.

131 Blackmar, *Manhattan for Rent*, p. 75.

132 Nettels, *National Economy*, p. 235.

133 Blackmar, *Manhattan for Rent*, p. 75.

134 Wilentz, *Chants Democratic*, p. 32.

135 Wilentz, *Chants Democratic*, pp. 26–32.

competitive businesses. It introduced a new enterprise system, which replaced 'established artisan practices with new forms of wage labor and distribution.'[136] Shopkeepers changed their merchandise, often adding British products to their supply, which forced many smaller artisans to alter their production habits and focus on cheaper production. Wilentz calls that rearrangement of production and labor relations the beginning of 'a peculiar metropolitan form of industrialization.'[137] By 1815, the growing elite of craft entrepreneurs dominated the labor market. They were less affluent than merchants, but still very rich in comparison to smaller merchant firms. 'Their furniture was of mahogany instead of the more common pine; fineries like gilt-edged mirrors, silver cutlery, and chinaware adorned their homes. Most probably kept at least one servant.'[138] During colonial times most manufactures were created in the workshops of masters with the help of apprentices and journeymen. It was then common routine for journeymen to become masters, continuing the patriarchal tradition. With the rise of commerce, many masters expanded their workforce by hiring more employees. The workers were usually paid as external wage earners and not accommodated in the house. Journeymen stayed for shorter periods of time and the turnover rate of workers in craft workshops was higher than ever before. The Philadelphia cabinetmaker Samuel Ashton, for example, employed his journeymen for an average of six months between 1795 and 1803. Since the shop employed five workmen at a time, this meant that Ashton had hired 49 different men in this eight-year period.[139] The traditional social structure where work was bound to property and the head of the household was the authority over house and workplace dependents such as family members, apprentices, servants and slaves began to erode

Some journeymen and apprentices also profited from those changes in hiring. In times of demand they could sell their work to the highest bidder or work for more than one employer. Those who had entrepreneurial talent could manage to make quite a comfortable living without going through the traditional custom of working several years for the same master.[140] New renting practices accommodated those wage laborers. With the increasing flow of new people moving to the city, many homes started to take in people for cash payments rather than as household workers. In highly demanded trades like

136 Wilentz, *Chants Democratic*, p. 30.

137 Wilentz, *Chants Democratic*, p. 36.

138 Wilentz, *Chants Democratic*, p. 36.

139 David Montgomery, 'The Working Classes of the Pre-Industrial American City, 1780–1830', *Labor History* vol. 9, no. 1, 1968, p. 7.

140 Blackmar, *Manhattan for Rent*, p. 61.

shipbuilding, masters began to build boarding houses to accommodate their workers, whose rent would then be deducted from their wages.[141]

The growth of commerce had strong effects on the working poor as well. The port areas became magnets for people looking for work and day labor. The demand for seamen, longshoremen, and carters rose significantly with the expansion of shipping. Construction and transportation that came with the growth of population also added work, as did the need for domestic servitude. James Henretta's study of Boston tax rolls found that in 1687, 69 percent of the city's adult male population belonged to the propertied classes. Of the seventeen percent listed as dependents, they usually worked as apprentices and servants in family homes. Only 14 percent were listed as non-property holders and non-dependents. In 1771, 29 percent were already listed as neither propertied nor dependent. It is reasonable to assume that in the years following the number continued to rise.[142]

Joseph H. Davis shows that by 1790 industrial production started rising at a rate of around five percent. His method of indexing the United States' industrial production permits a more refined look at the country's economic conditions, even though at the time the U.S. economy was still mainly based on agriculture. Davis assembled data on the physical outputs of 43 different industries, arguing that the industrial sector has 'historically derived demand directly from nonindustrial occupations, particularly farmers, merchants, and the construction trades.'[143] Davis' findings challenge common assumptions that there was no considerable increase in industrial production in the United States until the nineteenth century and show that the seaports played an important role in the development of industries between 1790 and 1825. The shipbuilding industry for instance was heavily affected by the decline of maritime trade after the Embargo Act of 1807.[144]

Dorothy Brady attaches the importance of the seaport cities to the introduction and diffusion of new industries, the rise of the cities as center of

141 Blackmar, *Manhattan for Rent*, p. 63.

142 J.A. Henretta, 'Economic Development and Social Structure in Colonial Boston', *William and Mary Quarterly*, Third Series, vol. XXII, Jan 1965, pp. 75–92, as cited by Montgomery, *Working Classes*, p. 14.

143 Joseph H. Davis, 'An Annual Index of U.S. Industrial Production, 1790–1915', *The Quarterly Journal of Economics* vol. 119. no. 4, 2004, p. 1180.

144 Davis, 'An Annual Index of U.S. Industrial Production', p. 1180. See also: D.A. Irwin and J.H. Davis, 'Trade Disruptions and America's Early Industrialization,' *NBER Working Paper No. 9944*, 2003. The authors show that while infant industries like cotton boomed in the years between 1807 and 1815, when the Embargo Act and subsequent non-importation measures slowed down the import of manufactures, other trade-related industries, like the shipbuilding industry, plunged.

specialization, and their role in introducing and leveling the consumption of fabricated consumer products. The introduction and diffusion of manufactural industries required techniques of specialized artisans such as local carpenters, blacksmiths, and other craftsmen to assemble parts and components used for the mills, waterwheels, printing machines, and other equipment. Although some of the hardware was imported, oftentimes craftsmen who lived in the cities and its nearby communities built additional parts. Large-scale importation of durable consumer items that came through port cities fostered the production of durable goods in those cities. Many craftsmen either tried to imitate products like carriages, coaches, watches, and pianos and adapt them to the American market or specialized in repairing them. The growth of consumerism brought by global trade increased demands in the cities and outlying areas, causing some craftsmen to increase their output and produce objects on larger scales. This was large-scale production even before the introduction of industrial machinery and helped to prepare a consumer market in which 'products of uniform design were readily accepted.'[145]

A World of Goods

In the late eighteenth century, because of the rise of global commerce, consumers in Europe and North America experienced a tremendous increase in the availability of goods. Markets were flooded with new commodities from different corners around the world. With the expansion of international trade, merchants eagerly expanded their palette of products, thereby contributing to a transformation of shopping behavior and consumerism. Two features that were unparalleled in history distinguish that development. For one, the range of commodities from different geographic regions as well as the sheer quantity of available goods had reached unprecedented dimensions. Second, the buyers of those goods began to encompass wider social circles than ever before. While in former times, it was mainly those in aristocratic and elitist circles who could afford luxury goods, consumption now extended to large parts of society. The products of the late eighteenth century were not only products of a globalizing world; they were also the consumer products of the emerging middling classes.

Historian Maxine Berg examines changes in supply and demand of consumer goods in Britain during the eighteenth century. She shows how global

145 D.S. Brady, 'Comment: Manufactures', in D.T. Gilchrist (ed.), *The Growth of Seaport Cities 1790–1825. Proceedings of a Conference Sponsored by the Eleutherian Mills-Hagley Foundation March 17–19, 1966*, Charlottesville, The University Press of Viriginia, 1967, pp. 92–97.

commerce and the increasing manufacturing of goods altered the supply of products, making them cheaper and more available for less affluent buyers. Manufacturers started to produce with higher frequency, which brought a steady supply of new goods onto the market, fueling people's desire for them. The products were shipped to Britain's global markets, where they stimulated a transatlantic consumer culture. Berg concludes that the creation of new technologies and labor that was triggered by the 'product revolution' must be seen as an important part of the Industrial Revolution.[146] Neil McKendrick, John Brewer, and J.H. Plumb have described the period as the 'birth of a consumer society' in England and emphasized the change of commodity values, many of which were formerly seen as 'luxuries' and within a decade, became understood as 'decencies' and even 'necessities.'[147]

Jan de Vries argues that rising consumer desire led to a change in household structures in Great Britain and parts of Northern Europe and North America as it caused an increase in the home production of market goods. To make money to buy things, women and children began to work longer and in new ways leading to two major transformations: the reduction of leisure time and the reallocation of labor from producing goods and services for direct consumption to goods produced for markets. The changes in household and labor force hitherto contributed to the beginning of industrialization. Households now bought products as well as provided labor for domestically produced products.[148]

de Vries's concept highlights the changes that happened in broad parts of society, where there was a shift from subsistence living to a desire to live

146 M. Berg, *Luxury and Pleasure in Eighteenth-Century Britain*, Oxford, Oxford University Press, 2005.

147 N. McKendrick, J. Brewer, and J.H. Plumb, *The Birth of a Consumer Society: The Commercialization of Eighteenth-Century England*, Bloomington, Indiana University Press, 1982.

148 J. de Vries, 'Between Purchasing Power and the World of Goods: Understanding the Household Economy in Early Modern Europe', in J. Brewer and R. Porter (eds.), *Consumption and the World of Goods*, London, Routledge, 1993, pp. 85–132. The linkage between consumerism and industrialization is also highlighted in the concepts of 'Proto-Industrialization' and the 'Industrious Revolution'. Proto-Industrialization, prominently expressed in the work *Industrialisierung vor der Industrialierung* by the German scholars Peter Kriedte, Hans Medick, and Jürgen Schlumbohm in 1970, emphasizes the growing participation of rural and peasant households in market craft production starting in the late seventeenth to the early nineteenth century. The increase preceded and paved the way for industrialization as it led to a higher specialization in certain areas in both agricultural and commercial craft production. Peter Kriedte, Hans Medick, and Jürgen Schlumbohm (eds.), *Industrialisierung vor der Industrialisierung: Gewerbliche Warenproduktion auf dem Land in der Formationsperiode des Kapitalismus*, Göttingen, Vandenhoeck & Ruprecht, 1978.

with more luxury. That shift took place in many regions in Europe and North America but was not necessarily a precedent of industrialization. Bayly points out that patterns of industrious revolutions without early industrialization were common in the Netherlands, Germany, and coastal North America and were also visible in some areas in Mexico and coastal Brazil before 1850.[149]

Most literature on eighteenth-century consumer society asserts a change in demand and desire.[150] Affluent groups but also smaller merchants and artisans as well as peasant households developed a hunger for the new consumer products. A story told by Benjamin Franklin to his friend Benjamin Vaughan in 1784 poignantly illustrates the growing enthusiasm and its associated changes in social and economic behavior.

> The skipper of a ship, employed between Cape May, New Jersey, and Philadelphia, had done us some small service, for which he refused payment. My wife, understanding that he had a daughter, sent her, as a present, a new-fashioned cap. Three years later, this skipper being at my house, with an old farmer of Cape May, his passenger, he mentioned the cap, and how much his daughter had been pleased with it; 'but,' says he, 'it proved a dear cap to our Congregation.' 'How so?' 'When my daughter appeared in it at a meeting, it was so much admired, that all the girls resolved to get such caps from Philadelphia; and my wife and I computed that the whole could not have cost less than an hundred pounds.' 'True,' says the farmer, 'but you do not tell all the story; I think the cap was nevertheless an advantage to us; for it was the first thing that put our girls upon knitting worsted mittens for sale at Philadelphia, that they might have wherewithal to buy such caps and ribands and you know that that inducement has continued, and is likely to continue and increase to a much greater value ...' Upon the whole I was reconciled but this little piece of luxury, since, not only the girls were made happier by having fine caps, but the Philadelphians, by the supply of warm mittens.[151]

149 Bayly, *Birth of the Modern World*, p. 52.

150 C. Carson, R. Hoffman, and P.J. Albert, *Of Consuming Interests: The Style of Life in the Eighteenth Century*, Perspectives on the American Revolution, Charlottesville, University Press of Virginia, 1994; L. Brekke, 'The "Scourge of Fashion" Political Economy and the Politics of Consumption in the Early Republic', *Early American Studies: An Interdisciplinary Journal* vol. 3, no. 1, Spring 2005, pp. 111–139; R.L. Bushman, *The Refinement of America: Persons, Houses, Cities*, New York, Knopf, 1992.

151 'Benjamin Franklin to Benjamin Vaughn, 27 July 1784', *The American Museum or Universal Magazine*, January 1790, p. 20. Cited in Brekke, *Scourge of Fashion*, pp. 111–112.

The emergence of new consumer desires is one of the crucial cultural changes caused by the expanding world trade of eighteenth century. Historical scholarship on eighteenth century America has emphasized the linkage between material culture, the rise of the middling class and its effects on politics.[152] The burgeoning middling classes bought new consumer goods not only because they were now affordable, but also because of their attached meaning of modernity and gentility. To own those global products meant to be fashionable, modern, and a participant in the social discourse surrounding those objects. As Berg argues, '[t]he new products were not the endless stuff of questionable taste that darkened Victorian parlours. They were the material products of enlightenment and modernity, of fashion and global commerce.'[153]

From the 1740s onwards there was a noticeable, steady increase in consumption of British products such as clothing, window glass, furniture, cutlery, metal ornaments, and French and other global products. Americans began orienting their styles and home interiors to English and French fashions for clothes, furniture, and tableware. Manufacturers produced their commodities frequently in new designs, marketing them as fashionable and attractive, fueling peoples' desire for new products. The American Revolution did not stop society's demand for British manufactures and British exports more than doubled from £2,649,000 in 1772 and 1773 to £5,700,000 in 1797 and 1798.[154]

The merchants were active in encouraging their contemporaries' desire for consumer goods. With the expansion of trade, more products reached America's cities than ever, enabling consumers to enjoy various products from all parts of the world. U.S. imports expanded rapidly in the years after 1790 and

---

152 T.H. Breen identified the expanding material culture of the colonial society and its impacts on the American Revolution. He argues that the separation movement was partially fueled by a new consumer society. People were now more engaged in making choices in their everyday lives, which for many was a liberating and empowering experience. T.H. Breen, *The Marketplace of Revolution: How Consumer Politics Shaped American Independence*, Oxford: Oxford University Press, 2004; On the linkage of consumerism and politics read also C. Shammas, *The Pre-Industrial Consumer in England and America*, Los Angeles, Figueroa Press, 2008; E. Hartigan-O'Connor '*Collaborative Consumption and the Politics of Choice in Early American Port Cities*' in J. Styles and A. Vickery, (*eds.*), *Gender, Taste, and Material Culture in Britain and North America, 1700–1830*, New Haven, Yale University Press, 2006, pp. 125–149; J. Cohen, '"The Right to Purchase is as Free as the Right to Sell": Defining Consumers as Citizens in the Auction-House Conflicts of the Early Republic', *Journal of the Early Republic* vol. 30, no. 1, 2010, pp. 25–62.

153 Berg, *Luxury and Pleasure*, p. 15.

154 Berg, *Luxury and Pleasure*, p. 286.

local consumption increased by almost four-fold between 1790 and 1815.[155] Since many consumer goods were recycled or handed down to others, an even greater circulation of these items can be assumed.

The imported products can be divided in three different types of groups: raw materials and crude food such as tea, coffee, indigo, dye wood and wood, wool, slates, spices, nuts, saltpeter, opium, and specie. Manufactured foods such as alcoholic drinks and sugar, molasses, chocolate, cheese, and salted meats. And manufacturers and semi-manufacturers such as textile manufactures, glass, earthenware, paint, gunpowder, books, paper, watches, saddlery, arms, and others. After 1815, manufactured foods accounted for the largest share of imports followed by manufactures and semi-manufactures. Raw materials and crude foods constituted the smallest part.[156]

With the increase of commerce and product availability, local consumption markets expanded in the seaport cities. Merchants contributed to that consumerism in three major ways: through the introduction of new commodities, the marketing of their products, and by being consumers themselves. As stated earlier, it was crucial for a successful trading voyage to stay informed on market demands so merchants kept track of which goods were easily sold and which were slow to go over the counter. Additionally, they kept an eye on competitors in fear of market gluts. Commodity memorandums were helpful lists, keeping one informed on tastes and demands in different markets.

The wide variety of Asian textiles was greatly enjoyed by American customers. The freights of fabrics brought back from Asia were usually large and included diverse cotton and silk textiles. Since most textiles were named after their place of origin, East India merchants and supercargoes had to remember vast numbers of different names and textiles. Samuel Ferguson's records contain a memorandum from 1797 listing India goods suitable for the American market. It lists 'Superfine Book Muslins, Jacconots, Gold End Mulls, Allibalies with gold ends, fine Deccae Stripe Doreas (or Mull Stripes, Deccae, Check Doreas, Cord Check Doreas, Hair Cords, Broken Check, Superfine Book Handkerchiefs, Superfine Ballasores and Good Madras Handkerchiefs'.[157]

---

155 North, *Economic Growth*, p. 228. The census from 1790 and 1810 records a population growth of less than 50 percent, which means that consumption increased considerably despite decreasing population numbers.

156 North, *Economic Growth*, p. 282 and p. 289.

157 Memorandum from Mr. Dobson, Series II: Business Records, Miscellaneous 1827–1836, Ferguson family papers. Manuscripts and Archives. The New York Public Library. Astor, Lenox, and Tilden Foundations.

The textiles were advertised in newspapers with their Indian names. The advertisement by Isaac Moses, a New York commission merchant, on 4 June 1793, is a great example. He announced 'INDIA SALES AT PUBLIC AUCTION' in the *Daily Advertiser* and claimed to have 'an extensive quantity of India goods, lately imported—Consisting of Gurrahs, Baftas, Chitabullys, Luckepores, Coffas of various description, Commercollys, Nymposakies, Guzeenahs, Tundats, Brown Baftas.'[158]

Merchants' advertisements of their products in newspapers and commercial advertisers give insight into the advanced consumer culture that was born out of the expansion of trade. Their marketing strategies reveal that they were quite active in promoting consumer desire and hence contributed to the social changes resulting from the growing consumerist economy. The expansion of printing was an important tool in product promotion. The number of newspapers, commercial advertisers, leaflets, and fashion magazines increased dramatically after 1780 and expanded to the city's hinterlands. Newspapers were filled with commercial notices that usually occupied at least half of the papers. The growing number of listings forced merchants and retailers to develop advertising strategies for their announcements to stand out to customers. Most merchants began with announcing the upcoming arrival of a ship and its port of departure so consumers knew to expect a variety of new goods, which fueled excitement. Some of merchants sent their goods to commission merchants but others sold them in their own stores.

Gouverneur & Kemble and Ferguson & Day sold most of their imports directly at their stores (at 26 Front Street and 92 Greenwich Street). One could read their announcements almost daily in the various New York papers between 1790 and 1820. Le Roy, Bayard & Co. also advertised the sale of imports at their store which was first at 202 Water Street, later at 3 Hanover Square, and then at 12 New Street. William Constable, in comparison, advertised relatively little as most of his imports were given for sale to commission merchants such as Isaac Moses.

Gouverneur & Kemble's advertisements of their East Indies goods give insight into the language and advertising strategies used to promote commodities to the public. In 1793, they advertised goods from Canton brought on the *Nancy* with a big headline 'INDIA SALES by Gouverneur & Kemble.' The advertisement also informed the reader about the origin of the goods and the name of the ship with a list of the imported goods. The first items mentioned were the teas; 'HYSON' was printed in capital letters to grab attention.[159] The ad also announced:

---

158 *The Daily Advertiser*, 4 June 1793, p. 3.

159 *The Daily Advertiser*, 4 June 1793, p. 3.

A small quantity of very fine short nankeens.
Black and coloured silks of all kinds, viz.
Lutestrings, taffitys, sattins, finchews, and
A small parcel sewing silk,
Tea China, with a large proportion of cups and saucers.
Nankeen fans, and a quantity of exceeding good grain sugar, very white, in matts.
They have also for sale,
Musenvado sugar in Hhds.[160]
Some very excellent claret, in boxes of 1 & 3 doz. each.
French Brandy in pipes, and a quantity of Barcelona hides.[161]

In the same edition of the newspaper, a listing by Le Roy, Bayard & Co. wrote that they had brandy, Tenerife wine, gin, rum, sugar, and Swedish iron for sale.[162] Also in the paper were advertisements for the sale of gold watches or miniature profile painting, hair work, textiles, household furniture, wines and groceries from every part of the world, theater shows, college courses and more. Taken together, that day's *Daily Advertiser* listed more than 160 advertisements, representing the vast array of products and services that New York's consumers had available to them. Most goods were described in extravagant language. Some advertisers even garnished their announcements with printed pictures such as a rose, a house, a ship, or shoes.

Further advertising strategies were months-long advertisement series. Gouverneur & Kemble arranged such a series after their ships *America* and *Sampson* arrived in New York in 1796. Half a year later, the 30 January 1797, issue still had the announcement of the sale of large amounts of teas from those ships (200 chests fine Hyson, 40 chests Gunpowder or Imperial, 30 chests Souchong, and 600 chests Bohea Tea). It also indexed yellow short nankeens, yellow and white nankeens, as well as a 'quantity of blue and white China plates in rolls, both flat and soup plates, in three different sizes,' as well as China window blinds and other goods.[163] In the spring of 1800, Gouverneur & Kemble listed a variety of different goods that read like the compendium of the firm's global activities. In one and the same ad they announce the sale of Chinese teas, chinaware, indigo, quicksilver, Russian duck, Martinique licorice, brandy, kid gloves, German goods ('Platittas, Britannias, Lawns or Estopillas Umes, Listados, Blue and white, Bagging Stuff, brown Silosias, Oznaburgs, and White

160 Hhd was the short form for a large cask or barrel.
161 *The Daily Advertiser*, 4 June 1793, p. 3.
162 *The Daily Advertiser*, 4 June 1793. p. 1.
163 *The Daily Advertiser*, 30 January 1797, p. 1.

Rolls'), Writing Paper, Wax Candles, Nails, Russian hemp, Russian iron, white and brown Havana sugar, Malaga wine, whale oil, seal skins, and 'Battle Gun Powder.'[164]

Ferguson & Day similarly announced the sale of cargo from Trieste brought by their brig *Concord* in the *New York Commercial Advertiser* on 6 October 1806. They tried to grab the reader's attention with a large headline that read 'CASTILE SOAP, BRIMSTONE & C,' followed by a list of goods that included 1000 cases marble soap, 124 cases refined brimstone as well as currants, orange peel, creme tartar, and gum arabic.[165]

These are just a few examples of the copious advertisements instigated by merchants who were eager to entice customers with their global products. Terms like 'just imported' or 'just landed' as well as the country of origin highlighted the newness and originality of their products. Buying goods from various world regions was fashionable and the advertisements fortified people's desire for those goods. Detailed descriptions, the enumerations of the various textiles and the long listings of different goods were means to evoke customer enthusiasm. Even if one did not have the money for them, just reading and knowing about the cornucopia of goods certainly created a feeling of cosmopolitanism and modernism in people.

Carl Robert Keyes's study on early American advertisements in Philadelphia shows in detail how advertisements were an important means to stimulate consumer demand. Keyes argues that early advertisements have long been ignored in historical scholarship and their value for the explanation of socio-economic and cultural developments underrated.[166] One major practice of eighteenth century advertisers was to create long lists of their products, which accentuated quality and refinement. By emphasizing different products, their colors and styles, these lists underscored abundance, which generated consumer imagination.[167] After 1780, a growing cultural emphasis on fashion, elegance, and good taste was evident.

Advertisements were one of *the merchants'* means to create desire and find buyers for their increasing palette of global products. But they themselves were also consumers of those new global goods. *The merchants* and their families exhibited a certain lifestyle and modernism displayed in their homes and clothing that many found desirable.

---

164 *New York Commercial Advertiser*, 17 March 1800, p. 1.

165 *New York Commercial Advertiser*, 6 October 1806, p. 3.

166 C.R. Keyes, 'Early American Advertising: Marketing and Consumer Culture in Eighteenth Century Philadelphia', PhD Thesis, Johns Hopkins University, 2007.

167 Keyes, *Early American Advertising*, p. 135.

Different sources give indication of *the merchants'* consumption habits: correspondence and shipping lists often contain goods that were specifically brought for their personal use, account books give insight into their daily spending, and their remaining estates list furniture and other luxury items they owned. Samuel Ferguson's correspondence discloses the consuming habits of an aspiring merchant. In his letters Ferguson often discussed new products and received news on the latest trends in England from his correspondents, especially his uncle Edward Ferguson. In one of those letters Edward writes: 'I dare say the ladies will have told you how to Crop your hair—to Reduce the stuffing at the Neck—and pull up the Shirt Neck above the Cravat. Black Coats are very fashionable with yellow buttons my thin Neck and Chaps won't do without a little filling so I shall keep it to the last.'[168] He even illustrated his letter with little drawings. Edward also sent fashionable articles to his nephew from England such as printed fabrics, hoses, galloons, lace sleeves, waistcoats, stockings, silk clocks, and handkerchiefs, as well as gooseberries and cranberries, hang beef, and newspapers.[169] Ferguson's uncle seems to have been a typical dandy and most of his letters are filled with gossip and reports about the newest trends and fashions, information on daily politics, and general societal morals. Since Ferguson was from England it is not surprising that he stayed informed on happenings and trends in his home country. When Ferguson was in England arranging to move across the Atlantic with his new spouse, Day supplied him with lists of things he had already organized for the house and those British household goods which were still needed for their house on Wall Street. In May 1802, Day wrote:

> [Y]ou of course will, if you marry, bring out a number of Additions among other things I would recommend a Coffee & Tea Urn as likewise some carpeting—I could wish 3 or 4 good Engravings, there was one which struck me very much when I was in London—which has for a Subject a Scene in the Children of the Wood description of the Contest between the person who saves the Children from being murdered by the Russian.

168 'Letter from Edward Ferguson to Samuel Ferguson', 22 February 1798. Series 1: Correspondence, To Samuel Ferguson 1796–1806, Ferguson family papers. Manuscripts and Archives. The New York Public Library. Astor, Lenox, and Tilden Foundations.

169 'Letter from Edward Ferguson to Samuel Ferguson', 18 July 1797, and 22 February, 1798, Series 1: Correspondence, To Samuel Ferguson 1796–1806, Ferguson family papers. Manuscripts and Archives. The New York Public Library. Astor, Lenox, and Tilden Foundations.

> I likewise want some Books which I will give you a List of either in this or my next.[170]

A request of Gouverneur & Kemble to their partners Smith & Atkinson to organize the shipment of articles from London for personal use for Isaac Gouvernour reveals a similar eye for British fashion trends:

> A Handsome set of plated Harness for a Chariott with the initials of his name engraved on it…A Bridle and Saddle of plated furniture in the same manner, a net gold serviceable Watch with chain for his Lady—initials A.G, A Convenient Tool Chest, usually for famillys [sic] residing in the Country when House carpenters are not always at hand, A Medicine Chest comprehending usefull [sic] articles with measure weights and to answer to the same purpose but neither to be very expensive.[171]

From Havre, Gouverneur & Kemble ordered their supercargo 'to bring a parcel of Champaign [sic], provided it is very cheap, and also some Window Glass of the sizes 8 by 6 and 9 by 7 which we are told comes much lower from there than from England.'[172] From China they advised their supercargo 'to bring us a few small Chests of fine Souchong tea and some of the finest Black Tea for our own use.'[173]

William Constable's accounts list his consumption habits during his stay in Britain from 1791 to 1795. His family's spending habits are recorded in a copy of his account at the hardware store of P. & M. Grayhurst at 65 Shand, from July 1792 to June 1793, as well as a detailed list of the furniture in his house in Bristol. Items the Constable family bought from Grayhurst, were, for instance, a 'Black & Gold Tea and Knife Tray, a Bronze Greek Tea Urn Plated furniture, a Mahogany tray and Polished Black Tin Dish covers.' In one year, he spent a sum of

170 'John Day to Samuel Ferguson', 24 May 1802. Series I: Correspondence, To Samuel and John Ferguson 1802, 1806, 1825–1827, Ferguson family papers. Manuscripts and Archives. The New York Public Library. Astor, Lenox, and Tilden Foundations.

171 'Gouverneur & Kemble to Smiths & Atkinson', 15 September 1796, Gouverneur and Kemble, Letter book, 1794 May–1796 June, New York Historical Society Mss Collection.

172 'Gouverneur & Kemble to Samuel Gouverneur', 13 June 1795, Gouverneur and Kemble, Letter book, 1794 May–1796 June, New York Historical Society Mss Collection. Underlining as in original.

173 'Gouverneur & Kemble to Joseph Gouverneur', 1 April 1797, Gouverneur & Kemble letter book. Manuscripts and Archives. The New York Public Library. Astor, Lenox, and Tilden Foundations.

£239.6S at the store.[174] A list of his home interior reveals Constable's affluence, which was expressed in the size of his house and its quality furniture and decoration: The house consisted of a dining room, a breakfast room, a library, a billiard room, a 'best bed room', 'Mr. and Mrs. Constable's room', a 'field bed room', a 'powdering room', Mrs. Constable's room, a nursery, a servants' room, and a great hall and kitchen.[175] Centered in the dining room was a set of mahogany dining tables consisting of two center tables and two round ends made out of Spanish wood. Eighteen mahogany chairs and two elbow chairs surrounded the table. Along the walls were two large mahogany side tables with wine coolers and a spirit draw cupboard. Above one of the side tables hung a large gold frame with ornaments. A large 'mock Turkey carpet' was spread out on the floor. A Jug-table on socket castors was also in the room. Japanned, flowered, and varnished curved cornices garnished the windows. French window curtains framed them. The breakfast room held two large mahogany pin tables surrounded by mahogany chairs with curved and inlaid backs of satin, a spider table, and a satin wood balloon table. It also featured a portable desk, a large hearthrug, a Brussels carpet, and the same window decorations as in the dining room. A mahogany library range gothic door with London glass and six patent locks opened to the library which exhibited a bookcase with three glass doors and green curtains, a pair of mahogany library steps, a mahogany enclosed basin stand, a mahogany dressing table, a library table and a small desk. Mahogany window blinds covered with green silk decorated the windows. A billiard table was in the center of the billiard room. The best bedroom had a large size four-poster bedstead with four carved mahogany posts. They were covered by a set of cornices, japanned, flowered, varnished and decorated with white dimity curtains. The bedroom had a large mahogany wardrobe with Piedmont mahogany drawers, shelves and sideboards, a French night table, six japanned chairs, a corner basin stand with soap linings, and a mahogany commode dressing table. The great hall was laid out with Venetian carpet and decorated with large cast brass rods. The cabinet and upholstery goods of the house were valued at £773.[176]

---

174 'Accounts 1792', Constable Papers, Accounts 1773–1803, Constable-Pierrepont family papers. Manuscripts and Archives. The New York Public Library. Astor, Lenox, and Tilden Foundations.

175 'William Constable to Thomas Andrews 13 March 1795', Constable Papers, Accounts 1773–1803, Constable-Pierrepont family papers. Manuscripts and Archives. The New York Public Library. Astor, Lenox, and Tilden Foundations.

176 'William Constable to Thomas Andrews 13 March 1795', Constable Papers, Accounts 1773–1803, Constable-Pierrepont family papers. Manuscripts and Archives. The New York Public Library. Astor, Lenox, and Tilden Foundations.

Constable's interior design resembles the furniture trends outlined in the *Cabinet Maker,* one of the many furniture design books that circulated in Britain after 1750.[177] Up to three furniture pattern books were printed every year, among them Chippendale's *Gentleman and Cabinet Maker's Director* (since 1754), Ince and Mayhew's *Universal System of Household Furniture* (since 1762), and Hepplewhite's *Cabinet Maker and Upholster Guide* (since 1788).[178] They were also very influential for American cabinetmakers on the East Coast who copied British trends.[179] Especially noticeable is the number of japanned furniture listed in Constable's inventory. The trend of japanning—the glazing of furniture with black lacquer that imitated Asian lacquer work—had emerged in Europe by the late seventeenth century but reached its peak in the eighteenth century. The Constable's seem to have copied the fashion of the time in the decoration of their London home.

Unfortunately, such a detailed inventory does not exist for Constable's house in New York. However, since Constable brought furniture from London to New York, the house interior was most likely similarly ornate as it was in England.[180] In March 1796, a survey of his Wall Street house was administered by the Bank of New York, which provides some insight into Constable's New York living. The three-story house had four rooms on the first floor which were all wainscoted from top to bottom. Two rooms on the first floor had marble fireplaces. The second floor consisted of four rooms, all wainscoted, of which two had marble fireplaces. The third story came with four rooms all fully wainscoted and with cornices. The garret had two bedrooms. All stairs were wainscoted with mahogany. The house came with a cellar, a well, and a cistern as well as a large yard. It had a back building, which consisted of two floors with two rooms each. The first room had a kitchen and a storeroom and the second floor had two bedrooms. The value of the house was estimated to be £4500 New York currency.[181] The house and lot were sold to the Bank of New York for £11,000 New York currency in 1796. Constable's estate inventory does not list the housing interior in detail but lists the value of certain housing items. Furniture and

177 On the *Cabinet Maker* read G. Hepplewhite, *The Cabinet Maker and Upholsterer's Guide,* New York, Dover Publications, 1969.

178 E. White, *Pictorial Dictionary of British 18th Century Furniture Design: The Printed Sources,* Woolbridge, Antique Collectors Club, 1990, pp. 18–19.

179 Hepplewhite, *Cabinet Maker,* p. 6.

180 'Thomas Andrews to William Constable, 24 March 1796', William Constable Correspondence, *Constable Pierrepont Family Papers,* New York Public Library.

181 'Accounts 1796', Constable Papers, Accounts 1773–1803, Constable-Pierrepont family papers. Manuscripts and Archives. The New York Public Library. Astor, Lenox, and Tilden Foundations.

particulars were recorded to have a value of $3555, linens $840, plates $940, his almost 1000 books $1597, slaves $4500, horse carriages $2500 and liquors $913. Constable also owned a portrait of George Washington by Gilbert Stuart, which Hezekiah Pierrepont obtained after his death and hung in his Brooklyn Heights home. Constable died a rich man and his house and household items are proof of his affluence as well as his taste and elegance.[182]

Houses and household products became an important status symbol during the late eighteenth and early nineteenth century. A change in housing habits took place in American society and it became increasingly important for Americans with capital and social status to have at least one room representing good taste that was separated from the living area so that guests could be welcomed there.[183]

Constable had become a man of affluence and his consumption of luxury items and their display in his house is not surprising. Ferguson & Day were a smaller merchant firm and yet their preoccupation with consumer products is just as prevalent. Day's interest for the carpet, which he had seen in England is a good example. *The merchants* shared their passion and enthusiasm for consumer items with their fellow New Yorkers. The boundary between upper and lower ranks faded by the late eighteenth century where formerly, the upper ranks distinguished themselves through the desire of different products. William Constable certainly had much more money to spend for his consumption habits than a regular New York artisan or tradesman but the consumer items they liked were the same. Even people with meager purchasing power participated in the discourse through reading magazines and commercial advertisers. Luxury consumption was now acceptable not only for the upper ranks but also for the middling sorts. A stroll around the city could fuel one's desire for goods that were sold in the retail stores and displayed in the houses and clothes of others.

Conspicuous consumption was important to the self-identification of the rising middling ranks. It is crucial to remember that the percentage of self-made men in New York had risen considerably after 1784. The men were artisans, craft entrepreneurs, and merchants who had worked their way up. Their display of modern products was a way to differentiate themselves from the

182 'Journal with inventory kept by James Constable, 1803–1807', William Constable Estate, Volumes, Constable-Pierrepont families papers. Manuscripts and Archives. The New York Public Library. Astor, Lenox, and Tilden Foundations.

183 E.A. Chappel, 'Housing a Nation: The Transformation of Living Standards in Early America', in C. Carson, R.Hoffman, and P.J. Albert (eds.), *Of Consuming Interests: The Style of Life in the Eighteenth Century*, Charlottesville, University of Virginia Press, 1994, p. 186.

lower ranks and appear modern, genteel, and en vogue. Edward Chappel points out that the changes in housing of affluent merchants and entrepreneurial tradesmen is representative of an emergence of middling people that identified themselves through shared expectations rather than ideological foundations.[184] Housing and fashion were expressions of these expectations. While 'they may not have used their well-built houses to distinguish themselves as a self-conscious class, their refined buildings, furnishings, dress, and manners represented a body of shared expectations. These were applied toward the purchase of entry into an existing genteel culture rather than formation of a new social tier,' Chappel writes.[185]

An increasing desire to be identified as a person of gentility and good taste is represented by their need to buy sets of ceramics, wear silks and fine cotton and participate in conversations about new products from distant places. Social status was now defined in relation to commodities and behavior. In his remarkable study, *The Refinement of America. Persons, Houses, Cities* Richard L. Bushman argues that since 1790, respectability spread widely through the middle levels of American society.[186] The middling people came to believe that they should be living a genteel life, a feeling boosted by increasing materialist culture. 'The division between rude and refined only roughly corresponded to wealth, education, family, work, or any other measure of social class. Genteel culture became an independent variable, cutting across society, and leading... to the confusion about class that has long been characteristic of American society.'[187]

The increase of available commodities altered social identity. New popular products transformed cultural habits and practices accompanied by new discourses on consumer items and fashion. Consumption became a means to express affiliation to a genteel culture. Alternative spaces emerged that revolved around the middling groups, different from conventional public spaces as they were openers of a civic culture less regulated by state interference and more by commercial interests. It was in these new spaces that some of the most drastic changes of the time occurred.[188]

---

184 Chappel, *Housing a Nation*, p. 189.

185 Chappel, *Housing a Nation*, p. 189.

186 R. Lyman, *The Refinement of America: Persons, Houses, Cities*, New York, Knopf, 1992.

187 Bushman, *Refinement*, p. xv.

188 Similar middling classes formed in other parts of the world, mostly in those connected to the world market. In Great Britain their existence was not as obvious as in the United States, as they were situated between a strong landowning aristocracy, poor agricultural laborers, and a growing urban working class. In Germany, a social group called the '*gebildete Stände*' formed which expressed similar interests as the middling classes in the

During the late eighteenth century, people were confronted with a new kind of modernity. Newer and newer goods from places all over the world were being sold in the city, merchants maintained business relations with distant world regions, and now even less affluent middling people could afford to own at least one or two pieces of fashionable products. Bayly writes that, '[a]n essential part of being modern is thinking you are modern.'[189] The new goods allowed an increasing number of people to feel modern. And if one was not in the financial situation to buy the wide range of new goods, they nonetheless participated in the discourse. The feeling of modernity bestowed a feeling of

---

United States. The Germans also bestowed significance on education and gentility and established political and moral societies. Consumption played an important part for its group identity and was discussed in magazines and newspapers.

Bayly's analysis, as well as different national case studies, point to the fact that global commerce and consumerism are contributing factors for the rise of these distinctive societal groups. In many regions, mostly those integrated to the world markets, existing structures were transformed by new cultural (consumerism), political (constitutions) and economic (commercialization) changes. More comparison research on these middling classes and the role commerce and consumerism played in their constitution and identity formation would be necessary in order to be able to analyze how eighteenth-century globalization affected social and cultural changes. A global historic approach that portrays these societies within a global context rather than in national comparative studies could shed more light on its distinctiveness in history. Such a project was suggested by R. Blänkner and I.U. Paul, ‚Neuständische Gesellschaft—Europäische Gesellschaft im Globalen Kontext, 1750–1830/40', in *Ungleichheiten, 47, Deutscher Historikertag in Dresden 2008, Berichtsband*, Göttingen 2009, pp. 218–222.

In this context it would be interesting to focus more on the communication among these middling classes across continents. An interesting research question would be the role these transoceanic discourses have played in the conflicts and crises across the Atlantic and how crucial they were for the transmission of knowledge on the fall of *Anciens Régimes*. One of the main features of *the merchants'* global actions was discourse. This study has focused on the economic aspects of their global exchanges, but in order to show how networks have played a decisive role for political and cultural change, further research is necessary.

For the German 'gebildete Stände' see H.E. Bödeker, 'Die „gebildeten Stände" im späten 18. und frühen 19. Jahrhundert: Zugehörigkeit und Abgrenzung. Mentalitäten und Handlungspotentiale', in J. Kocka (ed.), *Bildungsbürgertum im 19. Jahrhundert. Teil IV: Politischer Einfluss und gesellschaftliche Formation*, Stuttgart, Vandenhoeck & Ruprecht, 1989, pp. 21–52; L. Gall, *Von der Ständischen zur Bürgerlichen Gesellschaft*, Enzyklopädie Deutscher Geschichte, vol. 25, no. 2., Aktualisierte Auflage, München, Oldenbourg Wissenschaftsverlag, 2012.

189 Bayly, *Birth of the Modern World*, p. 10.

cosmopolitanism, and worldliness in society. A description of Salem merchants, by contemporary Harriet Matineau, poignantly captures that sentiment:

> They speak of Fayal and the Azores as if they were close at hand. The fruits of the Mediterranean are on every table. They have a large acquaintance at Cairo. They know Napoleon's grave at St. Helena, and have wild talks to tell of Mozambique and Madagascar, and stores of ivory to show from there. They speak of the power of the king of Muscat, and are sensible of the riches of the southeast coast of Arabia. Anybody will give you anecdotes from Canton and descriptions of the Society and Sandwich Islands. They often slip up the western coast of their two continents, bringing furs from the back regions of their own wide land, glance up at the Andes on their return: double Cape Horn, touch at the ports of Brazil and Guiana, look about them in the West Indies, feeling almost at home there, and land some fair morning in Salem and walk home as if they had done nothing remarkable.[190]

Economic historian Emma Rothschild has called the eighteenth century an 'epoch of almost obsessive preoccupation with newness.'[191] In the United States, that newness was manifested in all realms of life: in the economical realm, through commercial expansion and new economic institutions; in the political realm, through a new government and constitution; and in the social realm, through new social spaces and groups. It was also found in new sciences, the different organization of homes and households, and new consumer items. It extracted people from their previous life realities and fundamentally changed former world perceptions. New concepts, values, and world models were formulated from those new experiences and expectations.

Growing global business opportunities that allowed merchants to bring large varieties of goods and expand shipping were of course an important factor for these social changes. By integrating the American economy into a global market, more and more people benefitted from commercial enterprises. The extent of that commercialization was striking. Within a few decades it had permeated through an enormous part of society. Gordon Woods has pointed to the significance of this fact, writing:

190 S.Greenbie and M.L. Greenbie, *Gold of Ophir the China trade in the Making of America*, New York, Wilson Erickson, 1937 p. 51.

191 Emma Rothschild, 'Global Commerce and the Question of Sovereignty in the Eighteenth-Century Provinces', *Modern Intellectual History*, 1, Issue 01 (April 2004), pp. 3–25, p. 4.

> There were no great technological breakthroughs in this period between 1780 and 1820, certainly nothing comparable to the railroad or the telegraph. It still took weeks to travel from Boston to Washington, DC., in the late 1820s. Industrialization and urbanization had scarcely begun. As late as 1810 there were no urban center larger than 100,000. Even by 1830 New York was the only city larger than 100,000. Beyond the east coast the society was even more primitive. Cincinnati was the largest city in the West; yet by 1830 it still had less than 25,000 people. In the early republic there were no great waves of foreign immigrants. The heavy infusion of nineteenth-century European migrants was yet to come, in the period following 1830. As late as the Age of Jackson America was still predominantly a rural agricultural society, on the surface not all that different from rural agricultural eighteenth-century colonial America. Yet beneath that seemingly similar surface everything had changed. America may have still been largely rural, still largely agricultural, but now it was also largely commercial, perhaps the most thoroughly commercialized nation in the world. Hundreds of thousands of very ordinary people were very busy buying and selling in order to realize what Niles' *Weekly Register* in 1815 said was 'the almost *universal ambition to get forward.*' Every European like Frances Wright who saw firsthand this society 'teeming with business' was excited, awed, or frightened. There was nothing quite like it on such a scale anywhere in the world. And it seemed to have emerged out of nowhere.[192]

As this study has shown, it is questionable if these changes could have manifested themselves so rapidly without the favorable global cirumstances that benefitted American merchants.

192 Wood, *Significance of the Early Republic*, p. 13.

Conclusion

This study has exposed how global forces in the late eighteenth century established the formation of a group of merchants that, through wit and favorable circumstances, expanded their commercial activities around the world leaving an economic, political, and social legacy. Two conclusions are drawn from this analysis: First, it is necessary to consider the global context of the late eighteenth and early nineteenth century in domestic developments. Second, globalization processes were jointly produced by a variety of state and non-state actors; it is therefore essential to focus attention on private actors in the study of early modern globalization.

For the merchants of this study, three global events were particularly central to their success, allowing them to expand their businesses into new world regions: the discontinuation of the British East India Company's monopoly on the India trade, a result of the American Revolution; the French Revolution and the subsequent Napoleonic Wars; and the revolution in Haiti. The opening of the East Indies trade allowed American traders to expand into new commercial territory. Following the European trade routes and practices, *the merchants* eagerly sent their vessels to India and China to purchase mainly tea and textiles. Within a decade, after a variety of creative businesses and market expansions, they managed to make the East Indies trade a flourishing commercial branch. Participating in inner-Indian Ocean trade networks, voyaging to the Pacific in search of seals, and exploring the American frontier in pursuit of ginseng are just a few examples of the opening of new economic spaces. Another event also affected the success of American enterprises with its far-reaching global impact: the French Revolution. The consequent European Wars during which Americans stayed neutral, allowed merchants to considerably expand their businesses. As neutral carriers they were able to take over large parts of the supply of the European continent with products from the colonies, especially with sugar, coffee, and tea, commodities that had become vital in the daily routine of the European middling classes. The crude food and naval supplies from the United States were also in great need on the war-torn continent and the merchants eagerly sent their ships to meet the high demand. Additionally, the Haitian Revolution was a beneficial event that granted new business opportunities. Commerce with the West Indies had already picked up again, making it one of the main branches of America's foreign commerce. The revolts on some of the islands opened up business of a grand significance. Even though there was much precariousness in trading in the area, the money gained from supplying the islands and European naval forces with American foodstuffs was worth the risks.

All in all, merchants were great profiteers from the global crises that afflicted the world in the late eighteenth century. To describe them as 'actors of globalization' is appropriate considering their manifold global interactions that interweaved different regions and continents. They were both producers of global interaction and beneficiaries of a new global condition they learned to use to their advantage.

One feature most crucial to the success of merchants' vast commerce: the existence of a stable and reliable network of business partners and information providers that existed across continents and prevailed even during war and crisis. Those networks were necessary on local and regional levels, as they often eased a person's entry into the business world and provided necessary capital. They were also pivotal in trans-regional and trans-oceanic commerce in the way that they facilitated the supply of market intelligence, the organization of commodity flows, and the provision of credit. The analysis of commercial correspondence illustrated that the businesses were not risky speculations and that merchants were very well informed about market supply and demand and knew what to expect when they sent out a ship. Those networks also gave the private merchants an advantage over trading companies in their flexibility to send ships out or change itineraries according to market demands.

The merchants' work was not only crucial for the promotion of America's maritime commerce overseas, but it also left a legacy in New York's economic, political, and cultural landscapes. Even with their far-reaching global business enterprises, they were similarly occupied and involved with local developments. They played a role in the establishment and development of the city's political and financial institutions. Although merchants have often belonged to the urban elites and thus occupied important positions, the difference was that a growing number of smaller merchants and middling people benefitted from the development of corporate institutions like banks, insurance companies or turnpike corporations, allowing for the rise of self-made men.

Two urban developments directly related to the growth of global maritime commerce are the rise of middling ranks involved in the shipping industry and the increased consumerism among them. The growing middling class affected New York's cityscape: the growth of the seaport and commercial areas led to an expansion of the harbor and emergence of new residential areas. New buildings, wharves, and piers were built; a new city plan was developed and different neighborhoods surfaced, changing the city's visual appearance. Accompanying those transformations was a change to the city's social spaces as well. The century-old ties of the household to the workspace began to erode with the emergence of new forms of labor relations. Newspaper advertisements and retail stores promoted the rising number of consumer products that began entering New York's markets. Merchants were eager to find customers for their growing palette of diverse goods and found their audience in the rising middling classes who saw in those global products an expression of a genteel and urbane lifestyle and culture.

Vis-a-vis their multifaceted commercial activities, the terms 'trade' and 'commerce' seem almost too limited to adequately describe the copious practices and operations of the merchants' global undertakings—as do descriptions of them as 'traders,' 'shippers' or even 'merchants'. Because of the complexity and intricacies of their businesses, it seems necessary to expand the terminology used to describe their commercial actions, which the word globalization, although anachronistic, better captures. Contemporaries already felt a necessity to describe that extension of commerce and the increased inter-linkage of global markets and businesses. Historian Paul Cheney, for example, shows that eighteenth century French writers started to refer to the 'advances of trade' (*les progres du commerce*).[1] With regard to their complex operations and business fields, a merchant resembled more of what we would call today a business manager of a global corporation than a merchant or trader.

This book has argued that by the late eighteenth century, globalization appeared not only in the quantitative rise in the flow of commodities, people, and ideas but also in the qualitative change of economic, social, and political life. Merchants contributed to those qualitative changes in four aspects. First, they played a part in the establishment of a complex commercial network of commodity, finance, and information exchange across countries and continents. The high density by which these networks operated, especially in the Atlantic, and the fact that they operated according to self-appointed rules and structures without supervision from formal, state-controlled institutions demonstrates the rise of a commercial system regulated by private actors. Because the networks prospered in spite of war and crises they permitted a high degree of autonomy against the political powers and fostered free trade. Second, the expansion of trade caused a deep transformation of society as it both promoted the rise of a consumer society and affected changes in labor relations. Third, profits of the trade were channeled into the establishment of capitalist institutions like banks and joint stock companies that were then instrumental in the cyclical creation of new commercial possibilities and in the mitigation of barriers to entry for less affluent businessmen. Fourth, to ease trade and commerce, political instruments such as diplomacy and consular relationships were extended. The merchants benefitted from new policies that provided a framework for free and unfettered trade carried out by private actors.

1 P.B. Cheney, Revolutionary Commerce: Globalization and the French Monarchy, Cambridge, Harvard University Press, 2010, p.1.

Merchants were the 'men of the moment.' Their entrepreneurial energy helped transform the United States after 1784. While they did not partake in the realm of grand visions and ideas like the Founding Fathers, they were just as equally important in making the new republic function. Their practical and innovative spirit influenced the country's course over the decades following 1784, considerably altering America's place in the world. Their endless search to carve out new global spaces, explore new markets, and expand their businesses secured the country's role in international trade. They were quick adaptors of changing global processes and operators of global flows of goods and knowledge. They were negotiators of new spaces and actions on the international arena, which made them successful businessmen and allowed them to accumulate great wealth. On the local level, their entrepreneurship was just as important. Many merchants were improvers. They worked to create better circumstances and conditions for the growth of their businesses and contributed to the commercialization of society. This is not to say that most merchants were exceptionally altruistic or well-minded people. Much of the local change did not result out of ideology but from mercantile success and the influence that came with wealth. America's merchants were global businessmen and it is through their lives and work that we can begin to comprehend how deeply eighteenth century commerce impacted local and national development, which is why they are regarded as 'actors of globalization'.

Bibliography

Archival Sources

William Edgar papers. Manuscripts and Archives. The New York Public Library. Astor, Lenox, and Tilden Foundations.

Oliver Wolcott letterbook. Manuscripts and Archives. The New York Public Library. Astor, Lenox, and Tilden Foundations.

Ferguson family papers. Manuscripts and Archives. The New York Public Library. Astor, Lenox, and Tilden Foundations.

Bayard-Campbell-Pearsall families papers. Manuscripts and Archives. The New York Public Library. Astor, Lenox, and Tilden Foundations.

Gouverneur & Kemble letter book. Manuscripts and Archives. The New York Public Library. Astor, Lenox, and Tilden Foundations.

Constable-Pierrepont papers. Manuscripts and Archives. The New York Public Library. Astor, Lenox, and Tilden Foundations.

Jacob Le Roy & Sons Correspondence and Papers 1791–1832, New York Historical Society Mss Collection.

Gouverneur and Kemble, Letter book, 1794 May-1796 June, New York Historical Society Mss Collection.

Kemble family collection, 1758–1895, New York Historical Society Mss Collection.

Sub Rosa Club, Records 1795–1800, New York Historical Society Mss Collection.

Isaac Bell Papers 1787–1940, Rare Book & Manuscript Library, Columbia University in the City of New York.

Ships and Shipping of Old New York: A Brief Account of the Interesting Phases of the Commerce of New York and the Foundation of the City to the Beginning of the Civil War, New York City: Printed for Bank of Manhattan Company. Rare Book & Manuscript Library, Columbia University in the City of New York.

Pierrepont family papers, ARC.263, Brooklyn Historical Society.

Unpublished Dissertations

Brekke, L., 'Fashioning America: Clothing, Consumerism, and the Politics of Appearance', PhD Thesis, Harvard University, 2007.

Block, M.D. 'New England Merchants, the China Trade, and the Origins of California', PhD Thesis, University of Southern California, 2011.

Davis, W.A., 'William Constable. New York Merchant and Land Speculator, 1772–1803', PhD Thesis, Harvard University, 1955.

Keyes, C.R., 'Early American Advertising: Marketing and Consumer Culture in Eighteenth Century Philadelphia', PhD Thesis, Johns Hopkins University, 2007.

Tailby, D., 'Chapters of the Business Career of William Constable', PhD Thesis, Rutgers University 1961.

Van, R.T., 'Free Trade & Family Values: Kinship Networks and the Culture of Early American Capitalism', PhD Thesis, Columbia University, 2010.

diZerega Wall, D., 'At Home in New York: Changing Family Life Among the Propertied in the Late Eighteenth and Early Nineteenth Centuries', PhD Thesis, New York University, 1987.

Publications

Armitage, D. 'Is there a Pre-History of Globalization.' in Deborah Cohen and Maura O'Connor (eds.), Comparison and History, Europe in Cross-National Perspective, London, Routledge 2004, pp. 165–175.

Aslanian, S., '"The Salt in a Merchant's Letter": The Culture of Julfan Correspondence in the Indian Ocean and the Mediterranean', *Journal of World History*, vol. 19, no. 2, 2008, pp. 127–188.

Aslanian, S., *From the Indian Ocean to the Mediterranean. The Global Trade Networks of Armenian Merchants from New Julfa*, Berkeley, University of California Press, 2011.

Baasch, E., *Beiträge zur Geschichte der Handelsbeziehungen zwischen Hamburg und Amerika; Festschrift der Hamburgischen Amerika Feier*, Hamburg, L. Friederischen & Co., 1892.

Bannet, E.T., *Empire of Letters: Letter Manuals and Transatlantic Correspondence, 1688–1820*, Cambridge, Cambridge University Press, 2005.

Barret, W., *The Old Merchants of New York City*, New York, Carleton, 1864.

Bauer, J.K., *A Maritime History of the United States: The Role of America's Seas and Waterways*, Columbia, SC, University of South Carolina Press, 1988.

Bayly, C.A., *The Birth of the Modern World, 1780–1914: Global Connections and Comparisons*, Malden, MA, Blackwell, 2004.

Bean, S.S., *Yankee India: American Commercial and Cultural Encounters with India in the Age of Sail 1784–1860*, Salem, Peabody Essex Museum, 2000.

Beckert, S., and Rosenbaum J.B., *The Monied Metropolis: New York City and the Consolidation of the American Bourgeoisie, 1850–1896*, Cambridge, Cambridge University Press, 2001.

Beckert, S., and Rosenbaum J.B., *The American Bourgeoisie: Distinction and Identity in the Nineteenth Century*, New York, Palgrave Macmillan, 2010.

Ben-Atar, D., 'Alexander Hamilton's Alternative: Technology Piracy and the Report on Manufactures', *The William & Mary Quarterly*, vol. 52, 1995, pp. 389–414.

Bender, T., *New York Intellect: A History of Intellectual Life in New York City, From 1750 to the Beginnings of Our Own Time*, Baltimore, Johns Hopkins University Press, 1988.

Bender, T., 'Introduction. Historians, the Nation, and the Plentitude of Narratives' in Bender T. (ed.), *Rethinking American History in a Global Age*, Berkeley, University of California Press, 2002.

Bender, T., *A Nation Among Nations: America's Place in World History*, New York, Hill and Wang, 2006.

Berg, M., *Luxury and Pleasure in Eighteenth-Century Britain*, Oxford, Oxford University Press, 2005.

Berg, M. and Helen Clifford (eds.), *Consumers and Luxury: Consumer Culture in Europe 1650–1850*, Manchester, Manchester University Press, 1999.

Bhagat, G., *Americans in India, 1784–1860*, New York, New York University Press, 1970.

Black, M. and Olshansky J.R., *New York City's Gracie Mansion: A History of the Mayor's House*, New York, J.M. Kaplan Fund, 1984.

Blänkner, R. and Paul I.U., ‚Neuständische Gesellschaft—Europäische Gesellschaft im Globalen Kontext, 1750–1830/40', *Ungleichheiten 47: Deutscher Historikertag in Dresden 2008*, Berichtsband, Göttingen, 2009.

Bledstein, B.J., 'Introduction: Storytellers to the Middle Class', in Bledstein, B.J. and Johnson R.D. (eds.), *The Middling Sorts: Explorations in the History of the American Middle Class*, New York, Routledge, 2001, pp. 1–25.

Blumin, S.M., *The Emergence of the Middle Class: Social Experience in the American City, 1760–1900*, Cambridge, Cambridge University Press, 1989.

Bordo, M.D., Taylor A.M., and Williamson J.G. (eds.), *Globalization in Historical Perspective*, National Bureau of Economic Research Conference Report. Chicago: University of Chicago Press, 2003.

Brady, D.S., 'Comment: Manufactures', in Gilchrist, D.T. (ed.), *The Growth of Seaport Cities 1790–1825*, Proceedings of a Conference Sponsored by The Eleutherian Mills-Hagley Foundation March 17–19, 1966. Charlottesville: The University Press of Virginia, 1967, pp. 92–97.

Breen, T.H., '"Baubles of Britain": The American and Consumer Revolutions of the Eighteenth Century', *Past & Present*, no. 119, 1988, pp. 73–104.

Breen, T.H., *The Marketplace of Revolution: How Consumer Politics Shaped American Independence*, Oxford, Oxford University Press, 2004.

Brekke, L., 'The "Scourge of Fashion": Political Economy and the Politics of Consumption in the Early Republic', *Early American Studies: An Interdisciplinary Journal*, vol. 3, no. 1, 2005, pp. 111–139.

Brewer, J. and Porters R. (eds.), *Consumption and the World of Goods*, New York, Routledge, 1993.

Bushman, R.L., *The Refinement of America: Persons, Houses, Cities*, New York, Knopf, 1992.

Carson, C., Hoffman R., and Albert P.J., *Of Consuming Interests: The Style of Life in the Eighteenth Century, Perspectives on the American Revolution*, Charlottesville: Published for the United States Capitol Historical Society by the University Press of Virginia, 1994.

Chappel, E.A., 'Housing a Nation: The Transformation of Living Standards in Early America', in Carson, C., Hoffman R., and Albert P.J., (eds.), *Of Consuming Interests: The Style of Life in the Eighteenth Century*, Charlottesville, University of Virginia Press, 1994, pp. 167–323.

Charles, J., 'The Origins of the American Party System', *The William and Mary Quarterly* vol. 12, no.4, 1955, pp. 581–630.

Cheney, P.B., *Revolutionary Commerce: Globalization and the French Monarchy*, Cambridge, Harvard University Press, 2010.

Christian, D., *Maps of Time: An Introduction to Big History*, Berkeley, University of California Press, 2004.

Clark, P., *British Clubs and Societies 1580–1800: The Origins of an Associational World*, Oxford, Oxford University Press, 2000.

Clemens, P.G.E., 'The Consumer Culture of the Middle Atlantic, 1760–1820', *The William & Mary Quarterly*, vol. 62, no. 4, 2005, pp. 577–624.

Coatsworth, J.H., 'American Trade With European Colonies in the Caribbean and South America, 1790–1812', *The William and Mary Quarterly*, vol. 24, no. 2, 1967, pp. 243–266.

Cochran, T.C., 'The Business Revolution', *The American Historical Review*, vol. 79, no. 5, 1974, pp. 1449–1466.

Cohen, J., '"The Right to Purchase is as Free as the Right to Sell": Defining Consumers as Citizens in the Auction-House Conflicts of the Early Republic', *Journal of the Early Republic*, vol. 30, no.1, 2010, pp. 25–62.

Colás, A., and Mabee B., 'The Flow and Ebb of Private Seaborne Violence in Global Politics Lesson From the Atlantic World, 1689–1815', in Colás, A. and Mabee B. (eds.), *Mercenaries, Pirates, Bandits, and Empires: Private Violence in Historical Context*, New York, Columbia University Press, 2010, pp. 83–106.

Craig-McDonald, M., 'The Chance of the Moment: Coffee and the New West Indies Commodities Trade', *The William and Mary Quarterly*, vol. 62, no. 3, 2005, pp. 441–473.

Crosby, A.W., *The Columbian Exchange: Biological and Cultural Consequences of 1492*, Westwood, Greenwood Press, 1972.

Crothers, A.G., 'Commercial Risk and Capital Formation in Early America: Virginia Merchants and the Rise of American Marine Insurance, 1750–1815', *Business History Review*, vol. 78, no. 4, 2004, pp. 607–634.

Davis, J.H., 'An Annual Index of U.S. Industrial Production, 1790–1915', *The Quarterly Journal of Economics*, vol. 119, no. 4, 2004, pp. 1177–1215.

Davis, J.S., *Essays in the Early History of American Corporations*, New York, Russel & Russel, 1965.

Davison, R.A., 'Comment: New York Foreign Trade', in Gilchrist D.T., (ed.), *The Growth of Seaport Cities 1790–1825*, Proceedings of a Conference Sponsored by the Eleutherian Mills-Hagley Foundation March 17–19, 1966. Charlottesville, The University Press of Virginia, 1967, pp. 68–78.

DeConde, A., *The Quasi War. The Politics and Diplomacy of the Undeclared War with France*, 1797–1801, New York, Charles Scribner's Sons, 1966.

Diamond, J.M., *Guns, Germs, and Steel: The Fates of Human Societies*, New York, W.W. Norton and Company, 1998.

Dierks, K., *In My Power: Letter Writing and Communications in Early America*, Philadelphia: University of Pennsylvania Press, 2009.

Doerflinger, T.M., *A Vigorous Spirit of Enterprise: Merchants and Economic Development in Revolutionary Philadelphia*, Chapel Hill, University of North Carolina Press, 1986.

Domett, H.W., *History of the Bank of New York*, New York, G.P. Putnam's Sons, 1884.

Downs, J.M., *The Golden Ghetto: American Commercial Community At Canton and the Shaping of American China Policy, 1784–1844*, Bethlehem, PA, Lehigh University Press, 1997.

Downs, J.M., 'American Merchants and the China Opium Trade, 1800–1840', *The Business History Review* vol. 42, no.4, 1968, pp. 418–442.

Dubois, L. and Garrigus J.D., *Slave Revolution in the Caribbean, 1789–1804: A Brief History With Documents*, Boston, Bedford/St. Martins, 2006.

Dun, J.A., '"What Avenues of Commerce Will You Americans Not Explore!": Commercial Philadelphia's Vantage onto the Early Haitian Revolution'. *The William and Mary Quarterly*, vol. 62, no.3, 2005, pp. 473–504.

Duyckinck, W.C., and Cornell J., *The Ducyckinck and Allied Families*, New York, Tobias A. Wright, 1908.

Engel, U. and Middell M., 'Bruchzonen der Globalisierung', *Comparativ*, vol. 15, no. 5/6, 2005, pp. 5–38.

Estes, T., 'Shaping the Politics of Public Opinion: Federalists and the Jay Treaty Debate', *Journal of the Early Republic*, vol. 20, no. 3, 2000, pp. 393–422.

Federici, M.P., *The Political Philosophy of Alexander Hamilton*, Baltimore, Johns Hopkins University Press, 2012.

Fichter, J.R., *So Great a Proffit: How the East Indies Trade Transformed Anglo-American Capitalism*, Cambridge, Harvard University Press, 2010.

Fleming, R.H., 'Phyn, Ellice and Company of Schenectady', *Contributions to Canadian Economics*, vol. 4, 1932, pp. 7–41.

Fletcher, J., 'Integrative History: Parallels and Interconnections in the Early Modern Periods, 1500–1800', *Journal of Turkish Studies* vol. 9, 1985, pp. 37–57.

Flynn, D.O. and Giraldez A., 'Born With a "Silver Spoon": The Origin of World Trade in 1571', *Journal of World History*, vol. 6, no. 2, 1995, pp. 201–221.

Fontenoy, P.E., 'Ginseng, Otter Skins, and Sandalwood: The Conundrum of the China Trade', *The Northern Mariner/ Le Marin du Nord* vol. 7, no. 1, 1997, pp. 1–16.

Frank, C., *Objectifying China, Imagining America: Chinese Commodities in Early America,* Chicago, University of Chicago Press, 2011.

Fremont-Barnes, G., *The Wars of the Barbary Pirates: To the Shores of Tripoli: The Rise of the US Navy and Marines*, Oxford, Osprey, 2006.

Furber, H., 'The Beginnings of American Trade with India, 1784–1812', *The New England Quarterly*, vol. XI, 1938, pp. 235–265.

Gall, L., 'Von der Ständischen zur Bürgerlichen Gesellschaft', *Enzyklopädie Deutscher Geschichte,* 25. 2. Aktualisierte Auflage, München, Oldenbourg Wissenschaftsverlag, 2012.

Gallagher, M.A.Y., 'Charting a New Course for the China Trade, the Late Eighteenth Century American Model', *The American Neptune, A Quarterly Journal of Maritime History and Arts* vol. 57, no. 3, 1997, pp. 201–218.

Geyer, M., and Bright C., 'World History in a Global Age', *The American Historical Review*, vol.100, no. 4, 1995, pp. 1034–1060.

Gibson, J.R., *Otter Skins, Boston Ships, and China Goods: The Maritime Fur Trade of the Northwest Coast, 1785–1841*, Seattle, University of Washington Press, 1992.

Gilje, P.A., 'The Rise of Capitalism in the Early Republic', *Journal of the Early Republic,* vol.16. no. 2, 1996, pp. 159–181.

Goldstein, J., *Philadelphia and the China Trade, 1682–1846: Commercial, Cultural, and Attitudinal Effects*, University Park, Pennsylvania State University Press, 1978.

Gould, E.H., and Onuf P.S. (eds.), *Empire and Nation: The American Revolution and the Atlantic World,* Baltimore, Johns Hopkins University Press, 2005.

Gunn, G.C., *First Globalization: The Eurasian Exchange, 1500 to 1800*, Lanham, MD, Rowman & Littlefield, 2003.

Gunn, S., 'The Spatial Turn: Changing Histories of Space and Place', in Gunn, S. and Morris R.J. (eds.), *Identities in Space. Contested Terrains in the Western City since 1850,* Ashgate, Burlington, 2001.

Greenbie, S. and Greenbie M.L., *Gold of Ophir the China trade in the Making of America,* New York, Wilson Erickson, 1937.

Habermas, J., *The Structural Transformation of the Public Sphere: An Inquiry into a Category of Bourgeois Society,* Cambridge, MIT Press, 1991.

Hamilton, A., *The Papers of Alexander Hamilton, Vol. IX.* Syrett, H.C. and Cooke J.E. (eds.), New York, Columbia University Press, 1965.

Hammond, B., *Banks and Politics From the Revolution to the Civil War*, Princeton, Princeton University Press, 1957.

Hancock, D., *Citizens of the World: London Merchants and the Integration of the British Atlantic Community, 1735–1785*, Cambridge, Cambridge University Press, 1995.

Hancock, D., 'Commerce and Conversation in the Eighteenth-Century Atlantic: The Invention of Madeira Wine', *The Journal of Interdisciplinary History* vol. 29, no. 2, 1998, pp. 197–219.

Hancock, D., 'The British Atlantic World: Coordination, Complexity, and the Emergence of an Atlantic Market Economy, 1651–1815', *Itinerario* vol. 23, no. 2, 1999, pp. 107–127.

Hancock, D. *Oceans of Wine: Madeira and the Emergence of American Trade and Taste*, New Haven, Yale University Press, 2009.

Harrington, V.D., *New York Merchants on the Eve of the Revolution*, Gloucester, Peter Smith, 1964.

Hartigan-O'Connor, E. '*Collaborative Consumption and the Politics of Choice in Early American Port Cities*' in Styles, J. and Vickery A. (eds.), *Gender, Taste, and Material Culture in Britain and North America, 1700–1830*, New Haven, Yale University Press, 2006.

Hausberger, B., and Lehners J.P. (eds.), *Die Welt im 18. Jahrhundert*, Wien, Mandelbaum-Verlag, 2011.

Henretta, J.A., *The Origins of American Capitalism: Collected Essays*, Boston, Northeastern University Press, 1991.

Hepplewhite, G., *The Cabinet Maker and Upholsterer*, New York, Dover Publications, 1969.

Hont, I., *Jealousy of Trade: International Competition and the Nation State in Historical Perspective*, Cambridge: Belknap Press, 2005.

Hopkins, A.G. (ed.), *Globalization in World History*, London, Pimlico, 2002.

Hough, F.B., *A History of Lewis County, in the State of New York: From the Beginning of his Settlement to the Present Time*, Albany, Munsell & Rowland, 1860.

Howard, D.S. and Wright C.E., *New York and the China Trade*, New York, New York Historical Society, 1984.

Huebner, S., *Marine Insurance in the United States*, Philadelphia, University of Pennsylvania, 1905.

Hunter, B. 'Wheat, War, and the American Economy During the Age of Revolution', *The William and Mary Quarterly*, vol.62, no. 2, 2005, pp. 505–526.

Hyneman, C.S., *The First American Neutrality: A Study of the American Understanding of Neutral Obligations During the Years 1792 to 1815*, Urbana, University of Illinois, 1934.

Irigoin, A., 'The End of a Silver Era: The Consequences of the Breakdown of the Spanish Peso Standard in China and the United States, 1780–1850', *Journal of World History*, vol. 20, no. 2, 2009, pp. 207–244.

Islam, S., 'Americans in Calcutta Bazaars in the Early Nineteenth Century: Images and Interpretations', *Journal of the Asiatic Society of Bangladesh,* (Humanities) vol. 50, 2005, pp. 219–245.

Islam, S. 'Contributions of Asian Trade to the Early Transformation of the United States of America', in Journal of the Asiatic Society of Bangladesh (Humanities) vol. 54,1 (2009), pp. 1–26.

Jaher, F.C., *The Urban Establishment: Upper Strata in Boston, New York, Charleston, Chicago, and Los Angeles*, Urbana, University of Illinois Press, 1982.

Kennedy, C.S., *The American Consul: A History of the United States Consular Service, 1776–1914*, New York, Greenwood Press, 1990.

Kingston, C., 'Marine Insurance in Britain and America, 1720–1844: A Comparative Institutional Analysis', *Journal of Economic History*, vol. 67, no. 2, 2007, pp. 379–409.

Klein, D.B. and Majewski J., 'Economy, Community, and Law: The Turnpike Movement in New York, 1797–1845', *Law & Society Review*, vol. 26, no. 3, 1992, pp. 469–512.

Knight, R.J.B., and Wilcox M.H. *Sustaining the Fleet, 1793–1815: War, the British Navy and the Contractor State*, Woodbridge, Boydell Press, 2010.

Kriedte, P., Medick H., and Schlumbohm J. (eds.), *Industrialisierung vor der Industrialisierung: Gewerbliche Warenproduktion auf dem Land in der Formationsperiode des Kapitalismus*, Göttingen, Vandenhoeck & Ruprecht, 1978.

Lamikiz, X., *Trade and Trust in the Eighteenth-Century Atlantic World: Spanish Merchants and their Oversea Networks*, Woodbridge, Boydell Press, 2010.

Landon, H.F., *The North Country; A History: Embracing Jefferson, St. Lawrence, Oswego, Lewis and Franklin Counties, New York*, Indianapolis, Historical Pub. Co., 1932.

Lang, M., 'Globalization and Its History', *The Journal of Modern History* vol. 78, 2006, pp. 899–931.

Lanier, A.S., 'The French Spoliation Claims', *The Virginia Law Register*, vol.10, no.1, 1924, pp.12–23.

Lankevich, G.J., *American Metropolis: A History of New York City*, New York, New York University Press, 1998.

Liss, P.K. *Atlantic Empires: The Network of Trade and Revolution, 1713–1826*, Baltimore, Johns Hopkins University Press, 1983.

Lloyd, C., *What on Earth Happened? In Brief: The Planet, Life and People From the Big Bang to the Present Day*, London, Bloomsbury, 2009.

MacGill, C.E., *History of Transportation in the United States Before 1860*, Contributions to American Economic History: Carnegie Institution, Gloucester: P. Smith, 1948.

Main, J.T., *The Social Structure of Revolutionary America*, Princeton, Princeton University Press, 1965.

Mann, C.C., *1493 Uncovering the New World Columbus Created*, New York, Knopf, 2011.

Markovits, C., *The Global World of Indian Merchants 1750–1947. Traders of Sind from Bukhara to Panama*, Cambridge, Cambridge University Press, 2004.

Marzagalli, S., 'Establishing Transatlantic Trade Networks in Time of War: Bordeaux and the United States, 1793–1815', *The Business History Review*, vol. 79, no. 4, 2005, pp. 811–844.

Mathias, P., 'Risk, Credit and Kinship in Early Modern Enterprise', in McCusker, J. and Morgan K. (eds.), *The Early Modern Atlantic Economy*, Cambridge, Cambridge University Press, 2000, pp. 15–35.

Matson, C.D., *Merchants & Empire: Trading in Colonial New York*, Baltimore, Johns Hopkins University Press, 1998.

McCusker, J.J., 'Worth a War? The Importance of the Trade Between British America and the Mediterranean', in Marzagalli, S., Sofka, J.R. and McKusker J.J. (eds.), *Rough Waters: American Involvement With the Mediterranean in the Eighteenth and Nineteenth Centuries*, St. Johns. International Maritime Economic History Association, 2010, pp. 7–24.

McCusker, J.J., and Morgan K. (eds.), *The Early Modern Atlantic Economy*, Cambridge, Cambridge University Press, 2000.

McKendrick, N., Brewer J., and Plumb J.H. (eds.), *The Birth of a Consumer Society: The Commercialization of Eighteenth-Century England*, Bloomington, Indiana University Press, 1982.

McKeown, A., 'Periodizing Globalization', *History Workshop Journal*, vol. 63, 2007, pp. 218–230.

McNeill, J.R., and McNeill W.H., *The Human Web: A Bird's Eye View of World History*, New York, W.W. Norton, 2003.

Melton, J., *The Rise of the Public in Enlightenment Europe*, Cambridge, Cambridge University Press, 2001.

Merli, F.J. and Wilson T.A., *Makers of American Diplomacy, From Benjamin Franklin to Henry Kissinger*, New York, Scribner, 1974.

Middell, M. and Naumann K., ‚Die Konstruktivistische Wende: Der Spatial Turn und das Interesse an der Globalisierung in der gegenwärtigen Geschichtswissenschaft', *Geographische Zeitschrift* vol. 93. no. 1, 2005, pp. 33–44.

Middell, M. and Naumann K., 'Global History and the Spatial Turn: From the Impact of Area Studies to the Study of Critical Junctures of Globalization', *Journal of Global History*, vol. 5, 2010, pp.149–170.

Milburn, W., *Oriental Commerce: Volume II*, London, Black, Parry, & Company, 1813.

Mintz, S., *Sweetness and Power: The Place of Sugar in Modern History*, New York, Viking, 1985.

Moffat, B., *Pierrepont Genealogies: From Norman Times to 1913, with Particular Attention Paid to the Line of Descent from Hezekiah Pierrepont, Youngest Son of Rev. James Pierpont of New Haven*, New York, L. Middleditch Co., 1913.

Mohl, R.A., *Poverty in New York, 1783–1825*, Oxford, Oxford University Press, 1971.

Montgomery, D., 'The Working Classes of the Pre-Industrial American City, 1780–1830', *Labor History* vol. 9, no. 1, 1968, pp. 3–22.

Morgan, K., 'Business Networks in the British Export Trade to North America 1750–1800' in McKusker, J. and Kenneth Morgan (eds.), *The Early Modern Atlantic Economy*, Cambridge, Cambridge University Press, 2000, pp. 36–64.

Morrison, J.H., *History of New York Ship Yards*, New York, W.F. Sametz, 1909.

Murphy, R.C. and Mannion L., *The History of the Society of the Friendly Sons of Saint Patrick in the City of New York, 1784 to 1955*, New York, The Society of the Friendly Sons of Saint Patrick, 1962.

Muthu, S., *Enlightenment Against Empire*, Princeton, Princeton University Press, 2003.

Muthu, S., 'Adam Smith's Critique of International Trading Companies: Theorizing Globalization in the Age of Enlightenment', *Political Theory*, vol. 36, no. 2, 2008, pp. 185–212.

Nettels, C.P., *The Emergence of a National Economy, 1775–1815*, Armonk, N.Y., Sharpe, M.E. 1989.

North, D.C., *The Economic Growth of the United States, 1790–1860*, Englewood Cliffs, Prentice-Hall, 1961.

Nye, J.S. and Keohane R.O., 'Globalization: What's New? What's Not (And So What?)', in Nye, J.S. (ed.), *Power in the Global Information Age: From Realism to Globalization*, London, Routledge, 2004, pp. 191–200.

Nylander, J., *Our Own Snug Fireside. Images of the New England Home 1760–1860*, New York, Alfred A. Knopf, 1993.

O'Brien, P., 'Merchants and Bankers as Patriots or Speculators? Foreign Commerce and Monetary Policy in Wartime, 1793–1815', in McCusker, J. and Kenneth M. (eds.), *The Early Modern Atlantic Economy*, Cambridge, Cambridge University Press, 2000, pp. 250–277.

O'Rourke, K.H., and Williamson J.G., *Globalization and History: The Evolution of a Nineteenth Century Atlantic Economy*, Cambridge, MIT Press, 1999.

O'Rourke, K.H., and Williamson J.G., 'When Did Globalization Begin?' *NBER Working Paper Series,* Working Paper 7632, 2000.

Osterhammel, J., and Petersson N.P., ‚Die Wiederkehr des Raumes', *Neue Politische Literatur,* vol. 43, 1998, pp. 274–397.

Osterhammel, J., and Petersson N.P., *Geschichte der Globalisierung. Dimensionen, Prozesse, Epochen*, München, Beck, 2003.

Osterhammel, J., and Petersson N.P., *Globalization: A Short History*, Princeton, Princeton University Press, 2005.

Pearson R., and Richardson D., 'Business Networking in the Industrial Revolution', *Economic History Review,* vol. LIV, no. 4, 2001, pp. 657–679.

Perkins, E.J., *American Public Finance and Financial Services, 1700–1815*, Columbus, The Ohio State University Press, 1994.

Porter, K.W., 'John Jacob Astor, Business Man: 2 Volumes', Cambridge: Harvard University Press, 1931.

Price, J.M., 'What Did Merchants Do?: Reflections on British Overseas Trade, 1660–1790', *The Journal of Economic History*, vol. 49, 1989, pp. 267–284.

Richards, R., 'Introduction: United States Trade With China, 1784–1814', *The American Neptune: A Quarterly Journal of Maritime History and Arts*, vol. 54, 1994, pp. 5–9.

Rothschild, E., 'Global Commerce and the Question of Sovereignty in the Eighteenth-Century Provinces' *Modern Intellectual History*, vol. 1, no. 1, April 2004, pp. 3–25.

Schlesinger, A.M., *The Colonial Merchants and the American Revolution 1763–1776*, New York, Frederick Ungar Publishing, 1957.

Schlögel, K., *Im Raume lesen wir die Zeit: Über Zivilisationsgeschichte und Geopolitik*, München, Carl Hanser, 2003.

Schulte-Beerbühl, M. and Weber K., *Deutsche Kaufleute in London: Welthandel und Einbürgerung 1660–1818*, München, Oldenbourg Verlag, 2007.

Schulte-Beerbühl, M. and Weber K., 'From Westphalia to the Carribbean: Networks of German Textile Merchants in the Eighteenth Century', in *GHI Bulletin*, Gestrich, A. and Schulte-Beerbühl M. (eds.), London, German Historical Institute, 2011.

Shammas, C., *The Pre-Industrial Consumer in England and America*, Los Angeles, Figueroa Press, 2008.

Sinha, J.C., 'Indo-American Trade, Past and Present', *Journal and Proceedings of the Asiatic Society of Bengal*, vol. XXV, 1929, pp. 201–221.

Smith, R.W., 'The Foreign Intercourse Bill of 1798 and the Debate over Early American Foreign Relations', *Journal of the Early Republic*, vol. 36, no. 1, Spring 2016, pp. 125–149.

Sofka, J., 'The Jeffersonian Idea of National Security Revisited' in Marzagalli, S., Sofka J.R. and McCusker J.J. (eds.), *Rough Waters: American Involvement with the Mediterranean in the Eighteenth and Nineteenth Centuries, Research in Maritime History*, no. 44, (2010), pp. 161–183.

Spindler, R., *New York und der Amerikanische Indienhandel (1784–1812)*, Stuttgart, Steiner, 1994.

Steele, I.K., *The English Atlantic, 1675–1740: An Exploration of Communication and Community*, Oxford, Oxford University Press, 1986.

Stearns, P.N., *Consumerism in World History. The Global Transformation of Desire*, New York, Routledge, 2001.

Stelle, C.C., 'American Trade in Opium to China, Prior to 1820', *Pacific Historical Review*, vol. 9, no. 4, 1940, pp. 425–444.

Steward, S.C., *The Le Roy Family in America*, Boston, Randall Publisher, 2003.

Stout, K., *Genealogy of the Kemble (Kimble) Family in America*, Pullman, K. Stout, 1992.

Swift, J.W., Hodgkinson P., and Woodhouse S.W., 'The Voyage of the Empress of China', *The Pennsylvania Magazine of History and Biography*, vol. 63, no. 1, 1939, pp. 24–36.

Sylla, R., 'The United States: Financial Innovation and Adaptation', in Bordo, M.D. and Cortes-Condo R. (eds.), *Transferring Wealth and Power from the Old World to the New World.Monetary and Fiscal Institutions in the 17th through the 19th Centuries*, Cambridge, Cambridge University Press, 2001, pp. 231–258.

Synder, J.W. Jr., 'The First American Voyage to India', *Americana (American Historical Magazine)* vol. XXXII, no. 2, April 1938, pp. 284–304.

Tchen, J.K.W., *New York Before Chinatown: Orientalism and the Shaping of American Culture, 1776–1882,* Baltimore, Johns Hopkins University Press, 1999.
Tenbruck, F.H., *Die kulturellen Grundlagen der Gesellschaft,* Opladen, Westdeutscher Verlag, 1989.
Thomson, J.E., *Mercenaries, Pirates and Sovereigns: State-Building and Extraterritorial Violence in Early Modern Europe,* Princeton, Princeton University Press, 1994.
Trautsch, J.M., 'The Causes of the War of 1812: 200 Years of Debate', *The Journal of Military History,* vol. 77, 2013, pp. 273–293.
Trivellato, F., 'Merchants' letters across geographical and social boundaries', in Bethencourt, F. and Egmond, F. (eds.), *Cultural Exchange in Early Modern Europe: Volume III, Correspondence and Cultural Exchange in Europe 1400 to 1700*, Cambridge, Cambridge University Press, pp. 80–103.
Trouillot, M.R., *Silencing the Past: Power and the Production of History*, Boston, Beacon Press, 1995.
Tyrrell, I.R., *Transnational Nation: United States History in Global Perspective Since 1789*, Basingstoke, Palgrave Macmillan, 2007.
Van, D., *The Canton Trade: Life and Enterprise on the China Coast, 1700–1845,* Hong Kong, Hong Kong University Press, 2005.
de Vries, J., 'Between Purchasing Power and the World of Goods: Understanding the Household Economy in Early Modern Europe', in Brewer, J. and Porter R. (eds.), *Consumption and the World of Goods,* London, Routledge, 1993, pp. 85–132.
de Vries, J., 'Connecting Europe and Asia: A Quantitative Analysis of the Cape-Route Trade, 1497–1795' in Flynn, D.O., Giraldez A., and von Glahn R. (eds.), *Global Connection and Monetary History, 1470–1800*, Aldershot, Ashgate, 2003, pp. 35–106.
Vries, P., 'Global History', *Österreichische Zeitschrift für Geschichtswissenschaften*, vol. 20. no. 2, 2009, pp. 133–169.
Vierhaus, R., 'Umrisse einer Sozialgeschichte der Gebildeten in Deutschland', in Vierhaus, R., (ed.), *Deutschland im 18. Jahrhundert. Politische Verfassung, Soziales Gefüge, Geistige Bewegungen. Ausgewählte Aufsätze,* Göttingen, Vandenhoeck & Ruprecht, 1987.
Weber, K., *Deutsche Kaufleute im Atlantikhandel, 1680–1830: Unternehmen und Familien in Hamburg, Cádiz und Bordeaux*, München, Beck, 2004.
Weld, R.F., *Brooklyn Village, 1816–1834,* New York, Columbia University Press, 1938.
White, E., *Pictorial Dictionary of British 18th Century Furniture Design: The Printed Sources,* Woolbridge, Antique Collectors Club, 1990, pp. 18–19.
Wilentz, S., *Chants Democratic: New York City and the Rise of the American Working Class, 1788–1850*, Oxford, Oxford University Press, 2004.
Williams, G.H., *The French Assault on American Shipping, 1793–1813: A History and Comprehensive Record of Merchant Marine Losses*, Jefferson, McFarland & Co., 2009.

Wood, G.S., 'The Significance of the Early Republic' in Cray, R.D. and Morrison M.A. (eds.), *New Perspectives of the Early Republic*, Urbana, University of Illinois Press 1994, pp. 1–22.

Wood, G.S., 'Was America Born Capitalist?' *The Wilson Quarterly*, vol. 23, no.1, 1999, pp. 36–46.

Wright, R.E., *Origins of Commercial Banking in America, 1750–1800*, Lanham, MD. Rowman & Littlefield, 2001.

Wright, R.E., *Hamilton Unbound. Finance and the Creation of the American Republic*, Connecticut, Greenwood Press, 2002.

Index

www.ingramcontent.com/pod-product-compliance
Lightning Source LLC
Chambersburg PA
CBHW071249180926
51613CB00002B/185
* 9 7 8 9 0 0 4 3 4 4 3 8 9 *